20. –

N. n

A CATALOGUE OF THE CARICATURES
OF MAX BEERBOHM

1 Self-caricature. *c.* 1893
Merton College, Oxford (1402)

A
CATALOGUE
OF THE
CARICATURES
OF
MAX BEERBOHM

COMPILED BY
RUPERT HART-DAVIS

MACMILLAN
1972

First published 1972
MACMILLAN LONDON LTD
London and Basingstoke
Associated companies in New York Toronto
Dublin Melbourne Johannesburg & Madras

Printed in Great Britain by
R. & R. CLARK LTD, EDINBURGH

CONTENTS

ILLUSTRATIONS

(on pages 181 *to* 244*)*

INTRODUCTION

Nearly twenty years ago my dear friend Allan Wade, who had admired and collected Max's work since the Nineties, suggested that I should publish four volumes of the caricatures, each covering a decade of Max's prime. Max approved, and Allan made a selection for the first volume, which Max accepted with some modifications. But by the time *Max's Nineties* appeared in 1958, both Max and Allan were dead, and when I tried to assemble material for the second volume, *Max's Noughts*, I quickly realised that I had no idea what I was choosing from.

Clearly the drawings that Max exhibited or published during the 1900s represented only a fraction of his ten years' output; many caricatures were given to friends or sold privately, and I must search in the illustrated papers of the time, in other people's books, in museums and galleries throughout the world, and in the homes of private collectors. Once I began I found that I was covering the whole of Max's life, and this catalogue is the result. There is no end to such a task, but Max's hundredth birthday (24 August 1972) seems a suitable day on which to publish the results of my labours so far. Further drawings and better identifications will undoubtedly come to light, and I hope that possibly a later edition will benefit by them.

Writing was always a labour to Max, and after 1910, when he married and retired to Italy – ostensibly to gain peace for writing – he wrote very little, except when a World War drove him back to England. Drawing, on the other hand, was always his delight and relaxation, and in one form or another it occupied him pleasurably for most of his long life. 'I can draw caricatures at any moment,' he wrote to his future wife Florence, 'and how I rejoice in them! *They* are what I was put into the world to do.'

Some of his schoolboy and undergraduate drawings show wit and promise, but as a caricaturist he came of age somewhere about his twenty-first birthday in 1893, was at his best during the first quarter of this century, and then gradually declined. By 1930 he had, as he himself said, lost the sharpness that caricature demands, and the three sets of drawings that he did in 1930–31 (*Heroes and Heroines of Bitter Sweet*, the *Spectator* series, and the six for *Ladbroke's Racing Calendar*) are feeble portraits only. 'I seemed to have mislaid my gift for dispraise. Pity crept in,' he told S. N. Behrman. Thereafter he drew for his own pleasure only, occasionally producing a surprisingly good drawing, often an echo of an old one. His astonishing visual memory was as sure as ever, but the sting had departed.

To have included the mass of juvenilia that has survived – mostly at Charterhouse, Merton College, Oxford, the University of Texas, and in the collection of Mr Robert H. Taylor at Princeton – would have swollen the catalogue unwarrantably. I have made a representative selection of the best of it, and excluded the rest. I have also omitted all drawings done in books, letters and manuscripts: many of them are brilliant, but they are very numerous and widely scattered: I prefer to concentrate on the regular drawings, and leave the wider task to another. Other omissions are Max's 'improvements' of other people's illustrations, which often seem to me unworthy of him, and are anyhow out of place here; pages of multiple drawings from sketchbooks (with one or two exceptions); indeterminate doodlings; and lastly Max's few 'straight' drawings. These include the series of sketches of his wife Florence, done in the early days of their marriage, which are more like love-letters than caricatures; the beautiful drawing of his sister Dora in her nun's habit, which belongs to Max's great-nephew Ivan Moffat; his three illustrations to 'The Story of the Small Boy and the Barley-Sugar', which appeared in *The Parade*, edited by Gleeson White, in 1897; drawings of his dogs; costume-designs for *The Happy Hypocrite*; and the two pages of heads of Rossetti and his circle, one now belonging to Mrs Virginia Surtees and one to Mr Alan G. Thomas, which Max must have done as an *aide-mémoire* for his drawings of the Pre-Raphaelites.

The catalogue therefore covers only caricatures that were intended either to be framed or to be reproduced in book or periodical. Max seldom threw anything away – from indolence rather than intention – and when his remaining drawings were sold at Sotheby's in December 1960 they included a quantity of rough sketches and spoilt drawings. Since many of these are now preserved in British and American collections, it seems essential to record them, so as to distinguish them from the finished drawings.

Although I believe Max to be without equal among British caricaturists, I have not considered artistic appraisal as part of my task, and my approach has everywhere been literary and descriptive rather than aesthetic, with identification as my chief object. I have therefore omitted some of the usual ingredients of *catalogues raisonnés*, including measurements. I started by recording as many as I could, but soon found they were as useless to me as I was sure they would be to others, and since they were often difficult to obtain accurately, I decided to omit them.

Except for three early drawings, the plates in this volume represent Max in his prime. None of them appeared in any of his own books, and only one or two have been reproduced in a book of any kind. Their choice has depended on the excellence of the drawing, the availability of a clear photograph, and the continued interest of the subject.

Max was primarily a water-colour artist, and the full effect of his drawings can be seen only in the originals: black-and-white reproductions convey the joke and the draughtsmanship only. Unless otherwise described, every drawing that I have seen is executed in pen or pencil, or a combination of the two. The great majority have some added water-colour, varying from a light wash here and there to a complete colouring.

Every drawing that I have seen is signed MAX unless otherwise described.

An asterisk against a drawing's number means that I possess a reproduction of it. Although the asterisked numbers are in a majority (1629 out of 2093), I have preferred to mark them rather than the minority, since they represent positive objects which I can consult, whereas the drawings without asterisks vary from ones that have been faithfully described by their owners, through ones that I briefly saw and noted in auction-rooms, dealers' galleries, or owners' houses but can no longer consult, to drawings known only from catalogue-entries or other notes. Most of my reproductions are good clear photographs, but some of the early newspaper reproductions are so indistinct that, although they enable me to identify the drawing, they do not disclose what, if anything, Max wrote on it. Half a dozen owners have kindly sent me exact tracings of their drawings. It is possible, indeed likely, that in a number of places two or more entries may refer to the same drawing. Many of the exhibited drawings, particularly those with plain titles, or none, are difficult or impossible to identify, unless they have an exhibition-label on the back of the frame, and I have everywhere catalogued these unknowns as separate items. The discovery of additional drawings since my final numbering explains such items as 61A, and where an unknown has proved to be listed already I have removed it and substituted **Nil**.

In Part One the names of the subjects in the headings are given in the simplest possible form, almost always as they were when Max first caricatured them, disregarding all later ennoblements and decorations. Occasionally, however, it has seemed more sensible to use the later and better-known name: thus Lord Northcliffe and Lord Burnham, with cross-references at Harmsworth and Lawson. The heading, with the dates and brief description underneath, should make identification easy. On the rare occasions when Max spelt a subject's name wrong I have retained his misspelling, since it appears on the drawing, and printed the correct name in the heading above. (Praxiteles I felt bound to put right.) Drawings under each heading are in chronological order, with undatable ones at the end.

The titles of the drawings, unless enclosed in square brackets, are Max's own, transcribed from the drawings by myself or by the owners. A title in brackets without other indication has been taken from the exhibition catalogue, but experience shows that such titles are not necessarily on the drawing: whether supplied by Max or by the gallery, they often differ from the title on the drawing, or describe an untitled drawing.

A plain date means that Max wrote it on the drawing; n.d. (no date) means that the drawing is undated. Dates within square brackets are conjectural. In his early exhibitions Max almost always showed very recent work, often done at the last moment in time for the show. These drawings can therefore be conjecturally dated with some confidence, but from 1911 unsold earlier drawings began to be shown with new ones, and the last three Leicester Galleries exhibitions were wholly retrospective. In the 1928 exhibition Max's suggested dates for the earlier drawings are of doubtful accuracy.

Any further legend on the drawing is printed immediately below the title, in Roman type, except where Max italicised a word or words. Explanatory notes of mine follow, in italics. As Sir John Rothenstein has written, 'His drawings are so intimate as to be almost soliloquies; but soliloquies easily comprehensible to his friends.' Most of his friends are now dead, and the point of some drawings has died with them. I have explained as many as I can, but a few remain inscrutable. Some titles are self-explanatory, and where an asterisked drawing is not described it can be taken to be a simple portrait-caricature. 'Facing left' means the reader's left.

It is not always easy to account for two identical and equally finished drawings. Presumably Max did 1546 and 1547 so that the Sitwell brothers could each have one; Robert Ross, who was artistic adviser to the Johannesburg Art Gallery, probably persuaded Max to draw 885 for them as a copy of 884; others may have been done to please other friends.

The London galleries in which Max's caricatures were exhibited are shown in the catalogue as follows:

F.A.S.   The Fine Art Society in New Bond Street. In October 1896 Max contributed six drawings to an exhibition entitled 'A Century and a half of

English humorous art, from Hogarth to the Present Day'. So far as is known, this was his first public showing.

Carfax The Carfax Gallery, first at 17 Ryder Street and from 1907 at 24 Bury Street. Here Max held his first four one-man shows – in December 1901, May 1904, April 1907, and April 1908.

Baillie The Baillie Gallery in Baker Street, where Max contributed six drawings to a mixed show in February 1907.

N.E.A.C. The New English Art Club in Suffolk Street. Here Max showed fifteen drawings in Summer 1909, nine in Winter 1909, ten in Summer 1910, and seven in Winter 1911.

L.G. The Leicester Galleries in Leicester Square, where all Max's drawings were shown after 1911. One-man shows were held in April 1911, April 1913, May and September 1921, May 1923, April 1925, November 1928, September 1945 (the Guedalla Collection), May 1952, and (posthumously) June 1957.

Grosvenor The Grosvenor Gallery in Grosvenor Street, where fifteen of the caricatures that later formed part of *Rossetti and his Circle* were shown at a Modern Loan Exhibition in November 1917.

The American galleries are designated as follows:

New York The Berlin Photographic Co. in New York, where Max showed sixteen drawings in October 1912.

Grolier The Grolier Club in New York, which in March 1944 put on a Max exhibition consisting largely of the collection of A. E. Gallatin (now in Harvard College Library).

American Academy The American Academy of Arts and Letters in New York, which showed a collection of Max's caricatures, manuscripts and books in December 1952.

Achenbach The Achenbach Foundation for Graphic Arts in San Francisco, which in March 1964 mounted an exhibition, based chiefly on the collection of Professor Majl Ewing (now in the William Andrews Clark Memorial Library).

Cincinnati The Cincinnati Public Library, where the collection of Mr Alfred H. Perrin (now in the Lilly Library) was exhibited in April 1965.

Max published the following books of caricatures:

Caricatures of Twenty-Five Gentlemen	1896
The Poets' Corner	1904
(King Penguin edition, with extra plates, 1943)	
A Book of Caricatures	1907
The Second Childhood of John Bull	1911

Fifty Caricatures	1913
A Survey	1921
Rossetti and his Circle	1922
Things New and Old	1923
Observations	1925
Heroes and Heroines of Bitter Sweet	1931

Since his death there have appeared *Max's Nineties* (1958) and *Caricatures by Max* (1958), a selection of the drawings in the Ashmolean Museum at Oxford.

Wherever I have a reproduction of a drawing, without knowledge of its present location, this, unless otherwise explained, is due to the kindness of the late Mr Oliver Brown and his successors at the Leicester Galleries, who generously supplied me with all their remaining photographs of drawings they had shown in the past.

Of the 2093 drawings here recorded I have traced the whereabouts of only 1347. The details of present ownership are as exact as I can make them, but during the ten years and more that I have been working on the catalogue some drawings have changed hands, and some owners have died. I have endeavoured to pursue and note all such changes, but inevitably some have escaped me, and a few locations are simply the last ones known to me. To save space I have abbreviated some of the names of the chief institutional owners, thus:

Arents Collection (N.Y.P.L.)	The Arents Tobacco Collection in the New York Public Library.
Berg Collection (N.Y.P.L.)	The Henry W. and Albert A. Berg Collection in the New York Public Library.
Huntington Library	The Henry E. Huntington Library at San Marino, California.
Lilly Library	The Lilly Library of Indiana University, at Bloomington, Indiana.
Newberry Library	The Stone and Kimball Collection, The Wing Foundation, The Newberry Library, Chicago, Illinois.
U.C. (Berkeley)	The Library of the University of California at Berkeley.
U.C.L.A. (Clark)	The William Andrews Clark Memorial Library in the University of California at Los Angeles.
University of Texas	The Humanities Research Center Library of the University of Texas at Austin, Texas.

The largest and best private collection in the world was formed by Philip Guedalla. After his death in 1944, 164 of his drawings were shown at the Leicester Galleries in 1945, and Mrs Guedalla presented sixty of them to the Ashmolean Museum. She kept some for herself, and the rest were dispersed. In the United States the two leading private collections were those, already mentioned, of Mr Alfred H. Perrin of Cincinnati and the late Professor Majl Ewing of the University of California. The extent of present holdings can be seen in the Index of Owners. Three owners who wish to remain anonymous are listed as Private, followed in brackets by the exact or approximate location of their drawings.

From the confusion of Max's papers there emerged a number of notes to him from the

Leicester Galleries and accounts showing which drawings had been sold: hence 'known only from an L.G. note'. There were also some pages torn from booksellers' catalogues without any indication of the bookseller's identity: hence 'known only from bookseller's catalogue'; and some photographs of otherwise unknown drawings.

My debts of gratitude are widespread and deep. Max's sister-in-law Mrs Eva Reichmann has helped, encouraged and trusted me through the years, and I am deeply and affectionately grateful. To all the private owners of drawings, including Mr Alfred H. Perrin and the late Professor Majl Ewing, I am enormously indebted for their generosity with photographs, information, and permission to reproduce: they are too numerous to thank individually here, and I trust they will accept this comprehensive but heartfelt word of gratitude.

Similarly I give thanks collectively to the librarians, curators and other officials of the libraries and museums that own drawings. All of them have gone out of their way to help me, but I must single out for special thanks those generous and helpful persons to whom I have given most trouble: Professor F. W. Roberts and Mrs Mary M. Hirth of the University of Texas; Mrs Edna C. Davis of the William Andrews Clark Memorial Library; Professor W. H. Bond and Mrs Eleanor M. Garvey of Harvard College Library; Miss Marjorie G. Wynne of Yale University Library; the late Dr John D. Gordan and Dr Lola L. Szladits of the New York Public Library; Mr Alfred L. Bush of Princeton University Library; Mr Gerald Taylor of the Ashmolean Museum; Mr John P. Harthan of the Victoria and Albert Museum; Dr Roy Strong of the National Portrait Gallery; Dr Roger Highfield and Mr John Burgass of Merton College, Oxford; and Mr John Sunderland of the Witt Library in the Courtauld Institute.

In the auction-rooms and galleries I owe an enormous debt to Miss Janet Green of Sotheby's and to Mr Godfrey Pilkington and Miss Christabel Briggs of the Piccadilly Gallery. I am also greatly indebted to Mr John Lumley of Christie's; Mr Richard Kingzett of Agnew's; Mr Anthony d'Offay of the d'Offay Couper Gallery; the late Mr Oliver F. Brown and Mr Nicholas E. Brown of the Leicester Galleries. None of them was under any obligation to help me, but their contribution has been immense.

I have also received much assistance from Mr Robert J. Barry Jr of C. A. Stonehill Inc; Mr S. N. Behrman; Mr John Carleton; Mr John Carter; Sir Charles Clay; Dr Kathleen Coburn; Mr Edward A. Craig; Mr Arthur Crook; Dr Malcolm Easton; Professor Leon Edel; Mr Harry Fairhurst, Librarian of York University; Mr Lew D. Feldman; Professor John Felstiner; Mr John F. Fleming; Professor William E. Fredeman; Mr Roger Fulford; Mr Martin Gilbert; Mr John Gore; Mr Christopher and Captain Hugh Hammersley; my son Mr Duff Hart-Davis; Professor Roy Huss; Mr F. R. Kaye of Ladbroke & Co Ltd; Mr T. H. Kelly, Librarian of the *Daily Mail*; Mrs M. Lago; Sir Alan Lascelles; Professor Dan H. Laurence; Professor Roger Lhombreaud; Messrs Raymond Mander and Joe Mitchenson; the late Professor R. B. McElderry Jr; Professor Hamish Miles; Miss Winifred Myers; my cousin Viscount Norwich; Prince Michael Radziwill; the late Mr Siegfried Sassoon; Mr George Sims; Mr Herbert Stuart Stone Jr; Mr Frank Swinnerton; Mr Steve Tokaruk; Mr Oliver Van Oss, Headmaster of Charterhouse; and Dame Veronica Wedgwood O.M. I am most grateful to all of them – and to any others whom I may have forgotten to mention.

Mr Stephen Greene nobly risked posting his invaluable Max scrapbook across the Atlantic for my benefit. Mr Edmund Wilson has encouraged the enterprise from the start. Mr John Sparrow has translated and identified Latin and Greek quotations for me. Mr Simon Nowell-Smith has brought his specialised knowledge and unerring eye to bear on the book in manuscript, besides giving expert help with the lay-out. Mr Ernest Mehew, turning aside from his monumental edition of Stevenson's letters, has sternly criticised manuscript and proof, as well as locating drawings and their subjects, thus proving once again his genius for research. The late Mr Kenneth Bloomfield from his home in New Zealand twice flew to England by way of the United States, so as to examine and photograph drawings for me; his help was incalculable, and I grieve that he died before he could see the result. The proofs have been read by Mr and Mrs Henry Maas, Mr and Mrs Ernest Mehew, and Mr Nowell-Smith. Finally Mr Nicolas Barker took infinite pains to devise an effective typographical setting for a complicated manuscript, and my old friend and colleague Mr Richard Garnett has piloted the book through the press with great patience and navigational skill.

These are the people who have done most of the work. Everyone who uses this book should be as grateful to them as I am.

RUPERT HART-DAVIS

Marske-in-Swaledale
March 1972

The Catalogue

PART ONE

Real People

ARRANGED ALPHABETICALLY

A

ABDUL HAMID II
1842–1913   Sultan of Turkey
See 186, 1739, 1740

WILLIAM ABINGDON
1888–1959   Actor and stage-director

1★ **Mr Abingdon** [n.d.]
Known only from a photograph in Max's papers.

J. J. E. W. ADDISON
1838–1907   Judge

2★ **Judge Addison** [n.d.]
OWNER Piccadilly Gallery

HAMILTON AIDÉ
1826–1906   Littérateur

3★ [**Untitled Unsigned** c. 1889]
A drawing done at Charterhouse.
REPRO *John O' London's Weekly*, 1 Apr 1949

4 [**Titled as below**] 1926
A Memory of Mr Hamilton Aidé, poet, painter, playwright and private gentleman. The Great War, and even more its consequences, would have jarred unspeakably upon him. Always a darling of the Gods, he died before the beginning of it.
EXHIB L.G. 1928
OWNER Brinsley Ford

DOUGLAS AINSLIE
1865–1948   Poet and diplomat

5 **Douglas Ainslie or Passion** 1908
Pasted on is D. A.'s poem 'Passion' from the 'Westminster Gazette' of 25 Aug 1908.
OWNER Sold at Sotheby's 14 Dec 1960

CHARLES AITKEN
1869–1936   Director of National Gallery

6 [**Mr Charles Aitken** 1923]
Dated by Max in note to L.G.
EXHIB L.G. 1957

PRINCE ALBERT
1819–61   Consort of Queen Victoria
See 588

GEORGE ALEXANDER
1858–1918   Actor-Manager
See also 27

7★ [**Untitled** 1896]
Shows G. A. leaning against a wall, with a piece of paper in his hand.
REPRO *Twenty-Five Gentlemen*, 1896

8★ **'Rival Beauties' With acknowledgments to Mr George Wyndham and Mr George Alexander** 1907
EXHIB Carfax 1907
REPRO **Plate 26**
OWNER Piccadilly Gallery

9★ **Rival Beauties – Mr George Wyndham and Mr George Alexander** [n.d.]
Pencil sketch for 8.
OWNER Sir Rupert Hart-Davis

10★ [**The St James's** c.1909]
Full length, three-quarter face, leaning forward, hands by sides. G.A. was lessee and manager of the St James's Theatre from 1890 until his death.
REPRO *Vanity Fair*, 20 Jan 1909, where captioned as above

11★ **Mr George Alexander** [n.d.]
Full length, three-quarter face, holding a flower.
OWNER Victoria & Albert Museum

QUEEN ALEXANDRA
1844–1925   Consort of King Edward VII
See 493, 494, 497, 1727

KING ALFONSO XIII OF SPAIN
1886–1941
See also 186

12★ **The King of Spain** [1914]
EXHIB L.G. May 1921
REPRO *A Survey*, 1921, where dated as above

13★ **H.M. The King of Spain** 1930
REPRO *Ladbroke's Racing Calendar*, 1931

THE SECOND LORD ALINGTON
1859–1919   Conservative M.P.
See also 1382

14 [**Mr Humphrey Sturt** 1901]
EXHIB Carfax 1901

15★ **Lord Alington** 1909
EXHIB L.G. 1911
OWNER Keith Mackenzie

LAWRENCE ALMA-TADEMA
1836–1912   Painter

16★ **Mr Alma-Tadema** [1898]
Full-length profile facing left.
REPRO *Sketch*, 16 Nov 1898

17★ **Sir Lawrence Alma-Tadema** [1901]
Full-length profile facing left.
EXHIB Carfax 1901; L.G. 1957
OWNER Fred Uhlman

18★ [**Untitled** n.d.]
Half-length profile facing left. Known only from a photograph in Max's papers.

LORD ALTHORP
See Sixth Earl Spencer

THE FIRST LORD ALVERSTONE
1842–1915   Judge and politician
See also 672

19★ **Sir Richard Webster** [1900]
Sitting on a parliamentary bench, apparently asleep.
REPRO *Idler*, Jul 1900

20★ **The Lord Chief Justice** 1908
Sitting on a judicial bench, apparently asleep.
EXHIB Carfax 1908
REPRO *Bystander*, 6 May 1908
OWNER Mrs Leonard Marsili

PERCY ANDERSON
1851–1928   Artist and stage designer

21 **Mr Percy Anderson** [n.d.]
OWNER John Burridge

W. B. ANDERSON
d. 1948   Partner of Christie's
See 679

WILLIAM ARCHER
1856–1924   Dramatic critic, translator and playwright
See also 95, 612

22★ **Mr William Archer** [1896]
W. A. gazes in awe at a bust of Ibsen on a pedestal. He was one of I's first translators and champions in England.
REPRO *Chap-Book* (Chicago), 1 Oct 1896

23★ [**Untitled** 1898]
Full-length profile facing left, holding umbrella.
REPRO *Academy*, 3 Dec 1898; *Max's Nineties*, 1958

24★ [**Untitled** 1899]
Illustrating a long letter by W. B. Yeats on 'Mr Moore, Mr Archer and the Literary Theatre'. It shows George Moore as a tipsy Irish peasant with a shillelagh in one hand and a trailed coat in the other. W. A., dressed in kilt and glengarry, has one foot on Moore's coat, at which he is pointing in an admonitory way.
REPRO *Daily Chronicle*, 30 Jan 1899

25★ [**Untitled**] 1900
My dear W. A., Breaking a butterfly on a wheel is all very well, but – you must 'first catch your' butterfly! Yours ever Max. Tuesday, December 18, '00.
Refers to W. A.'s review of the dramatic version of Max's

'The Happy Hypocrite'. W. A., kilted and blindfolded with a tartan handerkchief, is bowling a wheel with his left hand and holding out a huge butterfly-net with his right. A butterfly is escaping behind him.

REPRO Lt-Col. C. Archer, *William Archer*, 1931

26★ A Touching Coronation Scene – Mr W. Archer & Mr A. W. Pinero [1901]

W. A., standing behind Pinero, is rather ineffectively crowning him with a laurel wreath.

EXHIB Carfax 1901
REPRO *Candid Friend*, 14 Dec 1901

27★ Mr William Archer Really Conversing [1904]

Max had complained that in Archer's book of interviews with twelve contemporaries, 'Real Conversations', 1904, all his interlocutors spoke with Archer's voice. The drawing shows W. A. seated shirt-sleeved in front of a mirror, writing in a tiny notebook. On his nose hangs a mask of George Alexander, and on the wall masks of A. W. Pinero, Sidney Lee, William Heinemann, Thomas Hardy, Stephen Phillips and George Moore.

EXHIB Carfax 1904, where catalogued as 'Mr William Archer conducting his Real Conversations'
REPRO **Plate 25**
OWNER University of Texas

28★ Henrik Ibsen receiving Mr William Archer in audience [1904]

W. A. kneels to kiss Ibsen's foot. The room is bare except for a bottle of champagne and a single glass on a chest of drawers. On the wall is a portrait of Ibsen, the outlines of which are repeated all over the wallpaper.

EXHIB Carfax 1904
REPRO *The Poets' Corner*, 1904 and 1943
OWNER Municipal Gallery of Modern Art, Dublin

29★ [Untitled] 1908

Mr Archer: 'One last word! In the event of one of the charwomen being temporarily incapacitated by illness or other cause, need the Trustees call an extraordinary meeting to appoint her *locum tenens*? Would it not be simpler, and therefore better, if such *locums tenens* were selected by co-optation among the other five charwomen – three to form a quorum? Do you see any possible danger in that?'
Mr Barker: 'Well, I'll think it over – in America.'

W. A.'s head is in the clouds, from which emerges the National Theatre of his dreams. He holds the tail of the cloak of Granville Barker, who is escaping with a bag labelled G. B.

EXHIB Carfax 1908; L.G. 1945 (Guedalla)
REPRO *Theatre Notebook*, Summer 1967
OWNER Ashmolean Museum, Oxford

30★ [Untitled Unsigned n.d.]

Rough pencil sketch for 29.

OWNER University of Texas

31 [William Archer at the American Hat-Shop ?1910]

[W. A: 'This is in very bad style']

Known only from a bookseller's catalogue, where titled as above. On 15 Jan 1910 W. A. wrote to Max: 'The hat was by far the cheapest I ever bought; and the American tariff has for once been successful in fostering art – but English art.'

32★ A Loathsome Proposal 1911

Wm. Archer (Secretary of Reformed Spelling League): 'I want to rip you up, and hack you about, and then stitch you together again, on an entirely new system.'
The Muse of the English Language: 'Oh. May I ask why?'
Wm. Archer: 'To please Mr Andrew Carnegie.'

EXHIB N.E.A.C. Winter 1911; L.G. 1913 and 1952
REPRO *Fifty Caricatures*, 1913
OWNER G. H. Elliot

33★ A Loathsome Proposal 1911

An almost exact replica of 32, identically dated and captioned, but with infinitesimal differences.

OWNER Lilly Library

34 Mr Max Beerbohm asking Mr William Archer whether he knows Brompton's Specific 1922

For Helen [Granville-Barker] from Max. Rapallo, 1922.
A very large W. A. looks down at a very small Max. Brompton's Specific was a cough medicine.

OWNER C. A. W. Beaumont

35★ W. A. and G. B. S., as in '95 or so 1931

For F. W.
W. A. very correctly dressed, and Bernard Shaw in his Jaeger knickerbocker suit.

OWNER Max Reinhardt

36★ [Untitled n.d.]

A tripartite drawing, the head (Archer's) by Max, the upper torso (female) by C. Ferrier, the legs (a female ballet-dancer's, sitting cross-legged) by Charles Conder. Each section signed by its artist. See also 1662.

OWNER Mrs Eva Reichmann

THE NINTH DUKE OF ARGYLL
See Lord Lorne

MATTHEW ARNOLD
1822–88 Poet

37★ Mr Matthew Arnold. To him, Miss Mary Augusta, his niece [later Mrs Humphry Ward]: 'Why, Uncle Matthew, oh why, will you not be always wholly serious?' [1904]

EXHIB Carfax 1904; L.G. 1957
REPRO *The Poets' Corner*, 1904 and 1943
OWNER The Earl of Drogheda

38★ [Untitled 1946]

M. A. without whiskers, illustrating a letter from Max.

REPRO Listener, 19 Sep 1946

OSCAR ASCHE
1872–1936 Actor-manager
See 377

THE FIRST LORD ASHBOURNE
1837–1913 Lord Chancellor of Ireland

39 [Lord Ashbourne 1901]

EXHIB Carfax 1901

40 [Lord Ashbourne]

EXHIB L.G. 1911

THE FIRST LORD ASHBY ST LEDGERS
See Ivor Guest

HERBERT HENRY ASQUITH
1852–1928 Prime Minister
See also 439, 614-16, 799, 982, 1443, 1591, 2031

41 [Mr Asquith (Jowett's Delight) 1901]

[H. H. A. (loquitur): 'Well, but look at Cicero! Didn't he save the State? And wasn't *he* at the Bar too?']

EXHIB Carfax 1901

42★ 'Porro Unum Est Necessarium' [But One Thing is Needful. *St Luke*, X, 42] 1908

Mr Asquith, having kissed hands on his appointment, sets to work, with characteristic industry and determination, to acquire personal magnetism.

H. H. A. is connected at nine points with a galvanic

battery and various electrical apparatus. On the wall are portraits of Gladstone, Palmerston, Campbell-Bannerman and Fox, all emitting rays.

EXHIB Carfax 1908
REPRO **Plate 13**
OWNER Mrs Marie Strang

43★ [The Treasury Bench (while the Secretary for War still was on it) Unsigned 1911]

Black monochrome on grey paper, highlights picked out in white: the only known Max drawing so executed. The figures, facing right, are from left to right: Lloyd George, Asquith, Churchill, Haldane, L. V. Harcourt, Birrell and Burns. Haldane, the Secretary of State for War, was made a Viscount in Apr 1911.

EXHIB L.G. 1911, where titled as above
REPRO **Plate 11**
OWNER Lord Conesford

44★ [The Treasury Bench (while the Secretary for War still was on it) 1911]

Almost identical with 43 (perhaps a sketch for it), but executed in pencil and wash, with the figures facing left.

REPRO **Plate 12**
OWNER Jeremy Thorpe

45★ The Parliament Bill 1911

The Tory Party: 'Mr Asquith, you're a traitor!'

H. H. A., arm-in-arm with John Bull and King George V, is abused by an elderly Tory.

EXHIB L.G. 1913 (not catalogued but exhibited) and 1952
REPRO *Daily Sketch*, 11 Apr 1913
OWNER J. E. MacColl

46★ Mr Asquith in Office 1913

'Come one, come all, this rock shall fly
From its firm base as soon as I.'
[Scott: *The Lady of the Lake*]

H. H. A., imperturbably smoking a cigar with a copy of 'Payne on Statics' at his feet, is ringed by a shackled peer, a German soldier, a militant worker, a suffragette and Sir Edward Carson.

EXHIB L.G. 1913
REPRO *Fifty Caricatures*, 1913
OWNER Lady Barlow

47★ [Manners] 1913

Mr Bonar Law (drawing attention to Mr George Robey): 'Now, *he* really *is* vulgar.'
Mr Asquith: 'I conceive, sir, that he could plead justificatory tradition.'

EXHIB L.G. 1945 and 1957
REPRO *A Survey*, 1921, where titled as above

48 **[Untitled]** 1916
Filled through and through with British phlegm
    (Than which no phlegm is phlegmier)
He seems quite likely to be sem-
    piternally our Premier.
EXHIB L.G. 1957
OWNER Savile Club

49★ **Ex Forti Dulcedo [Out of the Strong Sweetness.** *Judges*, **XIV, 14] Mr Asquith** 1920
EXHIB L.G. 1952 and 1957
OWNER Dudley Sommer

50★ **A Belated Reader of Mrs Asquith's Memoirs**
1920
'H'm! – Appears to have a very facile pen.'
Margot Asquith's 'Autobiography', 1920, caused a sensation with its alleged indiscretions and lack of reticence. See also 138.
EXHIB L.G. 1921
REPRO *A Survey*, 1921

51★ **The Old and the Young Self, in Balliol** 1924
Old Self: 'Oh, the Craven? Well, that is no ignoble prize, and I hope you will win it. But you remember what Cicero said (in a letter to Atticus, I think): "In studiis, sicut in aliis rebus, aurea quaedam mediocritas tenenda est." [We should adhere, in our studies, as in all other matters, to a certain golden mean.] If I were you, I would go down into the quadrangle and invite three friends to come and play a rubber of – what is that old-world game

which is so much in favour among the young men of your day? Whist, yes, to be sure.'
EXHIB L.G. 1925
REPRO *Observations*, 1925
OWNER National Liberal Club

MARGOT ASQUITH
1864–1945   Wife of above
See 50, 138

ALFRED AUSTIN
1835–1913   Poet Laureate
See also 1875

52★ **[Untitled** 1900]
A. A. stands on a big drum, holding two drumsticks. Beside him stands Kipling with a lyre.
EXHIB Achenbach 1964
REPRO *World*, Christmas No, 1900
OWNER U.C.L.A. (Clark)

SIR HORACE AVORY
1851–1935   Judge

53 **[Mr Justice Avory** 1931]
EXHIB L.G. 1952, where dated as above

ALLAN AYNESWORTH
1864–1959   Actor
See 377

B

FRANCIS BACON
1561–1626   Philosopher and statesman
See 1472

DOROTHEA BAIRD
1873–1933   Actress

54 **[Dorothea Baird as Trilby]**
In 1895 D. B. created the part in the dramatisation of George du Maurier's novel.
EXHIB L.G. 1957

STANLEY BALDWIN
1867–1947   Prime Minister
See also 439

55★ **The Old and the Young Self** 1924
Young Self: 'Prime Minister? *You*? Good Lord!!'
EXHIB L.G. 1925
REPRO *Observations*, 1925
OWNER Athenaeum Club

56★ **Back at Chequers** 1924
'Vision! – that's what's needed in these days: vision! I must try and see if I can't – well, *see* something.'

BALDWIN (continued)

EXHIB L.G. 1925
REPRO *Observations*, 1925
OWNER James Stern

57★ **'Vision'** 1925

Mr Baldwin 'sees' something – in itself a perfectly
lovely thing . . .

*In the clouds a saintly young man haloed 'Capital' offers a
bag of money to a saintly young man haloed 'Labour', who
refuses it.*

EXHIB L.G. 1925
REPRO *Observations*, 1925

ARTHUR JAMES BALFOUR
1848–1930   Prime Minister
See also 279, 335, 439, 612, 614, 615, 1443, 1615

58★ **[Untitled Unsigned** 1894]

*Full-length profile, single-line neck, very tall hat, umbrella
under arm.*

REPRO *Pall Mall Budget*, 5 Jul 1894

59★ **[Untitled]** 1894

*Very thin, single-line neck, eyeglasses on long cord, very
tall hat.*

REPRO *Pick-Me-Up*, 16 Mar 1895

60★ **Mr Arthur Balfour** [c. 1896]

*Very thin, wearing a very tall hat and carrying a dispatch
box.*

REPRO *Twenty-Five Gentlemen*, 1896; *Max's Nineties*, 1958
OWNER Godfrey Pilkington

61★ **[Untitled** 1900]

I *beg* your pardon: but *could* you tell me the way to
Downing Street?

*A. J. B. addresses a truculent-looking workman in the
street.*

EXHIB Achenbach 1964
REPRO *World*, Christmas No, 1900
OWNER U.C.L.A. (Clark)

61A★ **[Untitled** n.d.]

I *beg* your pardon. But can you tell me what that large
building is?

*He is asking a policeman and pointing to the Houses of
Parliament.*

OWNER Piccadilly Gallery

62 **[Mr Arthur Balfour, leading the House of
Commons** 1901]

EXHIB Carfax 1901

63★ **[Untitled** 1903]

'When we find that we have a Leader like that, our
hearts beat more quickly' (Mr George Wyndham, at
Manchester)

A. J. B. is holding a golf club in a limp hand.

REPRO *John Bull*, 15 Apr 1903

64★ **Mr Arthur Balfour** [1903]

*Almost identical with 63, but the limp hand is different and
holds nothing.*

REPRO *John Bull*, 1 Oct 1903, where captioned 'The
Premier at the Sheffield Conference'

65★ **[Untitled** 1905]

*Three-quarter-length profile facing left, limp hand extended
in front of chest. On 25 Dec 1905 Max wrote to his future
wife Florence: 'I am furious today because two drawings which I had lent to* Pearson's Magazine *for
reproduction . . . have come back battered and
scrawled over.' They were this one and 1252, and it is
possible that Max destroyed this one.*

REPRO *Pearson's Magazine*, Feb 1906

66★ **Mr Arthur Balfour wishing he 'had been born
in a simpler age'** 1907

EXHIB Carfax 1907
REPRO *A Book of Caricatures*, 1907
OWNER Robert H. Taylor

67★ **Mr Balfour** 1909

Profile, hatless, leaning back, left hand holding lapel.

EXHIB L.G. 1945 (Guedalla)
OWNER Ashmolean Museum, Oxford

68★ **[Untitled** ?1909]

*A. J. B. in a sylvan setting, on which Max copied out, al-
most verbatim, his 'Words for a Picture' called 'Harlequin',
first published in the 'Saturday Review' on 16 Apr 1898
and reprinted in 'Yet Again', 1909. On 31 Mar 1952
Max wrote to Oliver Brown of the Leicester Galleries:
This is a mystery to me. The writing occurs in one of
my books. It was a description of that Harlequin sign-
board that hangs in the Villino. What kind of rele-
vance it had at some moment to Arthur Balfour I
cannot remember or imagine.*

*The drawing is similar to others done around 1909, when
Max reprinted 'Harlequin'.*

EXHIB Cincinnati 1965
OWNER Lilly Library

69★ **Turning Away Wrath** 1910

Mr Arthur Balfour (to militant Tariff Reformer):
'But, my dear sir, when, where, have I said anything that could be twisted to imply that I – er –
don't like you immensely?'

T. R. may be intended for Sir Alfred Mond.
EXHIB L.G. 1911
REPRO *Tatler*, 26 Apr 1911
OWNER Lord Melchett

70★ Mr Arthur Balfour piping to the Provinces

A. J. B. speaking, between two local dignitaries.
EXHIB L.G. 1911
REPRO *Daily Mail*, 22 Apr 1911

71★ A Solution 1911

Mr Arthur Balfour: '. . . And so – though of course it is quite possible that you are none of you at all restive really – I have prevailed on dear Gerald to return to public life and lead you in my stead.'

Against a background of the Houses of Parliament A. J. B., in country clothes, presents his brother (a former President of the Board of Trade) to his Conservative colleagues, Lord Hugh Cecil, George Wyndham, Edward Carson, F. E. Smith, Austen Chamberlain, Henry Chaplin and Walter Long. After the split caused by the Parliament Bill, and amid cries of Balfour Must Go, A. J. B. resigned the leadership of the Conservative Party in Nov 1911.
EXHIB L.G. 1952
REPRO D'Offay Couper catalogue, Oct 1968
OWNER Piccadilly Gallery

72★ Mr Balfour 1912

Small flat hat, pince-nez, hands holding lapels.
REPRO *Bystander*, 8 May 1912
OWNER Merton College, Oxford

73★ Amurath and Amurazzle 1912

Mr Balfour: 'What virtuosity! How sure, how firm a touch! What verve! What brio! *What an instrument!*'

A. J. B., a violin under his arm, watches Bonar Law, who has succeeded him as Conservative leader, beating a big drum.
EXHIB L.G. 1913
REPRO *Fifty Caricatures*, 1913

74★ Mr Arthur Balfour 1912

For Viola [Tree] and Alan [Parsons] July 1912.

Almost identical with the final figure in 75.
OWNER David Tree Parsons

75★ Mr Balfour – a Frieze [c. 1912]

Five full-length drawings of A. J. B. leaning further and further back until his top hat falls off.
EXHIB L.G. 1913
REPRO *Fifty Caricatures*, 1913
OWNER L. G. Duke

76★ Mr Arthur Balfour 1920

Standing in front of fireplace, holding small book.
OWNER Miss Kaye Webb

77★ 'Enfin Seuls!' 1920

In a world comparatively at peace now, Mr Balfour tackles Benedetto Croce.
EXHIB L.G. May 1921
REPRO *A Survey*, 1921
OWNER National Gallery of Victoria, Melbourne

78★ The Old and the Young Self [Unsigned n.d.]

Young Self (faintly): 'Who are you? You look rather like Uncle Salisbury, shaved. And what is that curious thing you're holding? [a tennis racket] And won't you catch cold, with so little on? But don't answer: I don't really care. And don't let me talk: I don't fancy I've long to live; and I want to devote the time to thinking – not that I suppose my thoughts to be of much value, but – oh, do, please, go away.'
EXHIB L.G. 1925
REPRO *Observations*, 1925
OWNER Lord Cottesloe

79★ Quoting from one of his Gifford Lectures [n.d.]

Lord Balfour (whose turn it is to play [at Bridge]): 'If calculable probability be indeed common sense reduced to calculation, intuitive probability lies deeper. It supports common sense, and it supplies the ultimate ground – be it secure or insecure – of' etcetera, etcetera.
EXHIB L.G. 1925
REPRO *Observations*, 1925
OWNER Armand G. Erpf

80 Arthur Balfour [c. 1945]

One full-length drawing, one head and shoulders, both looking up.
OWNER Oliver R. W. W. Lodge

81★ [Untitled Unsigned 1951]

Pencil sketch, full-length profile facing left. Dated on back by Elisabeth Jungmann.
OWNER Sir Rupert Hart-Davis

GERALD BALFOUR
1853–1945   Conservative Politician
See 71

GEORGE BANCROFT
1868–1956   Barrister and playwright
See 85

SQUIRE BANCROFT
1841–1926 Actor-manager
See also 982

82★ [Untitled 1895]

In a box at the theatre.

REPRO *Pick-Me-Up*, 23 Mar 1895; *Max's Nineties*, 1958

83★ Sir Squire Bancroft [1903]

Profile in tall hat, bending to lean on small cane.

REPRO *John Bull*, 10 Sep 1903
OWNER University of Texas

**84★ A Solemn Scene in the Garrick Club. 1.30.
November 28, 1919**

What *was* the subject of that intensely animated
monologue? What – oh what? I dimly conjecture –
perhaps I am wrong – and yet – I seem to hear words
that were unheard at the time . . . [S. B. to Gerald du
Maurier:] 'My dear boy, I'm just off to Folkestone to
join her Ladyship, but – you remember the subject
of our conversation last night. I've only five or ten
minutes to spare, but I do wish most earnestly to
impress on you once more: Hampstead, you know,
my dear boy, yes, haw, delightful spot, rural, salu-
brious, filled with memories of your gifted father,
but – *but* – BUT your position, your leading position
in our great profession – how about *that*? Doesn't it
suggest, doesn't it *demand* for you the lease of a house
in – not necessarily in Berkeley Square, no – but
somewhere not utterly remote from the home of
our Sovereign? I do feel, more than ever in these
days when the very foundations of society are – er –
threatened, that we of the theatrical profession should
do what in us lies to' etc. etc.

For Alfred [Sutro] from Max.

REPRO Alfred Sutro, *Celebrities and Simple Souls*, 1933

**85★ Mr Bancroft on a visit to Mr George Bancroft,
at Oxford, in the Summer Term of 1891** 1926

EXHIB L.G. 1928 and 1957
REPRO George Bancroft, *Stage and Bar*, 1939 (on dust cover)
OWNER Judge Ifor Lloyd

86★ Sir Squire Bancroft [n.d.]

Full-length profile, wearing tall hat and frock-coat.

OWNER Victoria & Albert Museum

JOHN BARBIROLLI
1899–1970 Conductor

87★ [Untitled Unsigned n.d.]

OWNER Benjamin Sonnenberg

THE HON. MAURICE BARING
1874–1946 Writer
See also 612, 616

**88★ Mr Maurice Baring, testing carefully the
Russian sense of humour** 1908

*M. B. in fur coat and hat is questioning a glum peasant in
deep snow.* On 21 May 1921 Max wrote to M.B.: 'One of
the drawings I took over from here [Rapallo] to
England was called "Experts in the Mentality of the
Moujik". It represented you and Hugh Walpole and
Stephen Graham – all avoiding the subject of the
Moujik. But I had to lay the drawing aside; for H. W.
and S. G. were both away from London, and I
hadn't seen either of them for some years, and had
heard that they had *altered their appearances* a good deal
in the meantime; and a man who has to displease must
please be up-to-date.'

EXHIB Carfax 1908
REPRO **Plate 40**
OWNER Miss Elizabeth Williamson

89★ Mr Maurice Baring, telling a fairy story 1911

*M. B. is surrounded by eight ecstatic young women, saying
collectively:* 'Oh, my dear, isn't he RATHER illustrious?', 'Oh BEYOND price!', 'Did you ever hear
anything MUCH more divine?', 'Make him promise
NEVER to leave off!' *The title is written on the mount.*

EXHIB L.G. 1911
OWNER Miss Elizabeth Williamson

**90★ The Old and the Young Self – and 'The Puppet
Show of Memory'** 1924

Old Self: 'Now, my little dear, *you* mayn't remember
everything you've been and gone and done and
thought and seen today. But *I* do. And before you
go to sleepy-bye, I'll read it to you.'

*M.B.'s autobiography, 'The Puppet Show of Memory',
was published in 1922.*

EXHIB L.G. 1925; Achenbach 1964
REPRO *Observations*, 1925
OWNER Mr & Mrs Joseph M. Bransten

HARLEY GRANVILLE BARKER
1877–1946 Actor, playwright and producer
See also 29, 30, 181, 769, 2000–4

91 [Mr Granville Barker 1907]

*In a newspaper review of the exhibition, H. G. B. is
described as 'standing at his bookshelves'.*

EXHIB L.G. 1907

92★ [Untitled Unsigned ?1907]

A half-length drawing, with bookshelves suggested beyond. Possibly the same as 91, or a sketch for it.

EXHIB Achenbach 1964
OWNER U.C.L.A. (Clark)

93★ Ex Libris Granville Barker [?1907]

Max's bookplate for H. G. B., showing him on a library ladder, greeting a star over a range of bookshelves.

94★ H. G. B. 1923

Three-quarter-length profile facing left, hands in pockets.

EXHIB L.G. 1951
REPRO W. Bridges Adams, *The Lost Leader*, 1954
OWNER Garrick Club

95★ The British Drama (that eternal invalid) 1923

Dr Granville-Barker: 'And how are we today? . . . Yes, yes. The old complaint. Cerebral anaemia. And complicated by acute cinematitis . . . Municipal pillules are the only hope.'
[St John Ervine:] 'Let's give her a strong tonic every Sunday morning.'
[Arnold Bennett:] 'Hammersmith air's all *she* needs.'
[Lord Howard de Walden:] 'Get some very rich man to endow her.'
[Bernard Shaw:] 'Try Shaw's cathartics!'
[Henry Arthur Jones:] 'Inject red corpuscles!'
[A. B. Walkley:] 'Tue la!'
[Gordon Craig:] 'Give her a Mask!'
[William Archer:] 'I don't think there's much wrong with her!'
[John Masefield:] 'I think Craig might save her.'
[George Moore:] 'I was once her lover.'
H. G. B. is taking the patient's pulse. The others are small figures in the background.

EXHIB L.G. 1923; Achenbach 1964
REPRO *Things New and Old*, 1923
OWNER U.C.L.A. (Clark)

JAMES STRACHEY BARNES
1890–1955 Eccentric Italianate Englishman

96★ A kindly though aquiline surveyor – Mr James Barnes 1933

REPRO James Strachey Barnes, *Half a Life*, 1933
OWNER Signora Buona Barnes-Guidotti

WILSON BARRETT
1846–1904 Actor and writer
See also 493, 494

97★ [Mr Wilson Barrett as Marcus Superbus 1896]

In his own play 'The Sign of the Cross', first produced in London Jan 1896.

REPRO *Saturday Review*, Christmas No, 1896, where captioned as above; *Max's Nineties*, 1958
OWNER Lilly Library

98★ Mr Wilson Barrett [1900]

Full-length, head turned to right, enormous neck.

REPRO *Idler*, Sep 1900

99 Mr Wilson Barrett [n.d.]

OWNER Joseph L. Mankiewicz

100 [In memory of the famous Wilson Barrett. What would he have made of Tchekov? 1926]

EXHIB L.G. 1928, where dated as above

JAMES MATTHEW BARRIE
1860–1937 Novelist and dramatist
See also 679, 748, 769

101★ [Titled as below] 1908

Mr J. M. Barrie in a nursery – telling a story about a little boy who wished – oh, how he did wish! – to be a mother; and how the fairies sent the stork to him with a baby; and how he mothered it, and his mother grandmothered it; with many other matters of a kind to make adults cry and, crying, smile through their tears.

J. M. B. in a high chair is surrounded by five sobbing adults and four yawning or scowling children. The legend is written on the mount.

EXHIB Carfax 1908
REPRO **Plate 34**
OWNER Haro Hodson

102★ Mr J. M. Barrie 1912

J. M. B. holds an enormous pipe, which stands on the floor and emits clouds of smoke.

EXHIB L.G. 1945 (Guedalla) and 1957
REPRO *Caricatures by Max*, 1958
OWNER Ashmolean Museum, Oxford

103★ [Untitled n.d.]

Shows J. M. B. in youth, smoking a cigar.

OWNER Lilly Library

MARJORIE BATTINE
See 1427, 1624

AUBREY BEARDSLEY
1872–98   Artist
See also 708, 1307, 1650

104★ **[Untitled** 1894]
Full length, three-quarter face, hair over eyes, arms extended and drooping.
REPRO   *Pall Mall Budget*, 7 Jun 1894
OWNER   Victoria & Albert Museum

105★ **Aubrey Beardsley** [1894]
Full length, three-quarter face, hands by sides.
REPRO   R. A. Walker, *A Beardsley Miscellany*, 1949, where dated as above, presumably by Max
OWNER   Mrs N. R. H. Owen

106★ **[Untitled Unsigned** c. 1894]
Full length, head in profile, elegantly dressed, holding sheet of paper.
REPRO   *The Uncollected Work of Aubrey Beardsley*, 1925; *Caricatures by Max*, 1958
OWNER   Ashmolean Museum, Oxford

107★ **Aubrey Beardsley** [1896]
Full length, leading a toy dog on a string
REPRO   *Savoy*, Apr 1896; *Twenty-Five Gentlemen*, 1896; *Max's Nineties*, 1958

108★ **Mr Aubrey Beardsley** [1896]
Sitting on a yellow and orange curtained divan. Max sent this drawing to Herbert S. Stone & Co. in 1896 for publication in the 'Chap-Book' (Chicago), but it was not used there.
REPRO   **Plate 64**
OWNER   Newberry Library, Chicago

109★ **Aubrey** '96
Full length, three-quarter face, hands by sides. A rough sketch on a torn fragment of paper.
OWNER   Jay Hall

110★ **[Untitled** n.d.]
Full length, three-quarter face, standing on stage or table, hands extended and drooping.
OWNER   Princeton University Library

111 **[Aubrey Beardsley]**
EXHIB   L.G. 1945 (Guedalla)

112★ **Aubrey as I remember him** [n.d.]
Full-length profile, facing left, hand extended. Clearly a very late drawing.
EXHIB   L.G. 1952
OWNER   Lilly Library

THE SEVENTH EARL BEAUCHAMP
1872–1938   Liberal Politician
See also 612, 1529

113★ **Lord Beauchamp** 1909
REPRO   *English Review*, Oct 1909

114★ **Liberalism in its more strictly ornamental aspects** 1913
Shows Lord B with Lords Chesterfield, Ashby St Ledgers, Craven, and Spencer (with eye-holes in his collar, as in 1580).
EXHIB   L.G. 1913

L. A. G. BECKER
Charterhouse master
See 664, 664A

ERNEST BECKETT
See Lord Grimthorpe

THE HON. GERVASE BECKETT
1866–1937   Banker and M.P.

115 **Hon. Gervase Beckett** 1911
EXHIB   L.G. 1911
OWNER   Sir Martyn Beckett Bart

JULIUS BEERBOHM
1854–1906   Traveller and writer. Max's half-brother

116 **[Untitled** n.d.]
OWNER   Mrs Olivia Wigram

117★ **Mr Julius Beerbohm** [n.d.]
EXHIB   L.G. 1952
REPRO   **Plate 76**
OWNER   Piccadilly Gallery

118 **In Memory of my brother Julius** 1926
OWNER   The Marchioness of Bath

MAX BEERBOHM
1872–1956   Caricaturist and writer
See Self-Caricatures (1399–1467)

HAROLD BEGBIE
1871–1929   Author

119★ **Almost like Simony. Mr Harold Begbie loth to receive, even from Sir William Robertson Nicoll, payment for such work as his** 1913
EXHIB   L.G. 1913 and 1957
REPRO   *Fifty Caricatures*, 1913
OWNER Dr A. Herxheimer

CLIVE BELL
1881–1964   Art critic
See 560

HILAIRE BELLOC
1870–1953   Poet and writer
See also 144, 1599, 1605

120★ **Mr Hilaire Belloc** [c. 1906]
Sitting on the floor, arms extended.
EXHIB   L.G. 1928, where dated as above
OWNER Yale University Library

121★ **Mr Hilaire Belloc, striving to win Mr Gilbert Chesterton over from the errors of Geneva** 1907
EXHIB   Carfax 1907
REPRO   *A Book of Caricatures*, 1907

122★ **Mr Belloc's visit to the Vatican** 1920
The Pope [Benedict XV]: 'On m'a dit, mon fils, que vous êtes prophète.'
Mr Belloc: 'Je le suis, Votre Sainteté. J'ai d'ailleurs le don de faire de très jolis diagrammes. En voilà un où je démontre qu'en Angleterre la conversion nationale s'accomplira bien certainement entre les mois de Mai et de Juillet, 1922.'
EXHIB   L.G. May 1921
REPRO   *A Survey*, 1921
OWNER Mrs Andrew Caldecott

123 [Mr Hilaire Belloc]
EXHIB   L.G. 1952

ALEXANDER, COUNT DE BENCKENDORFF
1849–1917   Russian Ambassador in London
from 1903
See also 1567, 1568

124★ **Count Benckendorff** 1907
EXHIB   Carfax 1907; L.G. 1957
REPRO   *A Book of Caricatures*, 1907
OWNER Lt-Col. C. J. G. Meade

125 [Count Benckendorff]
EXHIB   L.G. 1911

126 [Count de Benckendorff 1912]
EXHIB   L.G. 1928, where dated as above

127★ **Count Benckendorff** [Unsigned 1954]
A pencil sketch dated on back by Elisabeth Jungmann.
OWNER Mr and Mrs Ernest Mehew

ERNEST ALFRED BENDALL
1846–1924   Dramatic Critic and Examiner of Plays
See 181

POPE BENEDICT XV
1854–1922   Pope from 1914
See 122

MR BENJAMIN
Presumably a stockbroker

128★ **In Angel Court. Mr Benjamin – Mr Chaine – Mr Arthur Cohen** 1907
EXHIB   Carfax 1907
REPRO   *A Book of Caricatures*, 1907
OWNER B. P. Holt

129★ **Mr Benjamin** [n.d.]
OWNER Mrs Eva Reichmann

ARNOLD BENNETT
1867–1931   Novelist
See also 95, 612, 1443

130 [Mr Arnold Bennett – Personally conducted tours from the cradle, through Bursley, to the grave]
Described in the 'Daily News' of 22 Apr 1911 as having the cradle on the left, the smoking chimneys of Bursley rear-centre, and on the right a tombstone reading 'Hic Jacet Persona Bennettiana, Aged 97, or thereabouts.'
EXHIB   L.G. 1911

131★ [Untitled Unsigned 1912]
Full length, three-quarter face, walking with stick.
REPRO   *Bystander*, 5 Jun 1912

132★ **A Milestone** 1913
Hilda Lessways (to the author of her being): 'Now

then, Mister Bennett, how much longer d'you mean to keep me and Clayhanger standing about here? I never heard of such goings on.'

The second volume of A. B.'s Clayhanger trilogy, H'ilda Lessways', appeared in 1911; the third, 'These Twain', not till 1916. Meanwhile A. B., in collaboration with Edward Knoblock, had scored a great theatrical success with 'Milestones', 1912.

EXHIB L.G. 1913
REPRO *Fifty Caricatures*, 1913
OWNER Robert H. Taylor

133* War-Experts discussing Mr Kennington's prophecy 1915

A. B. and H. G. Wells

OWNER Sir John Rothenstein

134* Mr H. G. Wells 'fraternally' urging Mr Arnold Bennett to try too 1922

[A. B.:] 'Parliament, eh? Well, get 'em to raise the screw to forty thou', and perhaps I'll think of it.'

A. B.'s words are typewritten in a bubble. H. G. W. unsuccessfully stood as Labour Candidate for London University in the General Election of Nov 1922.

EXHIB L.G. 1923 and 1945 (Guedalla)
REPRO *Things New and Old*, 1923; *Caricatures by Max*, 1958
OWNER Ashmolean Museum, Oxford

135* The Old and the Young Self 1924

Old Self: 'All gone according to plan, you see.'
Young Self: '*My* plan, you know.'

EXHIB L.G. 1925
REPRO *Observations*, 1925
OWNER University of Texas

136* Mr Arnold Bennett [n.d.]

Full length, with three sketches of A. B.'s head in margin.

EXHIB L.G. 1945 (Guedalla)
OWNER Ashmolean Museum, Oxford

A. C. BENSON
1862–1925   Writer, schoolmaster and Cambridge don

137 [Mr Arthur Christopher Benson vowing eternal fidelity to the obvious 1908]

EXHIB Carfax 1908

E. F. BENSON
1867–1940   Novelist

138 [Mr E. F. Benson pointing out to Mrs Asquith how much better it would have been to go on leaving it all to *him* c. 1921]

['Stat, stat Dodonia quercus'] [The oak of Dodona stands firm]

E. F. B. is supposed to have based the heroine of his 'Dodo' (1893) on Mrs Asquith, whose autobiography appeared in 1920. See also 50.

EXHIB L.G. May 1921

E. W. BENSON
1829–96   Archbishop of Canterbury
See 812

COUNT LEOPOLD VON BERCHTOLD
1863–1942   Austrian statesman

139* A survivor of the Great War – Count Berchtold 1926

EXHIB L.G. 1928
OWNER George Sassoon

LORD CHARLES BERESFORD
1846–1919   Admiral and M.P.

140* Lord Charles Beresford [1900]

REPRO *World*, Christmas Supplement, 1900
OWNER Sold at Sotheby's 22 Apr 1970

141* Lord Charles Beresford balancing personal grievances with national despairs, and so remaining breezy 1913

EXHIB L.G. 1913 and 1945 (Guedalla)
REPRO *Fifty Caricatures*, 1913
OWNER Ashmolean Museum, Oxford

THE FOURTEENTH LORD BERNERS
1883–1950   Composer and writer

142* Lord Berners, making more sweetness than violence 1923

EXHIB L.G. 1923
REPRO *Things New and Old*, 1923
OWNER Robert Heber-Percy

SARAH BERNHARDT
1844–1923   French actress
See 1291

BARON MARSCHALL VON BIEBERSTEIN
1842–1912   German Ambassador in London 1912
See 640

LAURENCE BINYON
1869–1943   Poet
See also 144, 679, 748, 1266, 1267

143★ **Mr Laurence Binyon** [n.d.]

EXHIB   Achenbach 1964
OWNER   U.C.L.A. (Clark)

THE FIRST EARL OF BIRKENHEAD
See F. E. Smith

AUGUSTINE BIRRELL
1850–1933   Author and politician
See also 43, 44, 679, 799, 1766

144★ **Won't it be rather like 'Rep'?** March 1916
On 11 Apr 1916 A. B. presided over a Poets' Afternoon in Byron's old house, 139 Piccadilly, at which leading poets (including Belloc, Chesterton, de la Mare and W. H. Davies) read their own poems in aid of the Star and Garter Home for Disabled Servicemen. Max's drawing must have been occasioned by a preliminary announcement. The poets here are Yeats, Masefield, Sturge Moore, Binyon, Hewlett, Belloc, Seaman and Newbolt. 'Rep' was used at many schools, including Charterhouse, to mean the recitation in class of something learned by heart.

REPRO   **Plate 33**
OWNER   Sir Charles Forte

ALFRED BISHOP
1848–1928   Actor

145★ **Mr Bishop** [1895]

REPRO   *Pick-Me-Up*, 19 Jan 1895

JACQUES-EMILE BLANCHE
1862–1942   French painter

146★ **M. Jacques Blanche combating M. Maurice Maeterlinck's reluctance to be painted** [1907]

In the exhibition catalogue and the book Max added 'eagerly' before 'combating'.

EXHIB   Carfax 1907
REPRO   *A Book of Caricatures*, 1907
OWNER   Art Institute of Chicago

147★ **Monsieur Jacques Blanche** 1908

REPRO   Simona Pakenham, *Sixty Miles from England*, 1967
OWNER   Merton College, Oxford

148   [**Monsieur J. E. Blanche**]

EXHIB   L.G. 1911

149★ **To my friend Jacques Blanche, with homage and apologies** [n.d.]

REPRO   Jacques-Emile Blanche, *Portraits of a Lifetime*, 1937

150★ **Monsieur Jacques Blanche** [n.d.]
For Charles Conder affectionately

OWNER   Mrs Eva Reichmann

151★ [**Untitled** n.d.]
[Cutting from newspaper pasted on] M. Jacques Blanche, si sévère pour ses confrères, s'est toujours montré pour le plus fort des disciples et des amis de James Mac Neil Whistler d'une parfaite et fraternelle équité.

J. B. in top hat and tail-coat beats a big drum while shouting SICKERT through a megaphone. French bystanders comment: 'Et c'est ça qu'on appelle l'équité!'

OWNER   British Museum (Prints and Drawings)

RAYMOND BLATHWAYT
1855–1935   Journalist
See also 1027

152★ **Mr Raymond Blathwayt** [**Unsigned** c. 1903]

REPRO   *Cassell's Magazine*, Feb 1903

153★ **Mr Raymond Blathwayt** [n.d.]

OWNER   Piccadilly Gallery

ISIDORE BLOCH
Secretary of the Dieppe Casino

154★ **M. Bloch** [n.d.]

OWNER   Piccadilly Gallery

ANDREW BONAR LAW
See Law

BARON BONELLI

155 Baron Bonelli [n.d.]
OWNER Sold at Sotheby's 14 Dec 1960

TANCRED BORENIUS
1885–1948   Finnish art historian

156 [Dr Borenius 1922]
Known only from an L.G. note, where dated as above.

JAMES BOSWELL
1740–95   Biographer
See 831

HORATIO BOTTOMLEY
1860–1933   Journalist and financier

157 [Mr Horatio Bottomley]
EXHIB L.G. 1913

158★ [Titled as below] 1926
Mr Horatio Bottomley being assured by Mr E. S. P. Haynes that he (Mr Bottomley) 'belongs perhaps more to the eighteenth than to the nineteenth or the twentieth century', that he is 'not exactly introspective like Rousseau, or aesthetic like Ruskin, or contemplative like Herbert Spencer', but that 'his virtues and his failings have been on the grand scale,' and that 'whenever he dies his funeral will be attended by many humble and obscure persons who have rightly or wrongly' entrusted to him their hard-earned savings.
Dear E. S. P. Forgive me – or rather forgive my secretary. He, in writing out the inscription above for me, made an idiotic clerical error (and is under notice of dismissal). The last words – from *entrusted* to *savings* – should run thus:– 'regarded him as their champion against the tyranny of Church or State'. (See *Fritto Misto*, p.79.) Yours, Max.
For E. S. P.
All the words within quotation marks are from p. 79 of Haynes's 'Fritto Misto', 1926.
OWNER Mrs Eva Reichmann

MARCEL BOULESTIN
1871–1943   Writer and restaurateur

159★ M. Marcel Boulestin [1905]
REPRO *L'Hypocrite Sanctifié*, 1905, M. B.'s translation of Max's *The Happy Hypocrite*, and M. B.'s *Myself, My Two Countries*, 1936, where dated as above.

160★ 'You should have seen me in rustic mood – picking up flowers!' [n.d.]
OWNER Private (Yale)

ARTHUR BOURCHIER
1864–1924   Actor-manager
See also 377

161 [Mr Arthur Bourchier 1901]
EXHIB Carfax 1901

162★ Mr Arthur Bourchier [n.d.]
Full-length back view, in top hat and tails.
OWNER Mrs Eva Reichmann

163★ Mr Arthur Bourchier [n.d.]
Full-length profile, hatless, in breeches.
OWNER Mrs Eva Reichmann

CHARLES BOYD
1869–1919   Journalist and Secretary of Rhodes Trust
See also 614, 615

164★ Mr Charles Boyd receiving a Rhodes Scholar 1907
He is effusively welcoming a very black Negro in cap and gown, beneath a portrait of Cecil Rhodes.
EXHIB Carfax 1907
REPRO *A Book of Caricatures*, 1907

MAJOR-GENERAL J. P. BRABAZON
1843–1922   Soldier

165 [Colonel Brabazon 1901]
EXHIB Carfax 1901; L.G. 1952

166★ General Brabazon 1907
EXHIB   Carfax 1908
OWNER Lilly Library

167 [Sunday morning in the country – General Brabazon]
EXHIB L.G. 1911

168★ '... but never surrenders' [n.d.]
For Jack [Bohun] Lynch from Max.
Max wrote to Ralph Brown: The never-surrenderer is – or rather was – General Brabazon, a dashing cavalry-officer, famous from the 'seventies onwards, and adjudged to be the handsomest and the most resplen-

dently dressed man of his day. He wore a tuft on the chin in defiance of Army Regulations.

OWNER U.C.L.A. (Special Collections)

GEORG BRANDES
1847–1927   Danish literary critic
See 1500

FRANK BRANGWYN
1867–1956   Artist

169* **Mr Frank Brangwyn, taking a five-minutes well-earned rest** [n.d.]
He stands beside a ladder at the foot of one of the enormous murals for which he was famous.

EXHIB L.G. 1925
REPRO *Observations*, 1925
OWNER Mrs Alfred Bendiner

170* **[Untitled Unsigned** n.d.]
Early draft of 169, with Rough Sketch *in Max's hand on right.*

OWNER Piccadilly Gallery

ALBERT BRASSEUR
1862–1932   French actor

171* **Monsieur Brasseur** [n.d.]
For Reg [Turner] – reluctantly.

REPRO *A Book of Caricatures*, 1907, where, after 'Brasseur', Max added 'in "La Veine"' [by Alfred Capus, Paris 1901, London 1902]
OWNER Private (Yale)

ROBERT BRIDGES
1844–1930   Poet Laureate
See 616, 1511

THE HON. G. C. BRODRICK
1831–1903   Warden of Merton College, Oxford

172* **[The Warden of Merton   Unsigned** 1890]
Title and date in another hand, which added: 'Picked up in a Merton College Lecture Room after a Divinity Lecture – drawn by Max Beerbohm'.

REPRO **Plate 4**
OWNER Merton College, Oxford

172A* **The Merton Fancy Ball. The Warden as an Eton Boy [Signed with monogram** ?c. 1890]

OWNER Robert H. Taylor

173* **Design for an equestrian statue to be placed in the playing fields of Eton [Unsigned** ?c. 1891]

REPRO *Country Life*, 7 Apr 1966
OWNER Merton College, Oxford

173A* **Sequel to the Tranby Croft Case. Outbreak amongst Dons. A Junior Bursar tries 'La Poucette' [Unsigned** 1891]
The Warden is taking the bank at what must have been Max's idea of Baccarat. Two other dons are playing, a third acting as croupier and a fourth watching. They are speaking as follows. The Warden: 'I wish you'd put your stakes over the line. I'm bound to confess I did not see that'. One of the players: 'There's another tenner here Sir'. The spectator: 'This is too hot'. The Tranby Croft baccarat case, in which the Prince of Wales was called as a witness, was tried in June 1891. 'La Poussette' was a French form of sleight of hand, mentioned at the trial.

OWNER Robert H. Taylor

174 **The Warden of Merton 14 Jan 1892** [*Signed*] **H. M. Beerbohm**

OWNER Mrs Julian Vinogradoff

175* **['Merton'** 1895]
Shows the Warden at table.

REPRO *Octopus*, Oxford, 25 May 1895, where titled as above

176* **The Warden of Merton** [1896]
Full-length profile facing right. Hands extended behind him. At least three other caricatures of the Warden are in Mr Taylor's collection.

REPRO *Twenty-Five Gentlemen*, 1896
OWNER Robert H. Taylor

177 **[The Warden of Merton** 1901]
EXHIB Carfax 1901

178* **The Warden of Merton** [n.d.]
Very similar to 176.

REPRO *Farrago*, Oxford, Oct 1930
OWNER Kenneth Knowles

THE HON. ST JOHN BRODRICK
1856–1942   Secretary of State for War 1901–03

179* **Mr St John Brodrick** [1901]
In catalogue and magazine it is captioned 'Mr St John

Brodrick, playing at soldiers'. A wooden dummy inspecting an endless line of wooden soldiers.

EXHIB Carfax 1901
REPRO *Pall Mall Magazine*, Feb 1902

180★ **Broderick Dhu** [c. 1901]

In Highland costume, brandishing dirk and claymore on a steep hillside among the stars. Roderick Dhu was the Scottish bandit-hero of Scott's 'Lady of the Lake'.

OWNER Merton College, Oxford

CHARLES BROOKFIELD
1857–1913   Author and Examiner of Plays

181★ **In St James's Palace** 1912

Mr Brookfield (with whom is Mr Bendall) trying hard to fall under the spell of the Modern Drama.

On the wall hangs a picture of a wasp-waisted girl, inscribed 'Yours affectionately, the Drama of the Eighties'. The lay-figure of the Modern Drama wears sandals and a toga, on the hem of which are embroidered heads of Shaw, Barker, Galsworthy, Masefield, and Stanley Houghton.

EXHIB L.G. 1913 and 1952
REPRO *Fifty Caricatures*, 1913
OWNER Mr and Mrs Robin Fox

182★ **Mr Charles Brookfield** [n.d.]

EXHIB L.G. 1957
REPRO *Theatre World*, Nov 1957
OWNER Harold Matthews

183★ **Mr Charles Brookfield** [n.d.]

EXHIB Achenbach 1964
OWNER U.C.L.A. (Clark)

ERNEST BROWN
1852–1915   Co-proprietor of Leicester Galleries
See also 1152, 1438

184 **'A view of' the Leicester Galleries – coupled with an offer of many apologies from Max** [n.d.]
OWNER Nicholas Brown

FORD MADOX BROWN
1821–93   Pre-Raphaelite painter
See also 1276

185★ **Ford Madox Brown being patronised by Holman Hunt** 1916

EXHIB Grosvenor 1917; L.G. Sept 1921
REPRO *Rossetti and his Circle*, 1922
OWNER Tate Gallery

OSCAR BROWNING
1837–1923   Schoolmaster, Cambridge don and historian

185A★ **Mr Oscar Browning [Signed with monogram** n.d.]

Full-length profile facing left, cigar in hand. A rough drawing done at Oxford.

OWNER Robert H. Taylor

186★ **Mid-Term Tea at Mr Oscar Browning's** 1908

Besides O. B. himself and ten lay-figure undergraduates, there are present, all in full-dress uniform, nine of the crowned heads of Europe: Franz-Josef of Austria-Hungary, Gustav V of Sweden, Nicholas II of Russia, George I of Greece, Alfonso XIII of Spain, Abdul Hamid II of Turkey, Wilhelm II of Germany, Victor Emanuel III of Italy, and Leopold II of the Belgians.

EXHIB Carfax 1908; L.G. 1911, 1945 (Guedalla) and 1957
REPRO **Plate 24**
OWNER King's College, Cambridge

ROBERT BROWNING
1812–89   Poet
See also 595, 1273

187★ **Mr Robert Browning taking tea with the Browning Society** [c. 1904]

EXHIB Carfax 1904; L.G. 1945 (Guedalla) and 1957
REPRO *The Poets' Corner*, 1904 and 1943; *Caricatures by Max*, 1958
OWNER Ashmolean Museum, Oxford

188★ **[Untitled Unsigned** c. 1904]

Pencil sketch for 187.

OWNER Armstrong Browning Library, Waco, Texas

GEORGE (BEAU) BRUMMEL
1778–1840   Dandy

189★ **Mr Brummell, constricting his waist-belt, incurs the envious displeasure of the King** [n.d. *Signed* **Max Beerbohm** *in type*]

EXHIB L.G. 1945 (Guedalla)
REPRO T. A. Cook, *Eclipse and O'Kelly*, 1907
OWNER Robert H. Taylor

FRANCIS BULKELEY-JOHNSON

190 Mr Bulkeley-Johnson 1909
EXHIB N.E.A.C. Summer 1909
OWNER St James's Club

EDMUND BURKE
1729–97 Statesman and philosopher
See 1010

F. C. BURNAND
1836–1917 Writer and editor of *Punch*

191★ [Untitled Unsigned 1895]
REPRO *Pick-Me-Up*, 26 Jan 1895

192 [F. C. Burnand 1901]
EXHIB Carfax 1901

193 [Mr Burnand (Sir Frank Burnand) – an impression]
EXHIB L.G. 1945 (Guedalla)

EDWARD BURNE-JONES
1833–98 Painter
See 1072, 1268, 1276

THE FIRST LORD BURNHAM
1833–1916 Newspaper proprietor
See also 493, 494, 514, 515, 623, 1423, 1443

194★ Sir Edward Lawson [1901]
Full-length profile facing right, wearing frock coat and top hat.
EXHIB Carfax 1901
REPRO *Candid Friend*, 26 Oct 1901
OWNER Sir John Rothenstein

195★ The New Tantalus June 1902
Lo! Tantalus in his eternal thirst
Still reaching at the fruit he may not grasp
Sir E. L., clad only in a cache-sexe, reaches for three coronets dangling on the ends of branches above his head.
OWNER Private (Yale)

196★ The Baptism of Sir Edward (then Mr) Lawson [n.d.]
REPRO Stanley Weintraub, *Reggie*, 1965
OWNER Merton College, Oxford

196A★ [Untitled Unsigned n.d.]
Sir E. L. has swarmed up a cross labelled INRI and is clutching it with knees, hands and nose. At its foot lies a skull.
OWNER Robert H. Taylor

197★ [The 'Daily Telegraph'-ic Peer 1903]
In a box at the theatre.
REPRO *John Bull*, 9 Jul 1903, where captioned as above

198★ Are we as welcome as ever? 1911
Shows Lord B with four other wealthy Jews (Sir Ernest Cassel, Alfred and Leopold Rothschild and Arthur Sassoon) walking along a corridor in the palace to meet their new sovereign.
EXHIB L.G. 1911
REPRO *Fifty Caricatures*, 1913

199 [Lord Burnham]
EXHIB L.G. 1911

200 [Lord Burnham]
EXHIB L.G. 1913

201 A memory of Lord Burnham in his electric landaulette at Eton (Speech-day, 1909) Royal in all but birth [n.d.]
EXHIB L.G. 1928
OWNER The Hon. Hugh Lawson

202★ Lord Burnham [n.d.]
Full-length profile facing left, in evening dress, holding top hat in front of him.
EXHIB L.G. 1952
REPRO *Times Ed. Sup.*, 2 May, 1952; Stanley Weintraub, *Reggie*, 1965
OWNER Merton College, Oxford

203★ [Untitled n.d.]
Full-length profile facing left, hatless in evening dress with a bright red face.
OWNER Huon Mallalieu

204★ A Sense of Security [Unsigned n.d.]
Lord B and King Edward VII contemplate a pig in a sty.
[Lord B:] 'We'll have him at Breakfast tomorrow, Sir!'
[Pig:] 'I don't believe it.'
OWNER Kenneth Rose

JOHN BURNS
1858–1943 Labour politician
See also 43, 44, 386, 799

205★ 'You've jolly well *got* to be free!' [n.d.]

BURNS (continued)

J. B. militantly approaching a terrified worker, who has his back to a wall.

OWNER National Portrait Gallery

ROBERT BURNS
1759–96 Poet

206★ **Robert Burns, having set his hand to the plough, looks back at Highland Mary** [1904]

EXHIB Carfax 1904, L.G. 1957
REPRO *The Poets' Corner*, 1904 and 1943
OWNER Mrs Rachel Ward

THEODORE BYARD
1871–1931 Director of William Heinemann Ltd

207★ **[Untitled Unsigned]** 1923

Scene: An upper room in the Garrick Club.
Time: Late afternoon of July 6th 1923 (Thermometer 85 in the shade)
[Page-boy to T. B., asleep on sofa:] ' 'Ere! Are you Mr Byard? Well, there's a gent arahnd the corner as wants ter dror a droring of yer! Hup yer get!'

REPRO *Times Lit. Sup.*, 19 Oct. 1956
OWNER A. Dwye Evans

208★ **At 21 Bedford Street** 1923

Myself (to Mr Byard and Mr [C. S.] Evans): 'Oh Gentlemen, I know I'm not very gifted – but I *am* poor.'

Max, in patched and ragged clothes, offers a few pages of manuscript to his affluent publishers.

REPRO *Things New and Old*, 1923 (extra plate in limited edition); *N.Y. Times Book Review*, 4 Nov 1923
OWNER S. R. Hurst

THE SIXTH LORD BYRON
1788–1824 Poet
See also 1875

209★ **[Untitled** 1900]

REPRO *World*, Christmas No. 1900

210★ **Lord Byron shaking the dust of England from his shoes** [1904]

EXHIB Carfax 1904; N.Y. 1912; L.G. 1945 (Guedalla) and 1957
REPRO *The Poets' Corner*, 1904 and 1943
OWNER Freda, Countess of Listowel

211★ **Our Abbey** July 1924

Lord Byron (to the Dean of Westminster [Ryle]): 'Mr Dean, you're a man of sense and pluck: you've defied all England, just as *I* did; and you've saved me from the company of that damned old noodle, Mr Wordsworth.'

The Abbey's refusal to allow a memorial to B on the centenary of his death was rescinded in 1969.

EXHIB L.G. 1925 and 1945 (Guedalla)
REPRO *Observations*, 1925
OWNER Art Gallery of New South Wales, Sydney

INGRAM BYWATER
1840–1914 Professor of Greek

212★ **Mr Bywater** [Unsigned c. 1892]
OWNER Merton College, Oxford

213★ **Mr Bywater** [Unsigned c. 1892]
OWNER Ashmolean Museum, Oxford

C

THE FIFTH EARL CADOGAN
1840–1915 Lord-Lieutenant of Ireland

214 **[Lord Cadogan** 1901]
EXHIB Carfax 1901

JEAN CAFTANGIOGLU
d. 1929 Greek politician

215★ **Jean Caftangioglu** [n.d.]
OWNER Lysandros Caftanzoglu

HALL CAINE
1853–1931 Novelist
See also 386, 493, 494, 857, 858, 1268, 1277, 1423, 1443, 1563

216* Hall Caine [Unsigned 1898]
H. C. carrying sandwich board with his own name on it. This drawing was reproduced all over America and caused H. C. much pain
REPRO *Sketch, 28 Sept 1898*

217* [Untitled 1899]
Half-length of H. C. orating.
REPRO *Daily Mail, 16 Jan 1899*

218* Mr Hall Caine [1899]
REPRO *Idler, Dec 1899; Max's Nineties, 1958*

219* One before whom even Professor Munyon is as a crushed worm [1901]
M was a famous American quack and advertiser of patent medicines. His London manager was Dr Crippen and his office typist Miss Ethel le Neve.
EXHIB Carfax 1901
REPRO *Pall Mall Magazine, Feb 1902*

220* [Untitled 1903]
Full-length profile, expostulating.
REPRO *John Bull, 2 July 1903*
OWNER University of Texas

221* A Pulpiteer: Mr Hall Caine 1907
H. C. stands puzzled in an enormous top hat.
EXHIB Carfax 1907
REPRO *Daily Mirror, 20 Apr 1907*
OWNER Piccadilly Gallery

222* Triennial Negotiations between Mr Heinemann and Mr Hall Caine 1909
EXHIB N.E.A.C. Summer 1909; L.G. 1952 and 1957
REPRO *The Incomparable Max, 1962*
OWNER Messrs William Heinemann Ltd

223* [Untitled c. 1909]
H. C. stands in profile with hair so long that it sweeps forward and obscures his body. Max sent this drawing to Ford Madox Hueffer with an undated letter, in which he wrote: 'Here is Greeba's Lord – mantled in his mane – "clothed round with the world's desire, as with raiment."' It was clearly intended for the 'English Review', which F. M. H. edited from Dec 1908 to Dec 1909, but never appeared there.
EXHIB Grolier 1944
OWNER Harvard College Library

224* 'The Pen is mightier than the Sword.' Duel between Messrs Hall Caine and R. H. Sherard [n.d.]

H. C. (large) has the pen, Sherard (small) the sword.
OWNER Charterhouse School

225* The Manxman [n.d.]
H. C. running with three legs (cf. the Arms of the Isle of Man) against a background of stars.
EXHIB L.G. 1952
OWNER Princeton University Library

226* [Untitled Unsigned n.d.]
Rough sketch for 225, simpler and without stars.
OWNER Mrs Eva Reichmann

227* Mr Hall Caine [n.d.]
REPRO **Plate 35**
OWNER Robert Beloe

PAUL CAMBON
1843–1924 French Ambassador in London 1898–1921

228* M. Paul Cambon 1912
Full length, three-quarter face, standing to attention, wearing curved bowler hat and monocle and holding a stick.
EXHIB L.G. 1957
REPRO *Bystander, 3 Jul 1912*
OWNER Sir Anthony Hooper Bart

229* [Untitled Unsigned n.d.]
Very similar to 228, perhaps a rough sketch for it.
OWNER Roy Huss

230* 'When Labour Rules,' or, What M. Cambon frightfully foresees, and Why M. Cambon is leaving us December 1920
Secretary for Foreign Affairs (holding his first weekly reception): 'Glad to see you, MOOSOO! You'll find I'm pretty well up in all the main points already. Capital o' France: Paris, pronounced Paree. Republican form o' government, founded 1792. Principal exports: wines, silks and woollen goods. Battle o' Waterloo, 1814. The Great War, 1914 to 1918. Take a chair.'
The Labour Minister is a large pipe-smoking plebeian.
EXHIB L.G. May 1921
REPRO *A Survey, 1921*

231 'When Labour Rules,' or, What M. Cambon frightfully foresees, and Why M. Cambon is leaving us December 1920
Rough sketch for 230.
EXHIB Achenbach 1964
OWNER Achenbach Foundation, San Francisco

232* A Feverish Effort to Regain 'Touch'. 'When Labour Rules,' or, What M. Cambon *really*

foresaw, and why M. Cambon left us Boxing Day 1921

Secretary for Foreign Affairs (holding his first weekly reception): 'Comme moi, Monsieur l'Ambassadeur, vous apercevez, sans doute, que la haute politique, le Quai D'Orsay, la rue Downing, et même ce qu'on appelle "Labour", ne sont que d'illusions – et non pas des plus intéressantes. Asseyez-vous. Causons des idées charmantes de votre illustre compatriote, Henri Bergson.'

The Labour Minister is a slim, bearded intellectual. In a letter to the editor, published in the 'Manchester Guardian' on 21 Jan 1922, Max explained that this drawing was an answer to the paper's criticism of 230 in an article entitled 'Is Max Losing Touch? on 9 Dec 1921.

REPRO *Manchester Guardian*, 21 Jan 1922; David Ayerst, *Guardian, Biography of a Newspaper*, 1971

THE DUKE OF CAMBRIDGE
1819–1904   Soldier grandson of George III

233★ **H.R.H. The Duke of Cambridge** [1896]
REPRO *Twenty-Five Gentlemen*, 1896; *Max's Nineties*, 1958

234★ **The Ghost of the Duke of Cambridge** 1926
EXHIB   L.G. 1928
OWNER   Samuel Hessa

EMILE CAMMAERTS
1878–1953   Belgian poet
See 390

SIR GORDON CAMPBELL
1864–1953   Patron of the Red Cross
See 679

MRS PATRICK CAMPBELL
1865–1940   Actress
See 1502–5, 1507, 1508

THE REV. R. J. CAMPBELL
1867–1956   Pastor of the City Temple
See also 386, 1443

235★ **The Rev. R. J. Campbell, standing in no need of advertisement**

EXHIB   L.G. 1911
REPRO   *Daily News*, 22 Apr 1911
OWNER   Mrs Margaret Horrabin

SIR HENRY CAMPBELL-BANNERMAN
1836–1908   Prime Minister
See also 42, 439

236 **Sir Henry Campbell-Bannerman, leading the Opposition** [1901]
Neither for Kruger nor for his enemies.
Shows C.-B. precariously balanced on a barbed-wire fence.
EXHIB   Carfax 1901; L.G. 1945 (Guedalla)
OWNER   R. R. Feilden

237★ **[Untitled** c. 1902]
REPRO   *Artist*, Feb 1902
OWNER   Mark Birley

238 **[Sir Henry Campbell-Bannerman]**
EXHIB   L.G. 1928

239★ **Campbell-Bannerman** [n.d.]
C.-B. is shown in two halves, with his hyphen between. A catalogue-note says: 'at the time when he was placating both wings of the Liberal Party'.
EXHIB   L.G. 1952
REPRO   **Plate 9**
OWNER   Jeremy Thorpe

KING CARLOS I
1863–1908
See also 488

240★ **His Majesty the King of Portugal** [1903]
REPRO   *John Bull*, 3 Sep 1903
OWNER   University of Texas

THOMAS CARLYLE
1795–1881   Writer
See also 595

241★ **Blue China** 1916
Shows T. C. with Whistler.
EXHIB   Grosvenor 1917; L.G. Sept 1921
REPRO   *Rossetti and his Circle*, 1922; *The Poets' Corner*, 1943
OWNER   Tate Gallery

JOSEPH COMYNS CARR
1849–1916   Critic and playwright

242 Mr J. Comyns Carr [1901]
EXHIB Carfax 1901; L.G. 1957
OWNER Sold at Sotheby's 14 Dec 1960

243★ Jo Comyns Carr – a memory 1926
OWNER Sir Rupert Hart-Davis

LORD CARRINGTON
See Lord Lincolnshire

EDWARD CARSON
1854–1935 Lawyer and politician
See also 46, 71, 614, 615, 904, 952, 1423

244★ Mr Carson Q.C. M.P. [pre-1900]
A very thin tall figure, with match-thin arms and legs, head set on triangular neck at an angle of ninety degrees. Seated in morning clothes, with chin on knee. E. C. was knighted in 1900.
REPRO *Cassell's Magazine*, Feb 1903

245★ Mr Carson Q.C. M.P. [pre-1900]
Exactly the same head and figure as in 244, but standing, in evening dress.
EXHIB L.G. 1928, where dated 1926, but its title and close
       similarity to 244 make this unlikely
OWNER Sir John Rothenstein

246★ Sir Edward Carson [1900]
A similar figure, slightly less thin, holding a sheet of paper.
REPRO *World*, Christmas Supplement, 1900
OWNER Mrs David Karmel

247★ Sir Edward Carson 1913
In morning clothes, wearing a large sword.
REPRO *Fifty Caricatures*, 1913
OWNER National Portrait Gallery

248★ Unison 1920
John Bull: 'I wonder if you quite realise how utterly
  sick and tired of you I am.'
Sir Edward Carson: 'I wonder if you quite realise how
  utterly sick and tired I am of meself.'
EXHIB L. G. May 1921
REPRO *A Survey*, 1921
OWNER Sold at Sotheby's 19 Jul 1967

MURRAY CARSON
1865–1917 Actor and playwright

249★ Mr Murray Carson [c. 1898]

Full face, frowning, arms folded, high collar and check overcoat.
EXHIB L.G. 1928, where dated as above

250★ [Untitled ?1899]
Two drawings, back and front, of M. C. as Richelieu in Bulwer's play, which Max reviewed in the 'Saturday Review' on 24 Jun 1899.
OWNER Irving Drutman

251★ [Untitled n.d.]
Rough pencil sketch, known only from a photograph in Max's papers. Shows M. C. in profile, robed as for Richelieu but hatless.

252 [Mr Murray Carson 1901]
EXHIB Carfax 1901

253★ [Untitled n.d.]
Full-length profile, wearing top hat and big fur-collared coat. Known only from a photograph in Max's papers.

254★ [Untitled Unsigned n.d.]
Rough pen-and-ink sketch for 253.
OWNER U.C.L.A. (Clark)

SIR CHAUNCEY CARTWRIGHT
1853–1933 Diplomat

255 [Sir Chauncey Cartwright, en retraite]
Known only from an L.G. note.

ENRICO CARUSO
1874–1921 Italian tenor

256★ Signor Caruso, cynosure 1912
EXHIB L.G. 1913
REPRO *Fifty Caricatures*, 1913
OWNER Yale University Library

SIR ERNEST CASSEL
1852–1921 Financier
See also 198, 493, 494, 499, 679

257 [Sir Ernest Cassel 1908]
EXHIB Carfax 1908

VISCOUNT CASTLEREAGH
See Seventh Marquess of Londonderry

GUIDO CAVALCANTI

c. 1230–1300 Italian poet
See 1188

LORD HUGH CECIL

1869–1956 Conservative politician
See also 71

258★ A Perfervid Subtlist [1903]

REPRO *John Bull*, 6 Aug 1903

259★ Lord Hugh Cecil hurling at the Labour Party the last enchantments of the Middle Age 1910

A reference to Matthew Arnold's rhapsody on Oxford in the Preface to his 'Essays in Criticism', 1865.

EXHIB L.G. 1911 and 1957
OWNER I. R. Fleming Williams

260★ Cecils in Conclave [n.d.]

Lord H. C. with his brothers, Lord Robert Cecil and the fourth Marquess of Salisbury.

EXHIB L.G. 1913
REPRO *Fifty Caricatures*, 1913
OWNER The Marquess of Salisbury

261★ The Cecils cross over 1921

Lord H. C. and his brother Lord Robert are stepping to the right out of a picture frame, inside which a tiny Lloyd George is saying:
'Let me have about me men that are fat,
Sleek-headed men and such as sleep o'nights'
          [*Julius Caesar*, I, 2, slightly misquoted]
In Feb 1921 both brothers crossed over from L. G.'s Coalition Government to the Opposition.

EXHIB L.G. May 1921, 1945 (Guedalla) and 1952
REPRO *A Survey*, 1921; *Caricatures by Max*, 1958
OWNER Ashmolean Museum, Oxford

262 The Cecils Cross Over [Unsigned n.d.]

Pencil sketch for 261. The brothers stepping out to the left, Lloyd George silent.

OWNER The Marquess of Salisbury

263★ An Oxford memory: 1890: Lord Hugh Cecil and Mr H. B. Irving walking away from the Union together. (Deeply impressive to a freshman's heart.) 1926

EXHIB L.G. 1928
OWNER The Marquess of Salisbury

LORD ROBERT
(LATER VISCOUNT) CECIL

1864–1958 Conservative politician
See also 260-2

264★ Lord Cecil 1924

In public and in private life as admirable as all Cecils are apt to be.

EXHIB L.G. 1925
OWNER L. J. Cadbury

265★ Lord Cecil 1931

REPRO *Spectator* Supplement, 21 Feb 1931
OWNER *The Spectator*

THOMAS CHAINE

See also 128

266 [Mr Thomas Chaine 1901]

For some account of T. C. see S. N. Behrman, 'Conversation with Max', pp. 200-1.

EXHIB Carfax 1901

AUSTEN CHAMBERLAIN

1863–1937 Conservative politician
See also 71

267★ Deep but dubious impression made on Parisian statesmen by Mr Austen Chamberlain in Paris 1924

'Ce n'est pas une toilette d'homme d'Etat sérieux, voyons!'
'Il ressemble à un Gentleman du dix-huitième siècle.'
'Il fait croire aux Incroyables du dix-neuvième.'
'L'amant, sans doute, d'une Duchesse!'
'Un jeune homme qui devrait se ranger!'
'A bas ce frère de Boni de Castellane!'
A. C. is immaculate in top hat and frock-coat, the Frenchmen very scruffy.

EXHIB L.G. 1925, 1945 (Guedalla) and 1952
REPRO *Observations*, 1925; *Caricatures by Max*, 1958
OWNER Ashmolean Museum, Oxford

268 Mr Austen Chamberlain [n.d.]

EXHIB Achenbach 1964
OWNER Mr and Mrs William von Metz

269 [Mr Austen Chamberlain]

EXHIB L.G. 1957

JOSEPH CHAMBERLAIN

1836–1914 Radical politician
See also 442, 493, 494, 514, 515, 1563

270★ [Untitled Unsigned n.d.]

A page of schoolboy drawings. Head and shoulders of J. C. in centre, complete with eyeglass and orchid. Round the edge tiny vignettes illustrating: As he started in life; As mayor of Birmingham he entertained the Prince; The family affections are most perfect in the family; The two best-abused men in England – see how philosophically they bear it; Lord Randolph, tho' not always on speaking terms with Mr Chamberlain, is his greatest admirer; He is most proud of his social position.

At the bottom J. C. is haranguing Gladstone and others.

REPRO Collie Knox, *People of Quality*, 1947
OWNER Collie Knox

271★ **Joseph Chamberlain** [1896]
Full-length profile facing left, standing on pavement, left hand under tail of frock-coat.

REPRO *Twenty-Five Gentlemen*, 1896; *Max's Nineties*, 1958

272★ **[Untitled** 1898]
Full-length profile facing left. Enormous nose, tiny top hat, orchid in buttonhole.

REPRO *Daily Mail*, 2 Jul 1898
OWNER Victoria & Albert Museum

273★ **[Untitled** 1900]
J. C. on stage as nigger minstrel wearing sombrero.

REPRO *World*, Christmas No, 1900

274★ **Mr Joseph Chamberlain, doing his best** [1901]

EXHIB Carfax 1901
REPRO **Plate 18**
OWNER Merton College, Oxford

275 **[Mr Joseph Chamberlain** 1901]

EXHIB Carfax 1901

276★ **[The Rt. Hon. Joseph Chamberlain, J.P., M.P.** 1901.]
Full-length three-quarter face, dressed as in 272 but hatless, with cigar in hand.

REPRO *Critic* (N.Y.), Nov 1901, where captioned as above

277★ **Mr Chamberlain** [?c. 1901]
Similar to 276, but wearing top hat.

OWNER Sold at Sotheby's 26 Apr 1972

278★ **England's Darling** [1903]
Profile, cigar in hand, laurel wreath on head.

REPRO *John Bull*, 1 Apr 1903
OWNER Birmingham University Library

279 **[Mr Chamberlain and Mr Balfour** 1904]
[A suggestion for an allegorical picture to be entitled 'Force of character supporting personal charm']

EXHIB Carfax 1904

280 **[Mr Joseph Chamberlain]**

EXHIB L.G. 1928

281★ **Vagrom Memories of Sloping Shoulders** 1946
J. C. with George Moore and Swinburne.

OWNER David Tree Parsons

282★ **Joseph Chamberlain as he is, and as opposed to the idea formed of him by romantic foreign cartoonists** [n.d.]
Two drawings: one as usual, the other of a beautifully elegant youth.

EXHIB L.G. 1945 (Guedalla)
OWNER Ashmolean Museum, Oxford

283 **[Joseph Chamberlain]**

EXHIB L.G. 1945 (Guedalla)

284 **[S. Sebastian of Highbury]**
Identified in note from Max to L.G.

EXHIB L.G. 1957

285★ **The Brummell of Politics** [n.d.]
Full-length three-quarter face, huge nose and orchid. Reading from sheet of paper.

OWNER Gallery of Fine Arts, Columbus, Ohio

285A **[As seen by me in Downing Street 41 years ago – Mr Joseph Chamberlain and Sir Charles Dilke]**

EXHIB L.G. 1928

HADDON CHAMBERS
1860–1921   Australian playwright
See also 335

286 **[Mr Haddon Chambers** 1901]

EXHIB Carfax 1901

287★ **Mr Haddon Chambers** [1907]

EXHIB Carfax 1907
REPRO *A Book of Caricatures*, 1907

C. R. CHAMPION DE CRESPIGNY
1878–1941   Soldier

288★ **General C. R. de Crespigny** [1930]

REPRO *Ladbroke's Racing Calendar*, 1931

HENRY CHAPLIN
1840–1923   Conservative M.P.
See also 71, 614, 615

289★ [**The Right Hon Henry Chaplin M.P.** 1896]
Full length in evening dress, opera hat and monocle.
EXHIB F.A.S. 1896
REPRO *Twenty-Five Gentlemen*, 1896, where captioned as above.

290 [**Mr Henry Chaplin** 1901]
EXHIB Carfax 1901

291★ [**Right Hon H. Chaplin** 1903]
Half length, hatless, long white shirt-front.
REPRO *John Bull*, 8 Oct 1903, where captioned as above

292★ **Mr Henry Chaplin** 1907
Full length, full face, in day clothes and bowler hat.
EXHIB Achenbach 1964
OWNER Mr and Mrs Joseph M. Bransten

293★ **Mr Henry Chaplin** [1907]
Full-length profile in voluminous fur-trimmed overcoat.
REPRO *A Book of Caricatures*, 1907

294 [**Mr Henry Chaplin** 1907]
EXHIB Baillie 1907

295 [**Mr Henry Chaplin** 1910]
EXHIB N.E.A.C. Summer 1910

296★ **Mr Henry Chaplin**
Three-quarter length, in evening dress.
EXHIB L.G. 1911
REPRO *Bookman*, Aug 1911

297 **The Happy Father-in-Law** 1913
Mr Chaplin (to Lord Castlereagh): 'You and I, my boy, we belong to the Old School.'
Lord C (later seventh Marquess of Londonderry) married H. C.'s daughter Edith in 1899.
EXHIB L.G. May 1921
OWNER Lord Hylton

298★ [**Untitled** n.d.]
Full length, right hand inside voluminous coat. Max's instructions to printer at foot.
REPRO *Fifty Caricatures*, 1913
OWNER Robert Beloe

299★ **Mr Henry Chaplin** [n.d.]
REPRO **Plate 16**
OWNER National Portrait Gallery

300★ [**Untitled Unsigned** n.d.]
[H. C. to young lady:] 'The cost of living is less in America.'
OWNER University of Texas

301 [**Mr Henry Chaplin**]
EXHIB L.G. 1952

THE HON. EVAN CHARTERIS
1864–1940 Barrister and writer
See also 612, 616, 807A, 1366

302★ **Mr Evan Charteris** 1907
EXHIB Carfax 1907
REPRO *A Book of Caricatures*, 1907

303★ **Evan Charteris** [**Unsigned** n.d.]
Pen-and-ink head.
OWNER Lilly Library

'CHEIRO' (COUNT LOUIS HAMON)
1866–1936 Writer and palmist

304★ **'Cheiro'** [n.d.]
OWNER Mrs Eva Reichmann

THE TENTH EARL OF CHESTERFIELD
1854–1933 Courtier
See also 114

305★ **Lord Chesterfield conserving the family traditions** 1908
Max wrote to A. E. Gallatin on 23 May 1911: 'I remember that I drew the cravatte and the button-hole first of all, and the rest was exhaled corollarily from *them*!'
EXHIB Carfax 1908; New York 1912; Grolier 1944
REPRO A. E. Gallatin, *Whistler's Pastels etc*, 1913
OWNER Harvard College Library

306★ **Lord Chesterfield** [n.d.]
REPRO *Fifty Caricatures*, 1913

307★ **The Old and the Young Self** 1924
Old Self: 'What? Because I'm wearing a billicock? But – but' (abandons attempt to give concise history of modern times) 'well, I think you're quite right, my dear boy.'
EXHIB L.G. 1925
REPRO *Observations*, 1925
OWNER Miss Joan Wilson

308 [**Lord Chesterfield**]
EXHIB L.G. 1928

G. K. CHESTERTON
1874–1936   Poet and Writer
See also 121, 612, 614, 615, 1423, 1443, 1490-2, 1599

309★ Mr G. K. Chesterton giving the world a kiss [1904]

Mrs Chesterton wrote in her diary on 12 May 1904: 'Went to see Max Beerbohm's caricature of Gilbert at the Carfax Gallery. "G. K. C. – Humanist – Kissing the World"'.

EXHIB Carfax 1904, where listed as 'Mr G. K. Chesterton, humanist'; American Academy 1952
OWNER Yale University Library

310 [Mr G. K. Chesterton 1907]

EXHIB Baillie 1907

311★ [Mr G. K. Chesterton]

Three-quarter length, reading in tiny book.

EXHIB L.G. 1911
REPRO *Daily News*, 22 Apr 1911, where captioned as above

312★ [Untitled Unsigned 1912]

Making an after-dinner speech, shirt showing under waistcoat.

EXHIB L.G. 1945 (Guedalla)
REPRO *Bystander*, 24 Jul 1912; *Caricatures by Max*, 1958
OWNER Ashmolean Museum, Oxford

313 Portrait of Mr Gilbert Chesterton 1913

For Brian and Dora Roberts with every good wish. 1935
Full length, the body an immense circle with an exaggerated watch-chain across it.

EXHIB L.G. 1913, where catalogued as '(Unfinished)'
OWNER Brian R. Roberts

314★ The Old and the Young Self. Mr G. K. Chesterton 1925

Young Self: 'Oh yes, I drank some beer only the other day, and rather liked it; and of course the Crusades were glorious. But all this about English public life being honeycombed with corruption, and about the infallibility of the Pope, and the sacramental qualities of beer, and the soul-cleansing powers of Burgundy, and the immaculate conception of France, and the determination of the Jews to enslave us, and the instant need that we should get straight back into the Middle Ages, and' – Old Self: 'Well, you haven't met Belloc.'

EXHIB L.G. 1945 (Guedalla), 1952 and 1957
REPRO *Caricatures by Max*, 1958
OWNER Ashmolean Museum, Oxford

315★ [Untitled Unsigned n.d.]

Full length, gesticulating in evening dress.

EXHIB L.G. 1952
REPRO *Britain To-day*, Jul 1952
OWNER U.C.L.A. (Clark)

316★ [Untitled Unsigned n.d.]

Half-length pencil sketch, profile facing right.

OWNER University of Texas

SIR GEORGE CHETWYND
1849–1917   Landowner

317 [Sir George Chetwynd c. 1897]

EXHIB L.G. 1928, where dated as above

318 [Sir George Chetwynd 1901]

EXHIB Carfax 1901

319★ Sir George Chetwynd [n.d.]

Full-length profile facing right, smoking big cigar, top hat and stick held behind back.

OWNER Robert Beloe

LORD RANDOLPH CHURCHILL
1849–95   Conservative politician
See also 270, 595

320★ Randolph [Unsigned c. 1890]

Drawn by Max at Charterhouse.

OWNER University of Texas

321★ [Untitled 1894]

REPRO *Pick-Me-Up*, 22 Dec 1904

322★ Lord Randolph – a recollection [c. 1897]

EXHIB L.G. 1928, where dated as above; 1945 (Guedalla)
OWNER Charterhouse School

323★ Lord Randolph Churchill. A memory only, but a very clear one 1916

EXHIB L.G. 1928
REPRO *Bystander*, 5 Dec 1928
OWNER Winston S. Churchill

324★ A more Fortunate Churchill 1920

Shade of Lord Randolph: 'Seems to be simply nothing they won't forgive *him* [Winston]!... And hang it all! – they *liked* ME!'

EXHIB L.G. May 1921
REPRO *A Survey*, 1921
OWNER Martin Wedgwood

325★ [Untitled Unsigned 1951]

Dated 19 Mar 1951 on back by Elisabeth Jungmann.

OWNER Sir Rupert Hart-Davis

WINSTON CHURCHILL
1874–1965   Prime Minister
See also 43, 44, 324, 493, 494, 514, 515, 797, 799

326★ **[Untitled** 1900]
W. C. blowing a large trumpet labelled MY OWN.
REPRO *World*, Christmas No, 1900

327★ **Saving the State** [1903]
REPRO *John Bull*, 22 Oct 1903

328★ **Mr Winston Churchill** 1907
REPRO *A Book of Caricatures*, 1907

329★ **Draughting a Bill at the Board of Trade** 1909
Mr Churchill: 'Oh, I *understand* all these figures right enough. What we've got to do, gentlemen, is to put some – er – *humanising ginger* into 'em.'
W. C. in an armchair surrounded by aged officials. Edward Marsh guards the door.
EXHIB   L.G. 1952 and 1957
REPRO   Randolph S. Churchill, *Winston S. Churchill*, vol. II, 1967
OWNER   Winston S. Churchill

330★ **[Untitled Unsigned** c. 1909]
Rough sketch for 329.
EXHIB   Achenbach 1964
REPRO   Achenbach catalogue, 1964
OWNER   U.C.L.A. (Clark)

331★ **Mr Winston Churchill** 1910
EXHIB   L.G. 1945 (Guedalla) and 1957
REPRO   *Caricatures by Max*, 1958
OWNER   Ashmolean Museum, Oxford

332★ **The Budget** 1910
Mr Winston Churchill (to the Duke of Marlborough): 'Come, come! As I said in one of my speeches, "there is nothing in the Budget to make it harder for a poor hard-working man to keep a small home in decent comfort."'
They stand before the immensities of Blenheim Palace.
EXHIB   N.E.A.C. Summer 1910, where titled 'Balm in Gilead'
REPRO   Randolph S. Churchill, *Winston S. Churchill*, vol. II, 1967
OWNER   The Duke of Marlborough

333 **Mr Winston Churchill**
EXHIB   L.G. 1911

334★ **[The Succession]**
Mr Churchill: 'Come, suppose we toss for it, Davey.'
Mr Lloyd George: 'Ah but, Winsie, would either of us as loser abide by the result?'

EXHIB   L.G. 1911
REPRO   *Daily Mail*, 22 Apr 1911

335 **[In case I am not spared to see them]**
[Front Row: Pinero, Alfred Sutro, Winston Churchill, Soveral.
Second Row: Augustus John, Lord Howard de Walden, George Wyndham, Kitchener, Bernard Shaw, George Moore, Duke of Westminster.
Back Row: L. V. Harcourt, G. S. Street, A. E. W. Mason, Haddon Chambers, H. B. Irving, Sir Charles Wyndham, F. E. Smith, Arthur Balfour.]
All presumably pictured in old age.
EXHIB   L.G. 1911

336★ **Mr Winston Churchill** 1912
In huge overcoat, smoking cigar, hat in hand.
EXHIB   L.G. 1945 (Guedalla)
REPRO   *Bystander*, 22 May 1912
OWNER   Mrs Philip Guedalla

337★ **A Study in Dubiety** 1913
Mr Edward Marsh wondering whether he dare ask his Chief's leave to include in his anthology of 'Georgian Verse' Mr George Wyndham's famous and lovely poem 'We want eight and we won't wait.'
This phrase of G. W.'s in a speech at Wigan in March 1909, referring to the number of Dreadnought warships which the Conservative Opposition thought necessary, was used as a slogan by the Party and Admiral Fisher. Churchill and Lloyd George thought four would be sufficient.
EXHIB   L.G. 1913
REPRO   *Blue Review*, May 1913; Christopher Hassall, *Edward Marsh*, 1959

338★ **The Churchill-Wells Controversy** – December 1920
Churchill: 'You were only 14 days in Russia!'
Wells: 'Your mother's an American!'
Both dressed as schoolboys. The controversy (in the 'Daily Express' of 5 and 12 Dec 1920) concerned H. G. W.'s claim in his recently serialised 'Russia in the Shadows' that the collapse in Russia was due to Capitalism rather than Bolshevism.
EXHIB   L.G. May 1921 and 1957
REPRO   *Graphic*, 21 May 1921
OWNER   Dudley Sommer

339★ **The Churchill-Wells Controversy** 1920
For Tania [Jepson] gratefully from Max.
An almost exact copy of 338, but without December.
OWNER   Harvard College Library

340 **Mr Winston Churchill seeming to be, after all, indispensable** 1920
EXHIB   L.G. 1928
OWNER   Lord Hylton

341 **The Elder and the Younger Pitt-Churchill**
1941
Two drawings showing W. C. in 1911 and 1941.
OWNER *Mr and Mrs Graeme Hendrey*

342 **Non Plus Ultra Finest Hour** 1941
For Sydney and Violet [Schiff] Christmas Eve 1941
with love from Max.
W. C. on horseback rides over a prostrate Hitler.
OWNER *Lady Beddington-Behrens*

343★ **[Untitled]** 1949
*Head and shoulders profile, smoking a cigar, whose smoke
forms a replica of his head.*
EXHIB L.G. 1952
REPRO *Liverpool Daily Post*, 1 May 1952
OWNER *National Gallery of Victoria, Melbourne*

THE SECOND MARQUIS OF CLANRICARDE
1832–1916 Reactionary Irish landlord and
art connoisseur

344 **[Lord Clanricarde and a Dealer** 1908]
EXHIB Carfax 1908; L.G. 1957

JOHN CLARE

345★ **Mr John Clare** [n.d.]
OWNER *Mrs Eva Reichmann*

JULES CLARETIE
1840–1913 French novelist and theatrical director

346 **A Rehearsal at the Théâtre Français [Unsigned**
c. 1910]
M. Jules Claretie: 'Mesdames, mesdames! N'oubliez
pas que vous faites parti de la maison de Molière!'
*Two actresses, one old, one young, are about to tear each
other's hair out. Dated by Max in a letter to Mr Halliday.*
EXHIB L.G. 1913 and 1952
OWNER *Maxwell Halliday*

SIR EDWARD CLARKE
1841–1931 Barrister and M.P.

347★ **Sir Edward Clarke** [1900]
REPRO *Idler*, Apr 1900

THE REV. T. B. CLAYTON
b. 1885 Founder of Toc H

348★ **Rev. T. B. Clayton** 1931
REPRO *Spectator* Supplement, 28 Mar 1931
OWNER *The Spectator*

GEORGES CLEMENCEAU
1841–1929 French Prime Minister
See 1804

C. B. COCHRAN
1872–1951 Theatrical impresario

349★ **Mr Charles Cochran** [c. 1931]
REPRO *Heroes and Heroines of Bitter Sweet* [1931]
OWNER *Lilly Library*

ARTHUR COHEN
See 128

SIR ARTHUR COLEFAX
1866–1936 Don, barrister and M.P.

350★ **Sir Arthur Colefax** [n.d.]
EXHIB L.G. 1923
REPRO *Things New and Old*, 1923

THE SECOND LORD COLERIDGE
1851–1927 Judge
See 1307

S. T. COLERIDGE
1772–1834 Poet

351★ **Samuel Taylor Coleridge, table-talking** 1904
EXHIB Carfax 1904
REPRO *The Poets' Corner*, 1904 and 1943
OWNER *Private (Maine and N.Y.)*

CONSTANCE COLLIER
1878–1955 Actress

352★ **[Untitled** n.d.]
REPRO *Theatre Notebook*, Winter 1966–67
OWNER *Ashmolean Museum, Oxford*

JOHN CHURTON COLLINS
1848–1908   Scholar and critic

353 Mr Churton Collins [c. 1900]
EXHIB   L.G. 1928, where dated as above
OWNER   Mrs Helen Stutchbury

SIR JEREMIAH COLMAN
1859–1942   Business man and philanthropist
See 679

SIDNEY COLVIN
1845–1927   Museum director and writer
See also 679

354★ Mr Sidney Colvin [n.d.]
EXHIB   L.G. 1911 and 1952
REPRO   *Bookman*, Aug 1911
OWNER   Lilly Library

CHARLES CONDER
1868–1909   Artist
See also 36, 614, 615, 1322, 1586, 1588, 1650, 1662

355★ Mr Charles Conder [n.d.]
REPRO   Bohun Lynch, *Max Beerbohm in Perspective*, 1921

356★ [Untitled 1905]
My dear Conder Couple★ Here is the drawing. But
only Utamaro could have done it worthily of the
design – and of the exploit that it records. Looking
forward to seeing you both after Paris. Yours
affectionately Max.
★ This includes Stella – *not the burglar.*
Shows an escaping burglar caught in the coils of C's hair.
The incident occurred in Dec 1905.
EXHIB   L.G. 1945 (Guedalla)
REPRO   *Caricatures by Max*, 1958
OWNER   Ashmolean Museum, Oxford

THE DUKE OF CONNAUGHT
1850–1942   Son of Queen Victoria

357★ 'The flourish set on youth' [Shakespeare,
Sonnet 60] 1923
Time (to the Duke of Connaught): 'Bless me if I
hadn't quite forgotten *you*!'
EXHIB   L.G. 1923 and 1957
REPRO   *Things New and Old*, 1923
OWNER   Birmingham City Art Gallery

JESSIE CONRAD
1873–1936   Wife of Joseph Conrad
See 363

JOSEPH CONRAD
1857–1924   Novelist
See also 612, 679, 814, 1172

358★ Mr Joseph Conrad 1909
Full-length profile facing right.
EXHIB   L.G. 1911
REPRO   *Bookman*, Aug 1911

359★ Somewhere in the Pacific 1920
Mr Joseph Conrad: 'Quelle charmante plage! On se
fait l'illusion qu'ici on pourrait être toujours presque
gai!'
J. C. contemplates a snake crawling through a skull on an
empty beach.
EXHIB   L.G. May 1921
REPRO   *A Survey*, 1921

**360★ 'A party in a parlour, all silent and all
damned' [Wordsworth, 'Peter Bell'] – and, as
usual, Mr Joseph Conrad intruding** 1920
The room, which has a skull in a glass case on the table, is
full of agonised sea-captains and their wives.
EXHIB   L.G. 1945 (Guedalla), where wrongly dated 1914
REPRO   *A Survey*, 1921
OWNER   Mrs Philip Guedalla

361★ Conrad in Bedford Street Feb 27 1924
J. C. sunk in an arm-chair in Heinemann's office.
REPRO   *Teachers' World*, 20 Aug 1924
OWNER   A. Dwye Evans

362★ The Old and the Young Self 1924
Young Self: 'Na volski primskch kalz gatscki lo
visck British Mercantile Marine zut li hasphor ta
glanimph por kumptlck?'
Old Self: 'Mais oui, mon enfant – and what's more,
I was a Master Mariner! And I've written some
books, too . . . but you are hardly old enough to
understand them.'
EXHIB   L.G. 1925 and 1952
REPRO   *Observations*, 1925
OWNER   Mrs David Karmel

**363★ Frontispiece for that dreadful work 'Joseph
Conrad and His Circle'** 1935
The circle encloses the head of Jessie Conrad, the author of
the dreadful work.
REPRO   **Plate 54**
OWNER   Benjamin Sonnenberg

SIR THEODORE ANDREA COOK
1867–1928   Journalist and author

364 **Sir Theodore Andrea Cook** [n.d.]
OWNER Sold at Sotheby's 14 Dec 1960

DUFF COOPER
1890–1954   Politician, ambassador and writer

365★ **Mr Duff Cooper assured by Lord Birkenhead that a brilliant début in the House of Commons is not necessarily fatal** 1925
EXHIB L.G. 1925
REPRO *Observations*, 1925

CONSTANT-BENÔIT COQUELIN (AÎNÉ)
1849–1909   French actor
See also 1291, 1293

366★ **'Moi qui ne parle jamais de moi . . .'** Dieppe 1904
OWNER Southern Illinois University

367★ **M. Coquelin in Dieppe** [1907]
For Reg [Turner] on his -nth birthday.
EXHIB Carfax 1907; American Academy 1952
REPRO *A Book of Caricatures*, 1907
OWNER Private (Yale)

368 **Coquelin Aîné** [n.d.]
EXHIB L.G. 1945 (Guedalla)
OWNER The Hon. Christopher Lennox-Boyd

ROSA CORDER
1853–1904   Painter and copyist

369★ **Mr—and Miss—nervously perpetuating the touch of a vanished hand** 1917
Max is believed to have intended these figures to represent R. C. and Charles Augustus Howell, who were suspected of copying and forging Rossetti pictures and drawings. She stands working at an easel in an empty room while he nervously listens at the door. Several Rossetti pictures on the walls.
EXHIB L.G. Sep 1921
REPRO *Rossetti and his Circle*, 1922
OWNER Tate Gallery

FANNY CORNFORTH
c. 1840–1914   Rossetti model
See 1272

LEONARD COURTNEY
1832–1918   Liberal M.P.
See also 1068

370 **Mr Leonard Courtney** [n.d.]
'The World came and fawned at my feet.'
The World, globe-headed, is kissing his foot. The chair-knobs are replicas of his face.
EXHIB L.G. 1957
OWNER G. H. Chipperfield

W. L. COURTNEY
1850–1928   Don, journalist and author
See also 378, 1443

371★ **Mr W. L. Courtney** [n.d.]
EXHIB L.G. 1911 and 1957
REPRO *Bookman*, Aug 1911

372 **[The Young Lions of 'The Daily Telegraph'. No. 1]**
[Mr W. L. Courtney, wondering whether 'it is not too much to say' that Mrs Thingumy's latest work ("Through Mire and Mist", by Elizabeth Thingumy, Trashby, Stodger & Co, six shillings) 'may unhesitatingly be pronounced' in some respects – though not, perhaps, he ventures to think, in all respects – a masterpiece, or a masterly achievement, or something of that sort.]
The title comes from the Preface to Matthew Arnold's 'Essays in Criticism', 1865, where it refers to arch-Philistines.
EXHIB N.E.A.C. Winter 1911, where titled as above; L.G. 1945 (Guedalla)

NOËL COWARD
b. 1899   Playwright and composer

373★ **Mr Noel Coward** [c. 1931]
REPRO *Heroes and Heroines of Bitter Sweet* [1931]
OWNER Lilly Library

EDWARD ANTHONY CRAIG (EDWARD CARRICK)
b. 1905   Artist son of Gordon Craig
See 379

EDWARD GORDON CRAIG
1872–1966   Stage designer
See also 95, 614, 615, 1836, 1884, 2019

374★ **Mr Gordon Craig, having failed to induce Signora Duse to secede from the theatre, tries his appeal on Mr Charles Frohman** 1908

CRAIG (continued)

EXHIB Carfax 1908; L.G. 1945 (Guedalla)
REPRO *Theatre Notebook*, Summer 1967
OWNER Ashmolean Museum, Oxford

375* **Mr Gordon Craig producing 'Hamlet'** 1913
Manipulating a tiny puppet in a toy theatre.
EXHIB L.G. 1913, 1952 and 1957
OWNER University of Texas

376* **Craig's New Protégé** [c. 1914]
E. G. C. (to new protégé): 'Don't, CITIZEN, oh
don't go in there! They'll upset your beautiful
WELL-ORDERED LIFE and play the deuce with
your JUST BALANCE!'
*E. G. C. in huge hat is stopping a stout man in morning
dress from entering the Realistic Theatre.*
REPRO *Mask*, Jan 1914; Gordon Craig, *Le Théâtre en
Marche*, 1964
OWNER Bibliothèque de l'Arsenal, Paris

377* **Mr Gordon Craig asking them for 'a sacrifice
worthy of their calling and their ideals'** 1920
*E. G. C. is surrounded by four commercial actor-managers –
Allan Aynesworth, Oscar Asche, Arthur Bourchier, and
Gerald du Maurier holding a golf-club.*
EXHIB L.G. May 1921
REPRO *A Survey*, 1921
OWNER James Fox

378* **Gordon Craig in clever contradictory mood**
1922
*At a banquet for the first International Exhibition of
Theatrical Art, 1922, E. G. C. is climbing over the
dinner-table. On his right sit Sir Cecil Harcourt-Smith
and W. L. Courtney, on his left Will Rothenstein and
Lord Howard de Walden. The title is a pasted-on cutting
from the 'Daily Herald' of 5 Jun 1922.*
REPRO Gordon Craig, *Le Théâtre en Marche*, 1964
OWNER Bibliothèque de l'Arsenal, Paris

379* **Preparing for the International Theatre
Exhibition, Victoria and Albert Museum, 1922
(Mr Martin Hardie; Mr Gordon Craig the elder;
Mr Gordon Craig the younger)** 1924
OWNER Victoria & Albert Museum

380 **[The Theatre Advancing Nothing, Mr Gordon
Craig approaches a Financier** 1925]
*Known only from a note in Max's papers. E. G. C.'s book
'The Theatre Advancing' appeared in 1923.*

381* **Mr Gordon Craig** 1925
*A full-length Thurberesque figure in profile facing left,
right hand extended.*
OWNER Sir John Rothenstein

[Titled as below] 1926
Two complementary drawings:
382* (1) Here are five friends of mine – Mr Nicholson,
Mr Rutherston, Mr Craig, Mr Morrison, and Mr
Ricketts. All are designers of fantastic and lovely
costumes. Yet they dress themselves thus:
All in drab modern clothes.
383* (2) Why not rather thus?
All in brightly coloured mediaeval dress.
EXHIB L.G. 1957
REPRO **Plates 60 and 61**
OWNER Birmingham City Art Gallery

384 **Gordon Craig visiting Max Beerbohm by
'Quiz'** [n.d.]
*Max shows how he thinks 'Quiz' would have depicted
them: a portly walrus-moustached Max and a withered
Craig, with a portion of the Rapallo balcony between them.*
OWNER Ronald Searle

THE FOURTH EARL OF CRAVEN
1868–1921
See 114, 1382

MANDELL CREIGHTON
1843–1901 Bishop and historian

385* **The Bishop of London** [1900]
REPRO *World*, Christmas Supplement, 1900
OWNER Sold at Sotheby's 26 Apr 1972

THE MARQUESS OF CREWE
1858–1945 Liberal politician and ambassador
See 612, 616

THE CROWN PRINCE OF GERMANY
1882–1951 Son of the Kaiser
See 1797

R. B. CUNNINGHAME GRAHAM
See Graham

LORD CURZON
1859–1925 Politician and viceroy
See also 436, 612, 679, 952, 1443, 1529

386* **The Encaenia of 1908, being an humble hint
to the Chancellor, based on the Encaenia of 1907,**

whereby so many idols of the market-place were cheerily set up in the groves of the Benign Mother 1908

C, as Chancellor of Oxford University, is shaking hands with Eugene Sandow, the strong man. The other graduands are Conan Doyle, Hall Caine, the Rev. R. J. Campbell, Prince Edward of York (later King Edward VIII), Sir Thomas Lipton, John Burns, G. R. Sims and Little Tich. The Encaenia of 1907 had honoured, among others, Mark Twain, 'General' Booth, Kipling, Hubert Herkomer and Prince Arthur of Connaught.

EXHIB Carfax 1908; L.G. 1911 and 1945 (Guedalla)
REPRO *Caricatures by Max*, 1958
OWNER Ashmolean Museum, Oxford

387★ **Once a proconsul, always a proconsul** 1909

EXHIB N.E.A.C. Summer 1909; L.G. 1911
REPRO **Plate 15**
OWNER All Souls College, Oxford

388★ **[Untitled Unsigned** c. 1909]

Rough sketch for 387.

OWNER Gallery of Fine Arts, Columbus, Ohio

389★ **Lord Curzon rehearsing an oration** 1912

REPRO *Bystander*, 7 Aug 1912
OWNER Mrs Dilys Sullivan

390★ **A Gracious Act. Lord Curzon of Kedleston reading to M. Cammaerts a translation (signed with his own hand) of a poem by M. Cammaerts** 1915

REPRO *The Book of the Homeless*, ed. Edith Wharton, 1916

391★ **The Old and the Young Self. Lord Curzon of Kedleston** 1924

The Young Self is humbly kissing the Proconsul's hand.

REPRO Ronaldshay, *Life of Lord Curzon*, vol. 2, 1928
OWNER A. M. Hamilton

392 **[Lord Curzon exemplifying 'the elder, the greater style' in an age not quite worthy of it]**

EXHIB L.G. 1928

393 **[Lord Curzon]**

EXHIB L.G. 1952

LIONEL CUST
1859–1929   Art expert and courtier
See also 679

394★ **A Gentleman Usher – Mr Lionel Cust** [1914]

EXHIB L.G. May 1921, where dated as above
REPRO *A Survey*, 1921

D

VISCOUNT D'ABERNON
1857–1941   Ambassador

395★ **Lord D'Abernon** 1930

Half length, full face, country clothes, loose collar.

OWNER Piccadilly Gallery

396★ **Lord D'Abernon** 1931

Almost identical with 395. Presumably a copy made by Max.

OWNER Keith Mackenzie

397★ **[Untitled]** 1931

Pasted on is a cutting from the 'Sunday Times' of 14 Jun 1931, describing a musical party at the Polish Embassy, at which the guests included 'Viscount and Viscountess D'Abernon, the latter in black.' In the drawing Lord

D.'A. is dressed in a blue tail-coat with yellow facings, a pink waistcoat and green trousers. Lady D.'A. is in simple black.

OWNER Lilly Library

W. J. DALY
1848–1924   Comedian

398★ **[Dutch Daly** 1894]

REPRO *Pick-Me-Up*, 29 Dec 1894, where captioned as above

GABRIELE D'ANNUNZIO
1863–1938   Italian poet, playwright and novelist

D'ANNUNZIO (continued)

399* The meeting of Signor D'Annunzio and M. Rostand 1911

M. Rostand: 'Je trouve qu'il n'a manqué que d'une chose – une: la simplicité.'

EXHIB N.E.A.C. Winter 1911; L.G. 1952
REPRO **Plate 74**
OWNER Allan Cuthbertson

400* Signor Gabriele D'Annunzio [1912]

In March 1912 Max wrote to Reggie Turner: 'I have done caricatures of Rodin and 'il' d'Annunzio today'

EXHIB L.G. 1913
REPRO *Fifty Caricatures, 1913*
OWNER Private (Yale)

401* 'Post Taedia Longa Laborum' [Long and tedious labours at an end – Ovid, 'Metamorphoses', XIV, 158] 1920

M. Paderewski: 'Ah, read me one of the poems of your youth!'

Signor D'Annunzio: 'Ah, play me one of your adorable sonatas!'

Both had recently been drawn from art into politics.

EXHIB L.G. May 1921
REPRO *A Survey, 1921*
OWNER Lilly Library

DANTE
1265–1321   Italian poet
See also 1188

402* Dante in Oxford [1904]

Proctor: 'Your name and college?'

EXHIB Carfax 1904
REPRO *The Poets' Corner, 1904 and 1943*
OWNER Mrs Eva Reichmann

MR JUSTICE DARLING
1849–1936   Judge

403* On Circuit [?Unsigned c. 1913]

Mr Justice Darling (to his Marshal): 'Oh, and get some bells sewn on this cap, will you?'

It is the black cap worn by judges when pronouncing sentence of death. D was famous for making jokes on the bench.

EXHIB L.G. 1913
REPRO *Fifty Caricatures, 1913*

CHARLES DARWIN
1808–82   Naturalist
See 595

ALPHONSE DAUDET
1840–97   French writer

404 [?Alphonse Daudet]

Known only from letter of Will Rothenstein in 'Times Lit. Sup.' of 22 Apr 1926, asking for its whereabouts.

NORMAN DAVEY
Writer

405* Mr Norman Davey quoting Catullus 1924

EXHIB L.G. 1925
REPRO *Observations, 1925*

JOHN DAVIDSON
1857–1909   Poet
See also 614, 615, 1650

406* John Davidson [1897]

Full-length profile facing left, right arm extended, cigar in mouth.

REPRO *Chap-Book (Chicago), 1 Feb 1897*

407 [Mr John Davidson 1901]

EXHIB Carfax 1901

408* Mr John Davidson 1907

Full-length profile facing left, wearing overcoat and holding bowler hat in front of face.

EXHIB Carfax 1907
REPRO *A Book of Caricatures, 1907*
OWNER Sherman Lurie

409* This would have amused my very dear John Davidson 1926

Half-length, full face, sitting at table, cigar in hand.

EXHIB L.G. 1928
OWNER George Sassoon

410* [Untitled Unsigned n.d.]

Pencil sketch of J. D. standing on top of the world and juggling with moon, stars and planets.

OWNER University of Texas

RANDALL DAVIDSON
1848–1930   Archbishop of Canterbury 1903–28
See also 612, 616, 1591

411 [**The Archbishop of Canterbury** 1908]
EXHIB Carfax 1908

412 [**The Archbishop of Canterbury**]
EXHIB L.G. 1911

THE REV. G. S. DAVIES
Charterhouse master
See 664

EDMUND DAVIS
1862–1939   South African millionaire and art patron
See also 1083

413* **Mr Edmund Davis – with Venice thrown in**
1907
EXHIB Carfax 1907
OWNER Piccadilly Gallery

414 **Mr Edmund Davis and France (But I anticipate**
– M. B.) 1913
EXHIB L.G. 1913
OWNER Mrs Dilys Sullivan

THE REV. ANTHONY C. DEANE
1870–1946   Canon of Windsor and writer

415* **A. C. D.** [1900]
REPRO *World*, Christmas No, 1900

PATRICK DE BATHE
1876–1930   Soldier and diplomat

416* **Mr Patrick de Bathe** [n.d.]
EXHIB L.G. 1957
OWNER Patrick Baldwin

COUNT BONI DE CASTELLANE
1867–1932   French dandy and writer
See also 267

417* **Count Boni de Castellane** [1895]
Full length, back view, looking over right shoulder,
exquisitely dressed.
EXHIB L.G. 1928, where dated as above, and 1957
REPRO *Bystander*, 5 Dec 1928
OWNER Sir Edward Maufe, R.A.

418 [**Comte de Castellane** 1901]
EXHIB Carfax 1901

419* **Count Boni de Castellane** 1912
After his rich American wife divorced him in 1906 he
changed from millionaire to pauper. In 1925 he published
'L'Art d'être Pauvre'.
EXHIB L.G. 1952
REPRO **Plate 75**
OWNER Sir Anthony Hooper Bart

420 [**Count Boni de Castellane**]
EXHIB L.G. 1913

W. G. DE GLEHN
1870–1951   Artist
See 1587

LORD DE GREY
1852–1923   Later second Marquess of Ripon
See also 1382

421 [**Lord de Grey** 1901]
EXHIB Carfax 1901

422* **Lord de Grey appraising a shepherdess** [1907]
EXHIB Carfax 1907; L.G. 1911, 1952 and 1957
REPRO *A Book of Caricatures*, 1907, where in the printed
caption 'Dresden' appears before 'shepherdess'

WALTER DE LA MARE
1873–1956   Poet

423* **Mr Walter de la Mare gaining inspiration for**
an eerie and lovely story 1925
EXHIB L.G. 1925 and 1945 (Guedalla)
REPRO *Observations*, 1925; *Caricatures by Max*, 1958
OWNER Ashmolean Museum, Oxford

A. TEIXEIRA DE MATTOS
1865–1921   Translator

424* [**Untitled** n.d.]
EXHIB L.G. 1913
OWNER Private (Yale)

425 **Teixeira de Mattos. A sea piece** [n.d.]
OWNER Martin Wedgwood

EDOUARD DE MAX
1869–1925   French actor

426 Monsieur de Max [c. 1904]
EXHIB L.G. 1928, where dated as above
OWNER Dr A. Herxheimer

BARONESS DE MEYER

427 [Baroness de Meyer]
EXHIB Edwardian Exhibition, Eastbourne, 1951

CHAUNCEY DEPEW
1834–1928   American lawyer and tycoon

428★ Mr Chauncey Depew [1895]
EXHIB L.G. 1928, where dated as above
OWNER Stephen Greene

THE FIFTEENTH EARL OF DERBY
1826–93   Politician
See 637

EDOUARD DE RESZKE
1855–1917   Polish bass
See 1664–66

LORD DESBOROUGH
1855–1945   Sportsman and Conservative M.P.

429★ Lord Desborough 1907
Three-quarter length, arms folded, head turned to left.
OWNER Keith Mackenzie

430★ Lord Desborough 1910
Same stance as in 429, but head turned to right. Standing on raft by river.
EXHIB N.E.A.C. Summer 1910; L.G. 1911
REPRO *Tatler*, 26 Apr 1911
OWNER Mrs Dilys Sullivan

GEORGES DE STAAL
1822–1907   Russian Ambassador in London
1884–1902

431★ M. de Staal [n.d.]
EXHIB L.G. 1928
OWNER Dr A. Herxheimer

THE EIGHTH DUKE OF DEVONSHIRE
1833–1908   Liberal politician

432★ [Untitled Unsigned n.d.]
Full-length profile facing left, wearing monocle and holding cigar. An undergraduate drawing.
OWNER Piccadilly Gallery

433 [The Duke of Devonshire, letting the grass grow under his feet 1901]
EXHIB Carfax 1901

434 [Lord Hartington as in 1886 1926]
EXHIB L.G. 1928 and 1957
OWNER Sold at Sotheby's 26 Apr 1961, where dated as above

435★ His Grace the Duke of Devonshire, K.G. [n.d.]
EXHIB Cincinnati 1965
OWNER Lilly Library

THE NINTH DUKE OF DEVONSHIRE
1868–1938   Politician and proconsul

436★ Lord Londonderry and Lord Curzon explaining to the Duke of Devonshire a joke of Mr Gosse's 1913
Gosse was Librarian of the House of Lords 1904–14.
EXHIB L.G. 1913
REPRO *Fifty Caricatures*, 1913
OWNER The Duke of Devonshire

437★ Further Economies in the Library of Chatsworth: the Duke, having disposed advantageously of his sofa, sleeps where the Caxtons stood 1914
His head rests on six books – 'Smiles on Self-Help', 'A Briton's First Duty', 'The Beggars' Opera', 'Life of Belisarius', 'Fort L'Honneur', and 'Life and Letters of Lazarus'.
EXHIB L.G. 1923
REPRO *Things New and Old*, 1923
OWNER The Duke of Devonshire

JOSÉ DE LA CRUZ PORFIRIO DÍAZ
1830–1915   President of Mexico

438★ 'Diaz, whom Queens had flattered' 1955
For Elisabeth with Max's love.
Queen Victoria is doing the flattering.
OWNER Mrs Eva Reichmann

C. G. COTSFORD DICK
1846–1911   Versifier

438A★ Mr Cotsford Dick [n.d.]

OWNER Mrs Eva Reichmann

SIR CHARLES DILKE
1843–1911   Radical politician
See 285A

BENJAMIN DISRAELI
1804–81   Prime Minister
See also 595, 872

439★ Prime Ministers in my day – and mostly tremendous luminaries in theirs 1929

Heads, in a diagonal line, of Disraeli, Gladstone, Salisbury, Rosebery, Balfour, Campbell-Bannerman, Asquith, Bonar Law, Lloyd George, MacDonald and Baldwin.

REPRO   *The Legion Book*, ed. H. C. Minchin, 1929
OWNER Oscar Pio

440 Curzon Street, 1880 [c. 1940]

Master Max (aged 8): 'I breakfasted with Lord
  Houghton today, sir. He seemed very young.'
The Earl of Beaconsfield, K.G.: 'The Disappointed are
  Always Young.'

Max stands to attention in a sailor-suit. Lord B sits upright in an arm-chair, wearing carpet-slippers.

OWNER Oliver R. W. W. Lodge

441★ A Recent Rapprochement in Elysium [n.d.]

Lord B[eaconsfield] and Mr G[ladstone]: 'For good
  or ill at least we did do *something*!'

EXHIB   L.G. 1945 (Guedalla)
REPRO   *Sunday Times*, 16 June 1955
OWNER John Grigg

AUSTIN DOBSON
1840–1921   Poet and essayist
See also 612, 748

442★ Scene: the Board of Trade. Time: Office-hours in the early 'eighties. Mr Austin Dobson and Mr Edmund Gosse caught in the act of composing a ballade by their President, Mr Jos. Chamberlain [c. 1904]

EXHIB   Carfax 1904; L.G. 1945 (Guedalla), 1952 and 1957
REPRO   *The Poets' Corner*, 1904 and 1943; *Caricatures by
         Max*, 1958
OWNER Ashmolean Museum, Oxford

ARNOLD DOLMETSCH
1858–1940   Musician
See also 1890

443★ Dr Dolmetsch [1901]

EXHIB   Carfax 1901
REPRO   *Artist*, Feb 1902
OWNER James M. Wells

LORD ALFRED DOUGLAS
1870–1945   Poet
See 1791

NORMAN DOUGLAS
1868–1952   Writer

444★ A flask of Bombarolina; and Mr Norman Douglas bent on winning an admission that the rites of the Church are all a survival of Paganism pure and simple 1923

EXHIB   L.G. 1923
REPRO   *Things New and Old*, 1923

ARTHUR CONAN DOYLE
1859–1930   Writer
See also 386

445★ [Untitled Unsigned n.d.]

The tail-end of a letter from A. C. D., with his signature, has been pasted on to the mount below the drawing.

OWNER Mrs Edward Kaye

JOHN DRINKWATER
1882–1937   Poet

446★ Mr John Drinkwater 1925

EXHIB   L.G. 1925
REPRO   *Observations*, 1925
OWNER Mrs Daisy Kennedy Drinkwater

MAJOR DRUMMOND
A Cotswold neighbour of the Rothensteins

447★ Major Drummond [Unsigned n.d.]

OWNER Lilly Library

THE FIRST MARQUESS OF
DUFFERIN AND AVA
1826–1902 Ambassador and Viceroy

448* **Lord Dufferin** [1901]
EXHIB Carfax 1901
REPRO *Pall Mall Magazine*, Feb 1902

449 **[Lord Dufferin]**
EXHIB L.G. 1928

PRINCE VICTOR DULEEP SINGH
1866–1918 Soldier

450 **[Prince Victor Dhuleep Singh** 1901]
EXHIB Carfax 1901

451 **[Prince Victor Dhuleep Singh]**
EXHIB L.G. 1911

GERALD DU MAURIER
1873–1934 Actor-manager
See also 84, 377, 679, 735

452 **[Gerald du Maurier** 1907]
Known only from a bookseller's catalogue.

453* **[Untitled Unsigned** n.d.]
Three-quarter-length pencil sketch, back view, head turned to left.
OWNER University of Texas

LORD DUNCANNON
1880–1956 Later ninth Earl of Bessborough

454* **Lord Duncannon** 1907
EXHIB Carfax 1907
OWNER Keith Mackenzie

E

SIR WILLIAM EDEN BART
1849–1915 Landowner, painter, and eccentric

455* **Sir William Eden** [1899]
Full-length profile facing left, hat held in front of him.
REPRO *Butterfly*, Jun 1899; *Max's Nineties*, 1958

456 **[Sir William Eden** 1901]
EXHIB Carfax 1901

457* **Sir William Eden, revisiting Paris** 1907
The shade of Whistler is flying over the city. In 1895 W. E. had sued Whistler in Paris for the non-delivery of a portrait.
EXHIB Carfax 1907
REPRO *A Book of Caricatures*, 1907
OWNER Art Institute of Chicago

458* **Sir William Eden and Mr Whistler** [n.d.]
REPRO **Plate 59**
OWNER University of Glasgow

459* **[Untitled** n.d.]
A huge Eden faces a tiny Whistler.
REPRO Timothy Eden, *The Tribulations of a Baronet*, 1933

460* **[Untitled** n.d.]
Sir William: 'There is something exceedingly fascinating in a turned up nose.'
Parker [his valet]: 'Yes, Sir Willum. Without doubt, Sir Willum. Something very taking indeed . . . Dinner-gong's gone ten minutes, Sir Willum.'
EXHIB L.G. 1952
OWNER Mrs Evelyn Isaacs

461* **[Untitled** n.d.]
Full-length profile facing left, knee-breeches, hands in pockets.
EXHIB Cincinnati 1965
OWNER Lilly Library

462 **Sir William Eden** [n.d.]
Three-quarter length, three-quarter face.

KING EDWARD VII
1841–1910
See also 204, 270, 1307, 1563, 1725-27

462A★ The Happy Prince by the Master [Signed with monogram n.d.]

Standing on one foot in a champagne glass, wearing a crown with three feathers and holding up a smaller glass of champagne. A drawing done at Oxford, its title referring to Oscar Wilde's 'The Happy Prince' (1888)

OWNER Robert H. Taylor

463★ H.R.H. The Prince of Wales [1896]

Wearing kilt, check coat and cap, smoking cigar.

REPRO *Twenty-Five Gentlemen*, 1896

464★ Stirring Scenes in the Prince's Life – the Victory of Persimmon [?1896]

The Prince, weeping tears of joy, leads in his first Derby winner (1896). Below the horse Max wrote 'Cruel of Persimmon!'

EXHIB L.G. 1957
OWNER Osbert Lancaster

Waddesdon Manor. Sunday, 17 July '98. 2 p.m.

Three drawings as under

465 (1) His Royal Highness, having retired to rest, re-emerges suddenly with the intention of finding his host, Baron Ferdinand de Rothschild, and drinking in the New Year. He misses his footing –

Purple-faced, carrying candle, with a bottle of champagne in his pocket, saying 'Three sheers for th' Queensh!'

466 (2) Early next morning he is found sleeping at the foot of the staircase.

Pale-faced, sitting on floor, candle upset, bottle broken in his pocket, he is discovered by manservant carrying a can of water.

467 (3) His Royal Highness is enabled to attend Divine Service. He is deeply touched by the reference to his patience in affliction.

Lying with drink, cigar and 'Sporting Life', listening through theatrophone.

OWNER Sold at Sotheby's 4 Mar 1959

468★ The Royal Sufferer July 1898

Seated, foot on rest, smoking large cigar, surrounded by doctors and nurses. He had broken his kneecap.

EXHIB L.G. 1945 (Guedalla)
OWNER Miss Joan Wilson

469★ The Convalescence of His Royal Highness [?1898]

Sitting on sofa, foot up, smoking big cigar. A cup of Bovril on table.

REPRO *Country Life*, 28 Sep 1967
OWNER Messrs Bovril Ltd

470★ [The Royal Box 1899]

Alone in box, looking through opera-glasses.

REPRO *Butterfly*, Nov 1899, where captioned as above

471★ If the Prince would only make no effort 1900

Full length, three-quarter face, spectacled and worried.

OWNER Princeton University Library

472★ The Prince in the Row [n.d.]

Profile on horseback.

OWNER Sir John Rothenstein

473★ H.R.H. The Prince of Wales, H.R.H. The Duke of Teck and an equerry at the play [n.d.]

OWNER S. Gorley Putt

474★ The Prince and his Friends [n.d.]

They are five, all Jewish. The most prominent is an exact replica of the Prince, except for his more rounded nose.

OWNER A. D. Peters

475★ The Prince of Wales [n.d.]

Full-length back view, head turned to left, holding grey top hat.

REPRO *Apollo*, Apr 1970
OWNER Piccadilly Gallery

476 Edward VII, or rather (for he was stouter in 1901 and afterwards) A. E., P. of W. [n.d.]

OWNER Oliver R. W. W. Lodge

477★ In the 'sixties and 'seventies [n.d.]

Peace hath her victories as well as war.

Shows the Prince in holiday clothes, a girl on his arm.

OWNER Phillip N. Davis

478★ King Edward VII is duly apprised of his accession [?1901]

The King descends the stairs in his pyjamas, towards the kneeling Lord Chancellor (Halsbury) and Archbishop of Canterbury (Temple). A parody of the well-known scene of Queen Victoria's accession.

EXHIB L.G. 1945 (Guedalla) and 1957
REPRO **Plate 21**
OWNER Mrs Rau

479 [The King's determination to tread ever in his Mother's Footsteps]

EXHIB L.G. 1945 (Guedalla)

480★ The First Gentleman in Europe 1901

To the first but one 1905.

Squat full-length, broader than he is tall.

REPRO Piccadilly Gallery catalogue, Christmas 1967
OWNER Malcolm Borthwick

481★ **The First Gentleman in Europe** [n.d.]
Full length, smoking cigar, grey top hat in hand.
OWNER Sir John Elliot

482 **A Constitutional Monarch** [n.d.]
Huge head with a tiny crown on top.
OWNER Lady Hastings James

483★ **We understand that His Majesty is so well pleased with the new stamps and coins that he has decided to abandon neckwear** 1902
EXHIB L.G. 1952 and 1956; Achenbach 1964
REPRO *Bandwagon*, Jun 1952; Achenbach catalogue
OWNER Eric Ambler

484★ **The New Coinage** 1902
Whilom Favourite (reading): ' "Edwardus VII D.G. Omn: Brit: Rex Fid: Def: Ind: Imp" . . . Ah! He'll always be Tum-Tum to *me*!'
For Albert [Rutherston] 1906
EXHIB L.G. 1957
OWNER David Rutherston

485★ **Quite like 'the Marguerite'** [1903]
'His Majesty, with his usual forethought, permitted the officers to appear in "No. 3 uniform", which consists of frock coats and caps.' *Daily Mail*, 20 April 1903.
EXHIB L.G. 1952
REPRO *Sunday Times*, 4 May 1952

[The Edwardyssey 1903]
Nine drawings as under, commemorating the King's round of ceremonial visits to the Continent, March–May 1903.
486★ **Marianne Calypso dallies with him. The sailors grow impatient**
[Marianne:] 'À ce moment c'est un Monsieur Loubet qui m'entretient. Mais je voudrais bien être honnête femme . . . C'est vraiment vrai que t'es pas bourgeois – toi aussi? . . . Tiens! T'en as l'air. Mais c'est un gentil gros tête . . .'
Emile Loubet (1838–1929) was President of France 1899–1906.

487★ **Edwardysseus will not hearken to the Syrens**
'His Majesty then ate a piece of cake and drank a glass of port wine a hundred years old, while four nuns sang Kathleen Mavourneen.' *Daily Mail*, April 17, describing the visit to the Convent of Dom Successio.

488★ **Meanwhile, Carlos the Cyclops detains Edwardysseus in his horrid cave**

Carlos I (1863–1908) was King of Portugal from 1889 until his assassination.

489★ **Leo Circe tries her vile incantations on him**
Leo XIII (1810–1903) was Pope from 1878.

490★ **After many other curious, lamentable and delectable adventures, Edwardysseus is washed ashore on his own island. To him appears, in the guise of a Highland shepherd, his mother, Pallas Victoria, and puts him on his way.**
The Queen-shepherdess is kilted and accompanied by a toy sheep.

491★ **Edwardysseus reaches Windsor Great Park – but is unrecognised by the faithful Eumaeus-Knollys, by George-Telemachus, and by Jacko-Argus**
Sir Francis Knollys (1837–1924) was the King's Private Secretary. Telemachus is the Prince of Wales (later King George V), Jacko a dog.

492★ **Edwardysseus smiles his well-known Hanoverian side-long smile, and is instantly recognised by the faithful Eumaeus-Knollys, by George-Telemachus, and by Jacko-Argus**

493★ **Penelope-Alexandra is here seen, grievously beset by those pushful ones who covet the throne of Edwardysseus. In the background, resentful but helpless, stand George-Telemachus and Jacko-Argus**
Queen Alexandra, knitting, ignores the suitors – Sir Ernest Cassel, Sir Thomas Lipton, Lord Burnham, Joseph Chamberlain, Alfred Harmsworth, Hall Caine, Winston Churchill, Wilson Barrett and Lord Rosebery.

494★ **The Happy Ending. 'Whosoever shall smoke the cigar of Edwardysseus, him will I wed.'**
The Queen on her knees to the King who is smoking a gigantic cigar. The suitors discomfited.
EXHIB } the whole {L.G. 1945 (Guedalla) and 1957
OWNER } series {Benjamin Sonnenberg

495★ **Illustrating the force of ancient habit** [c. 1903]
King Edward's Visit to the Convent of Dom Successio. King Edward: 'Enfin, Madame: faites monter la première à gauche.'
See 487 above.
REPRO **Plate 22**
OWNER Mrs David Karmel

496★ **[Untitled]** 1906
For Mabel [Beardsley]
Full length, wearing kilt, sporran and tiny glengarry. Cigar in hand.

EXHIB Grolier 1944
REPRO A. E. Gallatin, *Sir Max Beerbohm: Bibliographical Notes*, 1944
OWNER Harvard College Library

497* Christmas 1909. The King and Queen spent, as usual, a quiet, homely Christmas – Daily newspaper

They sit glumly holding hands on a sofa, beneath a small bunch of mistletoe.

EXHIB L.G. 1945 (Guedalla) and 1952
OWNER Fitzwilliam Museum, Cambridge

Royalty, Jewry, and Gold, or How History repeats itself without becoming monotonous [n.d.]

Two drawings as under:

498* A.D. 1199–1216 The King [John] drawing the Jew's teeth.

499* A.D. 1901–!! The Jew [Sir Ernest Cassel] stopping the King's.

OWNER Piccadilly Gallery

500 The King! God bless him! [c. 1911]

Max later annotated: Done by Max in about 1911 and now belonging to Ludovic and Moira Kennedy, 1952.

The King in uniform on horseback.

EXHIB L.G. 1952
OWNER Ludovic Kennedy

501* In the Rue Caumartin 1912

Shade of the Seventh Edward: 'After all, this is the most fitting of my memorials.'

He is pointing at the Restaurant Edouard VII.

OWNER Gallery of Fine Arts, Columbus, Ohio

502* Princeps Triplumiferus 1916

A little-known portrait in oils of Edward VII (then Prince of Wales) by D. G. Rossetti. Circa 1873.

It appears to have appeared to Mr Charles Augustus Howell that his illustrious friend would be able to command even higher prices if his work were sealed with the approval of some really fashionable member of the Reigning House. He bethought him of the Prince of Wales.

As usual, his resourcefulness was more than a match for difficulties.

On such-and-such an afternoon of the following week the Prince's brougham drew up sharp at the wrought-iron gate of 16 Cheyne Walk. His Royal Highness was escorted by Mr Rossetti and by Mr Howell to the drawing-room, where he partook of the sandwiches and other refreshments that had been sent on previously in a hamper from Marlborough House. It would seem that he was, as always, full of affability and bonhomie, and rather more than usually brilliant – though mainly of course in that interrogative vein of which he was a master.

He enquired whether Mr Hhwossetti were an Italian; whether he did not think that the shape of Italy on the map was very like that of a boot; when he had first come to London; *where* he was born in London; whether his father still lived at that addhhwess; *when* and of *what* his father had died; how old his mother was; how it was that so many of the organ-ghhwinders in London were Italians; whether the monkeys on the organs were Italian monkeys; whether it were not more difficult to paint in oils than in watercolour; the date of the invention of oil paints; what Mr Hhwossetti was laughing at; whether he knew Sir Charles Eastlake; whether . . . but this page would not contain a tithe of the searching questions that His Royal Highness put, punctuating the replies with that deep-throated *What-What* or *Yess-Yess-Yess* – which is so affectionately remembered by all who were privileged to come near him.

The brief meal having been consumed, an adjournment was made to the Studio, where his Royal Highness held a review of Mr Rossetti's recent work, including La Ghirlandata, Sibylla Calmifera, Reverie, Water-Willow and many others. It appears that he criticised these from a human, rather than from a merely technical, standpoint, and expressed a particular wish to meet Mrs Morris. He said that he had asked a few friends to dine with him next Sunday at the Star and Garter, and that he would be pleased to include that lady among his guests. It was explained to him by Mr Howell that Mr Morris was a man of uncouth and headstrong nature, with leanings to Republicanism, Monogamy, and other damnable heresies, and that really his wife went nowhere. It was said by Mr Howell that her sole privilege was that whenever Mr Rossetti was well on with a new portrait – when he had had (say) seven sittings – Mrs Morris was allowed by her husband to come and superintend with her counsel the later stages of the work.

It does not appear that she appeared at the eighth or any other sittings accorded by the Prince to Mr Rossetti; and it does appear that at length these sittings terminated somewhat abruptly – the Prince declaring forcibly (as had so often before, and has so often since, been declared by lesser men) that Mr Howell's word was inferior to his bond. Be this as it may, the portrait had been finished. It is one of the best examples of Rossetti's later and more luscious manner, an altogether admirable likeness, and an enduring monument not less to the genius of Mr Howell than to the early prime of Edward, the Peace-Giver.

Much of the beauty of the work is, alas, lost here through the limitations of the three-colour process.

EXHIB   L.G. 1957
REPRO   *Country Life*, 13 Jun 1957
OWNER   Mrs Joan Riddle

503* The rare, the rather awful visits of Albert Edward, Prince of Wales, to Windsor Castle 1921

EXHIB   L.G. 1923, 1945 (Guedalla) and 1952
REPRO   *Things New and Old*, 1923
OWNER   Mrs Philip Guedalla

504* All Things to All Men. The late King Edward at Balmoral 1921

Highland costume, smoking cigar in pouring rain.

EXHIB   L.G. 1945 (Guedalla)
OWNER   Ashmolean Museum, Oxford

[Proposed Illustrations for Sir Sidney Lee's forthcoming Biography] 1921
Eight drawings as under:

505* H.R.H. in the 'forties
A boy examining a globe of the world.

506* H.R.H. in the 'fifties
A youth between two stern-faced elders.

507* H.R.H. in the 'sixties
An elegant young man. Crinolined girl in background.

508* H.R.H. in the 'seventies
Cigar, striped shirt. Girl in background.

509* H.R.H. in the 'eighties
Evening dress. Girl in background.

510* H.R.H. in the 'nineties
Check suit, bowler hat, cigar. Girl in background.

511* H.M. in the 'noughts
Frock-coat and stock. Girl in background.

512* A. E. in the 'teens
Playing the harp in robe, halo and wings.

EXHIB ⎫ the ⎧ L.G. 1923, where the A.E. of 512 is
⎬ whole ⎨ interpreted as Angel Edward
OWNER ⎭ series ⎩ H.M. the Queen

513* [Edward VII] of Blessed Memory [Max 1921]
The bracketed parts are typewritten. Almost identical with 511, perhaps a sketch for it, without girl.

OWNER   Jeremy Clutterbuck

514* [Untitled Unsigned 1922]
A fresco containing heads (and sometimes shoulders) of King Edward, Joseph Chamberlain, Soveral, Henry James, Lord Rosebery, Reggie Turner, Pinero, Will Rothenstein, George Moore, Kipling, Lord Burnham, and Winston Churchill. For Max's three other frescoes, see 515, 614, 615, 1281–1283, 1837 and 1838.

REPRO   S. N. Behrman, *Portrait of Max*, N.Y., 1960
OWNER   University of Texas

515* [Titled as below] 1922
Sketch for a fresco [*514*], which has since been executed by me, quite seriously, on a ladder, in the Villino Chiaro. The faces are the faces that have always come easiest to me – lines of least resistance to the budding frescoist.
Offered to the Phillipsian Album.
  The faces as in 514, except that Henry James is missing.
OWNER   Norman Kark

516 [King Edward – Unforgotten 1929]
Known only from a note in Max's papers.

517* [Untitled] 1933
[Mr Gladstone, pointing to letter E on blackboard:]
  'And *this* letter, Sir – what is this one?'
[The Prince, a stout bearded boy:] 'Aitch'
[Queen Victoria:] 'What did I tell you, Mr Gladstone, *from* the very first? There's *nothing* to be got by it.'
  From 'The Q. and Mr G.' [*The Queen and Mr Gladstone* by Philip Guedalla, 1933], vol. I, p. 383. It would without doubt be a great object gained if, without reference to any other means, the Prince of Wales could through your majesty's influence or otherwise be induced to adopt the habit of reading' – Mr G. 4 Nov 1872.
  But 'She', replies the Q. on Nov 18 (page 385), 'has only to say that the P. of W. has *never* been fond of reading and from his earliest years it was *impossible* to get him to do so.' . . . Still, one does rather wish, dear Philip, doesn't one? that another effort had been made. Max. Rapallo 1933.
EXHIB   L.G. 1945 (Guedalla) and 1957
OWNER   J. C. Thomson

518* [Untitled c. 1945]
Full-length profile facing left, bare-headed, frock-coat, buttonhole. To the left and below are Max's instructions to the reproducer.
REPRO   *Lilliput*, Sep 1945
OWNER   Merton College, Oxford

519* L'Oncle de l'Europe 1946
(Happily for him, not spared to see his niece in the present year of grace).

Full-length profile facing left, evening dress, smoking cigar.
OWNER David Tree Parsons

520* An Illustrious Personage 1949
Very similar to 519, but a larger head and no cigar.
EXHIB L.G. 1952
OWNER Fitzwilliam Museum, Cambridge

521 'Vell pullt, poys!' [1951]
To Mr L. E. Jones – compared with whom Proteus was hide-bound.
An illustration to the parody of Max in L. E. J.'s 'A La Carte', 1951, it shows the King saying 'Vell pullt, poys!' to a pasted-on photograph of racing eights. It is believed to be the last full-dress coloured caricature that Max attempted.
OWNER Mrs Nancy Morse

522* The Old Familiar Figure 1953
For Elisabeth [Jungmann] with Max's love.
  Very similar to 520.
OWNER Mrs Eva Reichmann

523* [Untitled Unsigned n.d.]
Head and shoulders profile facing left. Possibly a sketch for leading figure in 514.
OWNER Giles St Aubyn

524* His Most Gracious Majesty [n.d.]
Half-length profile, facing left, top hat in hand.
EXHIB L.G. 1952
OWNER Mr and Mrs R. Grenfell

525 [King Edward VII]
EXHIB L.G. 1957

525A* H.R.H. The Prince of Wales, K.G., etc etc [n.d.]
Full-length three-quarter face. Top hat, overcoat.
REPRO Sotheby catalogue 26 Apr 1972
OWNER Sold at Sotheby's 26 Apr 1972

KING EDWARD VIII
b. 1894   Later Duke of Windsor
See also 386, 1591, 1725

526* Dons of Magdalen at great pains to incur no imputation of flunkeyism 1912
All studiously avoiding the undergraduate Prince of Wales in their midst.
EXHIB L.G. 1913
REPRO *Fifty Caricatures*, 1913
OWNER Mrs Norman D'Arcy

527* Pathetic attempt on my part at a cartoon which would be acceptable by some organ of the comic press 1921
[John Bull:] 'H.R.H. Sir, you have deserved well of Country and Empire! We hope that *they* have deserved well of *you*! We wish you long life, health, prosperity, and all that your heart desires! We ask you to transmit to your royal parents our most loyal regards. In you we recognise a chip of the old block. We wish King Edward, and Queen Victoria too, were also alive to see you as we see you to-day. Rough we may be, but our hearts are in the right place. Come rain, come shine, we shall not forget you. We most heartily desire that all good fortune shall attend you throughout life's journey.' How's that?
J. B. is shaking the Prince's right hand, while Britannia holds his left. A multi-coloured chorus of girls waves in the background. J. B.'s speech is written in capital letters in five sections between the legs of the main characters: each of the first four sections ends: '[to be continued]'
EXHIB L.G. May 1921
OWNER Mrs Katherine Lyon Mix

528* 'Long choosing and beginning late' [Milton, *Paradise Lost*] 1922
(Extract from *The Times* – November 10, 1972.)
Ex-'Prince' Weds
An interesting wedding was quietly celebrated yesterday at the Ealing Registry Office, when Mr Edward Windsor was united to Miss Flossie Pearson. The bridegroom, as many of our elder readers will recall, was at one time well-known as the 'heir-apparent' of the late 'King' George. He has for some years been residing at 'Balmoral,' 85 Acacia Terrace, Lenin Avenue, Ealing; and his bride is the only daughter of his landlady. Immediately after the ceremony the happy pair travelled to Ramsgate, where the honeymoon will be spent. Interviewed later in the day by a *Times* man, the aged mother-in-law confessed that she had all along been opposed to the match, because of the disparity between the ages of the two parties – the bride being still on the sunny side of forty. 'I had always,' she said, 'hoped that my Flossie was destined to make a brilliant match.' Now that the knot was tied, however, the old lady was evidently resigned to the *fait accompli*. 'I believe,' she said, 'that Mr Windsor will make a good husband for my girl, for I must say that a nicer, quieter gentleman, or a more pleasant-spoken, never lodged under my roof.'
EXHIB L.G. 1923, where it caused a press outcry and was
    withdrawn from view
OWNER Dame Daphne du Maurier

529* Untitled 1923
For Mr and Mrs Thomas Hardy from Max
Shows the Prince rushing towards Thomas Hardy, both

arms extended, saying 'Mayn't I call you Tom?' *Pasted on is a cutting from the* 'Evening News' *of 14 Jun 1923, announcing the Prince's visit to T. H.*

OWNER Dorset County Museum, Dorchester

530* **The Prince of Wales in New York** 1924

Mrs Garfield T. Placker (shrilly): 'Prince, you were right through that Great War: you know what a life-and-death struggle is; and all I ask is that you'll win me mine for the Social Leadership. Lunch with me and Mr Placker tomorrow.'

Mrs Schanamaker Dobbs (raucously): 'Don't you heed that plebeian, Prince! You've read your C. Darwin and know what's meant by Survival of the Fittest. I'm the fittest. Snatch a kiss from me right here in the eyes of all, and that'll settle the survival.'

(*Ceterae similia cantant.* [The others sing the same song])

EXHIB L.G. 1925 and 1945 (Guedalla)
REPRO *Observations*, 1925
OWNER Mrs Philip Guedalla

GUS ELEN
1862–1940 Cockney singer and comedian

531* [**Untitled** 1894]

REPRO *Pick-Me-Up*, 15 Sep 1894

ROBINSON ELLIS
1834–1913 Professor of Latin

532 [**Untitled Unsigned** c. 1893]

OWNER Merton College, Oxford

ST JOHN ERVINE
1883–1971 Author, playwright and critic
See 95

THE SECOND VISCOUNT ESHER
1852–1930 Politician and writer

533* **Pertness Rebuked** 1911

Lord Esher: 'Never mind who I am. Just go and do what I tell you.'

Lord E in frock-coat lectures Britannia on a cliff-ringed beach.

EXHIB L.G. 1911
REPRO *Tatler*, 26 Apr 1911
OWNER The Hon. Christopher Brett

MAJOR ESTERHAZY
1847–1923 Forger of the Dreyfus *bordereau*

534* **Major Esterhazy** [c. 1896]

EXHIB L.G. 1928, where dated as above
REPRO **Plate 72**
OWNER Keith Mackenzie

C. S. EVANS
1883–1944 Director of William Heinemann Ltd
See 208, 1447, 2017

THE REV. H. J. EVANS
Charterhouse master
See 664, 665

F

THE FIRST EARL FARQUHAR
1844–1923 Master of King Edward VII's household

535 [**Lord Farquhar** 1901]

EXHIB Carfax 1901

536 **Lord Farquhar recking nought of men's wonder as to what he may once have done that he should seem so very pleased and proud** 1913

EXHIB L.G. 1913 and 1957
OWNER The Earl of Drogheda

LADY FAUDEL-PHILLIPS
d. 1916 Sister of the first Lord Burnham
See 1366

THE FIRST DUKE OF FIFE
1849–1912 Son-in-law of King Edward VII

537 The Duke of Fife [n.d.]
In evening dress with a tartan face.
EXHIB L.G. 1911 and 1952

SIR ROBERT FINLAY
1842–1929   Barrister and M.P.

538★ **[Untitled** 1903]
'Qu'on me craint, ça c'est certain. Mais est-ce qu'on m'aime? Voilà ce qui m'agite.' Léon Gambetta
REPRO *John Bull*, 18 Jun 1903

SCOTT FISHE
Actor and singer

539★ **Mr Scott Fishe** [1895]
REPRO *Pick-Me-Up*, 5 Jan 1895

CLYDE FITCH
1865–1909   American playwright

540★ **Mr Clyde Fitch** [1896]
Holding a top hat in one hand and a tasselled cane in the other.
REPRO *Chap-Book* (Chicago), 15 Sep 1896
OWNER Newberry Library, Chicago

541★ **Mr Clyde Fitch** [*Signed*] **Max Beerbohm** 1898
Full-length profile facing left, top hat and cane in right hand.
REPRO Christie's catalogue 19 Mar 1971
OWNER Piccadilly Gallery

542★ **Jackwood** 1898
C. F. holding tennis racket. Jackwood Hall, in Kent, was rented by the American actor Nat Goodwin and his wife Maxine Elliot. Max and C. F. were frequent guests.
OWNER Mrs Leonard Marsili

543★ **Fitch** 1907
Full-length profile facing left, bareheaded. On his left hand two rings, and his left sleeve is triple-cuffed.
OWNER University of Texas

544★ **Mr Clyde Fitch** 1907
Full-length profile facing right, top hat in left hand, cane in right.
REPRO *A Book of Caricatures*, 1907
OWNER William Shawn

545 Count Fitchay (attributed to Maclise) [n.d.]
Refers to Count D'Orsay, an earlier dandy.
EXHIB New York 1912; L.G. 1945 (Guedalla)
OWNER R. R. Feilden

546 [Clyde Fitch 1938]
EXHIB L.G. 1952, where dated as above

547★ **Clyde Fitch** [n.d.]
Full length, three-quarter face, top hat and cane in right hand. Jewelled ring, cuff-links and buttonhole.
REPRO *Theatre Notebook*, Spring 1967
OWNER Yale University Library

548★ **[Untitled Unsigned** n.d.]
Full length, three-quarter face, hands by sides.
OWNER University of Texas

549★ **[Untitled Unsigned** n.d.]
Pen sketch, full length, back view, head turned to left.
OWNER University of Texas

EDWARD FITZGERALD
1809–83   Poet and scholar
See 1518, 1519

THE HON. EVELYN FITZGERALD
1874–1946   Stockbroker

550 [Hon. Evelyn Fitzgerald 1909]
EXHIB N.E.A.C. Winter 1909; L.G. 1911 and 1957

COLONEL FLETCHER

551 [Colonel Fletcher 1908]
EXHIB Carfax 1908

JOHNSTON FORBES-ROBERTSON
1853–1937   Actor-manager

552 [Mr Forbes Robertson 1901]
EXHIB Carfax 1901

E. M. FORSTER
1879–1970   Writer

553★ **Mr E. M. Forster** 1940
OWNER King's College, Cambridge

HELEN FORSYTH
d. 1901   Actress

554 Miss Forsyth, copied from 'Strand Magazine', vol. IV, p. 511, 'types of English Beauty', 1892 1919
Framed with 1187, q.v.
EXHIB   L.G. 1945 (Guedalla)
OWNER   Mrs Philip Guedalla

JOHN KNIGHT FOTHERINGHAM
1874–1936   Historian and astronomer

554A★ [Untitled Unsigned n.d.]
Full-length profile facing left, mortar-board in hand. A drawing done at Oxford, identified on back in another hand.
OWNER   Robert H. Taylor

GEORGE FRAMPTON
1860–1928   Sculptor

555★ Mr George Frampton 1908
Half-length profile facing left, pencil sketch.
EXHIB   Carfax 1908
OWNER   University of Texas

556 [Sir George Frampton]
EXHIB L.G. 1911

ANATOLE FRANCE
1844–1924   French writer
See 1483

EMPEROR FRANZ-JOSEF OF AUSTRIA
1830–1916
See 186

CHARLES FROHMAN
1860–1915   American theatrical impresario
See also 374

557★ [Untitled Unsigned n.d.]
Pencil sketch for the figure of C. F. in 374.
OWNER   University of Texas

558★ [Untitled Unsigned n.d.]
Another sketch for 374, but half length and hatless.
OWNER   University of Texas

ROGER FRY
1866–1934   Art critic
See also 982, 1266, 1267, 1586, 1588

559★ 'We needs must love the highest when we see it' [Tennyson, *Guinevere*]. Mr Roger Fry 1913
R. F. appreciating a toy soldier in an art gallery.
EXHIB   L.G. 1913
REPRO   *Fifty Caricatures*, 1913
OWNER   King's College, Cambridge

560★ Significant Form [n.d.]
Mr Clive Bell: 'I always think that when one feels one's been carrying a theory too far, *then's* the time to carry it a little further.'
Mr Roger Fry: 'A *little*? Good heavens, man! Are you growing old?.
EXHIB   L.G. May 1921 and 1952
REPRO   Clive Bell, *Old Friends*, 1956
OWNER   Mrs Barbara Bagenal

561★ A Law-Giver. Roger, first King of Bloomsbury 1931
EXHIB   L.G. 1952
REPRO   *Illustrated London News*, 10 May 1952
OWNER   National Portrait Gallery

HARRY FURNISS
1854–1925   Caricaturist

562★ [Untitled 1894]
REPRO   *Pick-Me-Up*, 13 Oct 1894

563★ Mr Harry Furniss
EXHIB   L.G. 1911
OWNER   Princeton University Library

CHARLES FURSE
1868–1904   Artist
See 1307, 1533

HAMILTON FYFE
1869–1951   Author and journalist

564 [Ariel, Mr Hamilton Fyfe; Prospero, Mr Thomas Marlowe]
H. F. wrote for the 'Daily Mail', of which T. M. was editor.
EXHIB L.G. 1913

G

W. J. GALLOWAY
1866–1931 Conservative M.P.

565★ Mr W. J. Galloway [*Signed* **RUTH** c. 1906]

For explanation of signature, see note to 1485.

REPRO *Vanity Fair*, 11 Jan 1906, where captioned 'He is very affluent'.
OWNER Mrs Katherine Lyon Mix

JOHN GALSWORTHY
1867–1933 Novelist
See also 181, 614, 615, 703, 748, 769, 1599

566★ Mr John Galsworthy envisaging Life and giving it – for he is nothing if not judicial – credit for the very best intentions 1909

Life is a hairy porcine creature on its hind legs.

EXHIB N.E.A.C. Summer 1909
REPRO H. V. Marrot, *Life and Letters of John Galsworthy*, 1935
OWNER Birmingham University Library

567★ [Untitled Unsigned n.d.]

Pencil sketch for 566.

OWNER University of Texas

568★ Breezy Jack of Biarritz 1924

'Seen *The Times* this morning? That's the stuff to give 'em, what? Shall give 'em some more, by Jove. Cheery-o! Right-o!'
For J. G. from Max. But why be breezy at Biarritz, when you might be roisterous at Rapallo?

Pasted on is a cutting from 'The Times' of 22 Mar 1924, headed 'The Three Years Average'. 'The breezy letter, which appears in an adjoining column, from MR GALSWORTHY on the dismal subject of the income-tax speaks for itself.'

REPRO H. V. Marrot, *Bibliography of John Galsworthy*, 1928
OWNER Lilly Library

J. L. GARVIN
1868–1947 Journalist

569★ Mr Garvin giving ideas to the Tory Party

EXHIB L.G. 1911
REPRO *Daily News*, 22 Apr 1911

570★ Atlas II

Mr J. L. Garvin: 'But ye see, bhoys, the little thing's so abshurdly loight! What I wanted was something to st-heady me.'

On the back of his neck he is balancing the world, which is much smaller than his head.

EXHIB L.G. 1913
REPRO *Daily News*, 11 Apr 1913

571★ Mr J. L. Garvin 1931

REPRO *Spectator* Supplement, 7 Mar 1931
OWNER *The Spectator*

KING GEORGE I OF GREECE
1845–1913
See 186

KING GEORGE IV
1762–1830
See also 189

572★ [Untitled 1894]

REPRO *Yellow Book*, vol. III, Oct 1894
OWNER William Bealby-Wright

KING GEORGE V
1865–1936
See also 45, 491–93, 1079, 1725

573★ H.R.H. The Prince of Wales [1899]

Shows the Prince in naval costume. Sometime between 1901 and 1910 Max erased the original title, 'H.R.H. The Duke of York', and substituted the above.

EXHIB L.G. 1945 (Guedalla)
REPRO *Butterfly*, Mar 1899; *Max's Nineties*, 1958
OWNER Ashmolean Museum, Oxford

574★ Duties and Diversions of the sweeter, simpler reign. King George inspecting an infant school

EXHIB L.G. 1913
REPRO *Fifty Caricatures*, 1913

575★ Amenities at Potsdam 1913

The very evident distress of either sovereign at the other's politeness.

GEORGE V (*continued*)

The King is in Prussian military uniform, the Kaiser in frock-coat and rounded bowler.

EXHIB L.G. 1957
OWNER S. J. Wingate

576* **A Sailor King** 1914

REPRO **Plate 23**
OWNER Mrs Philip Guedalla

577* **A Suggestion. Instead of incessantly visiting factories, work-shops, mills, pits, soup-kitchens, lime-kilns and the like, why should not the King and Queen stay comfortably at home and let people pop in to inspect *them* with benevolent interest?** 1924

Two matching drawings framed together. In one the Queen sits knitting among women and children of the lower orders; in the other, beneath busts of the Prince Consort and King Edward VII, the King writes at his desk, surrounded by male workers.

OWNER George Sassoon

ALFRED GILBERT
1854–1934   Sculptor

578* **Mr Alfred Gilbert** [c. 1896]

EXHIB L.G. 1928, where dated as above
OWNER Victoria & Albert Museum

W. S. GILBERT
1836–1911   Librettist and playwright

579* **W. S. Gilbert** [1894]

REPRO *Pick-Me-Up*, 27 Oct 1894; *The Poets' Corner*, 1943
OWNER Luke Gertler

580 **[Mr W. S. Gilbert** 1901]

EXHIB Carfax 1901

HAROLD GILMAN
1878–1919   Artist

581* **[Untitled** n.d.]

OWNER Art Gallery of New South Wales, Sydney

F. K. W. GIRDLESTONE
Charterhouse master
See 664, 665, 1630

CATHERINE GLADSTONE
1812–1900   Wife of W. E. G.
See 596

HERBERT GLADSTONE
1854–1930   Liberal politician

582* **[Untitled** 1900]

He is opening a front door marked LIBERAL PARTY, disclosing spiders' webs.

EXHIB Achenbach 1964
REPRO *World*, Christmas No, 1900
OWNER U.C.L.A. (Clark)

W. E. GLADSTONE
1809–98   Prime Minister
See also 42, 270, 439, 441, 517

583* **[Untitled Unsigned** n.d.]

A powerful early sketch, probably done at Charterhouse or Oxford.

REPRO **Plate 3**
OWNER Piccadilly Gallery

[Mr Gladstone goes to Heaven 1898]

Eleven drawings as under:

584* I. St Peter, having had his orders for some time, refuses admittance to Mr Gladstone. Mr Gladstone then commences to speak – 'It was a great effort, worthy of a great occasion,' wrote the Reporting Angel. 'Never had the Old Man Eloquent spoken with more fire and force, nor employed his inexhaustible resources of dialectic to greater effect.' The O.M.E. is here proving that Heaven was one of his birth-places. The simple ex-fisherman gradually falls under 'the wizard-spell of his eloquence' and in order to avoid the peroration, unbars the gates of gold and pearl.

585* II. The same evening, Mr Gladstone addresses a mass-meeting of Angels. He pays an eloquent and graceful tribute to God.

586* III. The old Adam. On leaving the meeting, Mr Gladstone picks up a fallen angel.

587* IV. Next morning, Mr Gladstone narrowly escapes an awkward rencontre with General Gordon.

588* V. Cut by the Prince Consort!

589* VI. Homer recognises his footstep.

590* VII. He passes beneath Horace's window. [Horace:] *'Ego docebo te perdere mea carmina!'* [*I'll teach you to ruin my poems!*]

591* VIII. He meets Mr Parnell. 'Oh Mr Parnell, *don't*

be so hasty! Give me two hours and a half, and I can explain all to you!'

592* IX. The Last Straw. Mr Gladstone reading the name of one of the principal streets [Disraeli Avenue].

593* X. His departure from Heaven. 'Certainly not! I presume you are paid your wages?' [To St Peter, holding out his hand for a tip]

594* XI. The End. Peace with Sulphur. 'And one clear call for me!' [Tennyson, *Crossing the Bar*] *He shakes hands with the Devil.*

EXHIB   the   L.G. 1945 (Guedalla) and 1957
REPRO   whole   *Max's Nineties*, 1958
OWNER   series   Junior Carlton Club

595* **If they were flourishing in this our day** 1936
W. E. G. and fifteen other eminent Victorians, shorn of all eccentricities of hair, beard, whiskers and clothes; instead dressed and coiffured in the drab uniformity of 1936. The others are Sir William Harcourt, Lord Leighton, Irving, Darwin, Whistler, Lord Randolph Churchill, Oscar Wilde, Browning, Herbert Spencer, Rossetti, Swinburne, Ruskin, Disraeli, Carlyle and Tennyson.
REPRO *Manchester Guardian*, 13 Mar 1936

596* **[Mr and Mrs Gladstone – from a photograph n.d.]**
EXHIB   L.G. 1945 (Guedalla, where titled as above)
OWNER   Professor M. R. D. Foot

J. M. GLOVER
1861–1931   Music critic and conductor

597* **Mr James Glover** [n.d.]
REPRO   J. M. Glover, *Jimmy Glover and his Friends*, 1913

JOHANN WOLFGANG VON GOETHE
1749–1832   German poet

598* **Goethe, watching the shadow of Lili on the blind** [c. 1904]
EXHIB   Carfax 1904; N.Y. 1912; L.G. 1945 (Guedalla) and 1957
REPRO   *The Poets' Corner*, 1904 and 1943
OWNER   Freda, Countess of Listowel

599 **[Goethe at his window in Rome ?1918]**
[From the watercolour by Tischbein.]
See Max's essay 'Quia Imperfectum' (1918) in 'And Even Now', 1920.
OWNER   Sold at the Parke-Bernet Galleries, N.Y., 1967

NAT GOODWIN
1857–1919   American actor

600* **Mr Nat Goodwin** [n.d.]
REPRO   *Radio Times*, 3 Dec 1954
OWNER   Douglas Cleverdon

GENERAL GORDON
1833–85   Soldier
See 587

COSMO GORDON-LENNOX
1869–1921   Actor and playwright

601 **[Mr Cosmo Gordon-Lennox** c. 1898]
EXHIB   L.G. 1928, where dated as above

602* **Mr Cosmo Gordon-Lennox** 1907
Full length, three-quarter face, wearing straw hat and large buttonhole, holding cane with handle in his mouth.
EXHIB   Carfax 1908; L.G. 1952
OWNER   Peter Hughes

603 **[Mr Cosmo Gordon-Lennox]**
EXHIB   L.G. 1911

604* **Mr Cosmo Gordon-Lennox** [n.d.]
Full-length profile facing right, wearing straw hat and carrying cane.
OWNER   Harvard College Library

605 **Mr Cosmo Gordon-Lennox** [n.d.]
Wearing tail coat and white tie, coral waistcoat-buttons and studs, lighted cigarette in holder in right hand.
OWNER   Simon Towneley

G. J. GOSCHEN
1831–1907   Liberal politician

606 **[Mr Goschen** c. 1894]
Max added in catalogue: Mainly remembered as having been forgotten by Lord Randolph Churchill.
EXHIB   L.G. 1928, where dated as above

607* **Mr Goschen** [1898]
Profile facing right. Top hat, eyeglass, hands together in front of him.
REPRO   *Daily Mail*, 9 Jul 1898

608★ Mr Goschen [n.d.]

Very similar to 607, but with umbrella under arm.

OWNER National Portrait Gallery

609★ Lord Goschen [1903]

Almost identical with 608, but facing left.

REPRO *John Bull*, 13 Aug 1903
OWNER University of Texas

EDMUND GOSSE

1849–1928 Critic and writer
See also 436, 442, 679, 703, 748, 807A, 1116, 1599, 1643

610 [Mr Edmund Gosse 1901]

EXHIB Carfax 1901

611 [Mr Edmund Gosse, judged by his Peers 1904]

E. G. was appointed Librarian to the House of Lords in 1904.

EXHIB Carfax 1904

612★ The Birthday Surprise 1919

'This is no moment for coyness or mock-modesty'
For E. G. affectionately from Max

E. G. being presented (by Lord Crewe) with a bust of himself to commemorate his seventieth birthday. The quotation is from E. G.'s printed letter (dated Sep 1919) to 200 friends who had sent him good wishes. The others in the drawing are Lord Beauchamp, Logan Pearsall Smith, G. K. Chesterton, L. V. Harcourt, George Moore, Kipling, Lord Curzon, Maurice Baring, Arnold Bennett, Lord Howard de Walden, the Archbishop of Canterbury (Davidson), Lord Londonderry, Conrad, Hardy, John Morley, Lord Spencer, Mr Ryman, Lord Haldane, Sir Frank Swettenham, Pinero, William Archer, Maurice Hewlett, Austin Dobson, Evan Charteris, Ray Lankester, and Arthur Balfour, in whose house the presentation took place.

EXHIB L.G. 1957
REPRO Evan Charteris, *Life and Letters of Sir Edmund Gosse*, 1931
OWNER Savile Club

613★ A Lacuna 1921

Mr Edmund Gosse (to his interlocutor in *Avowals* [by George Moore, 1919]): 'But, my dear Moore, of *course* you will – of *course* they shall! Only, you don't tell us when your seventieth birthday *is*!'
G. M. stares up at the bust of Gosse (see *612*), while E. G. consults 'Who's Who'.

EXHIB L.G. May 1921; Grolier 1944
REPRO *A Survey*, 1921
OWNER Harvard College Library

614★ [Untitled Unsigned c. 1922]

A fresco containing heads and shoulders of Gosse, Ray Lankester, Carson, Gordon Craig, Cunninghame Graham, Steer, Tonks, John Davidson, Shaw, G. K. Chesterton, Masefield, Lytton Strachey, Asquith, Galsworthy, Sargent, Conder, William Nicholson, Henry Chaplin, Arthur Balfour, Charles Boyd and G. S. Street. For Max's three other frescoes, see 514, 515, 615, 1281–1283, 1837 and 1838.

REPRO *The Faces of Authorship*, Texas, 1968
OWNER University of Texas

615★ [Untitled Unsigned n.d.]

Sketch for 614 on squared paper. Same figures less G. S. Street.

REPRO Parke-Bernet catalogue, 2 Nov 1966
OWNER University of Texas

616★ The Old and the Young Self 1924

Young Self: 'Are you saved?'

The Old Self is surrounded by his distinguished friends – Lord Londonderry, Lytton Strachey, J. C. Squire, Edward Shanks, W. B. Yeats, Maurice Baring, the Archbishop of Canterbury (Davidson), Edward Marsh, Lord Lincolnshire, Lord Crewe, Pinero, Robert Bridges, Evan Charteris, Haldane and Asquith.

EXHIB L.G. 1925, 1945 (Guedalla), 1952 and 1957
REPRO *Observations*, 1925; *Caricatures by Max*, 1958
OWNER Ashmolean Museum, Oxford

617★ Edmund Gosse [c. 1940]

Three-quarter length, profile facing left, pencil.

REPRO *Transatlantic Dialogue*, ed Mattheisen and Millgate, Texas, 1965
OWNER Oliver R. W. W. Lodge

618★ Mr Gosse and the Rising Generation [n.d.]

Mr Gosse loquitur: 'Diddums!'

E. G. nervously holds a rather grown-up-faced baby in a library.

OWNER Mrs Martin Robertson

619★ [Edmund Gosse in a Cavalry Mess n.d.]

E. G., between two Cavalry officers, has his hand on a small bookcase. Pasted on to various parts of the drawing are printed exerpts from a 'pen sketch' of E. G. – 'He has outgrown his early delicacy . . . is tall . . . blue eyes, at least so far as I could judge through his eye-glasses . . . well-furnished with, it goes without saying, an intellectual head . . . and, to complete the inventory, a heavy fair moustache . . . encyclopaedic learning . . . Mr Gosse among his many gifts, has that of adaptability, and I should say that he could make himself quite at home in a cavalry mess.'

REPRO Evan Charteris, *Life and Letters of Sir Edmund Gosse*, 1931

620★ Mr Edmund Gosse [n.d.]
Full-length profile facing right, right hand raised.
EXHIB L.G. 1952
OWNER Robert H. Taylor

621★ [Untitled Unsigned n.d.]
Full-length profile facing left, frock-coat, check trousers, spats, left arm extended.
REPRO Lord David Cecil, *Max*, 1964
OWNER Lord David Cecil

621A★ A Memory of Edmund Gosse, the vibrant, the brilliant 1943
Almost identical with 621.
REPRO *Abinger Chronicle*, Aug–Sept 1943

FRANCIS CARRUTHERS GOULD
1844–1925 Caricaturist
See also 1424

622★ [Untitled Unsigned n.d.]
A rough sketch, perhaps for the figure of F. C. G. in 1424.
OWNER University of Texas

DR W. G. GRACE
1848–1915 Cricketer

623★ Portrait of dear old W. G. – to the left is the Grand Stand, and to the right the funeral of one of his patients [n.d.]
W. G. is holding a tiny bat in one hand, and in the other a cheque for £10,000, signed Lawson. This was the result of the shilling collection organised by the 'Daily Telegraph' (of which Sir Edward Lawson was the proprietor) in 1895, when W. G. made his hundredth century.
REPRO *Sphere*, 8 Nov 1963
OWNER Marylebone Cricket Club

R. B. CUNNINGHAME GRAHAM
1852–1936 Scottish writer, horseman and Socialist politician
See also 614, 615, 1599, 1749, 1750

624★ Mr Cunninghame Graham [1899]
Full length, hair on end, top hat in hand, tasselled cane held upright on hip.
REPRO *Academy*, 28 Jan 1899; *Max's Nineties*, 1958

625★ Mr R. B. Cunninghame Graham 1910
[*One Cockney tough to another:*] 'Bly me, Bill, if 'e didn't corl us *comrids!*'

EXHIB N.E.A.C. Summer 1910
OWNER Sir Anthony Hooper Bart

626 [Mr Cunninghame Graham]
EXHIB L.G. 1911

627★ [Untitled 1921]
Six studies for a caricature of C. G. on one sheet.
EXHIB L.G. 1952, where dated as above
REPRO Bohun Lynch, *Max Beerbohm in Perspective*, 1921
OWNER Dartmouth College, Hanover, N.H.

628★ The Old and the Young Self. Mr Cunninghame Graham 1924
The Young Self, riding a rocking horse, greets the Old Self, leaping in through the window as a centaur.
EXHIB L.G. 1925
REPRO *Observations*, 1925
OWNER Sold at Sotheby's 17 Nov 1954

629★ Mr Cunninghame Graham [n.d.]
A later and more polished version of 624.
REPRO **Plate 77**
OWNER Admiral Sir Angus Cunninghame Graham

CORNEY GRAIN
1844–95 Entertainer

630★ [Untitled Unsigned 1894]
REPRO *Pick-Me-Up*, 8 Dec 1894

PERCY GRAINGER
1882–1961 Australian pianist and folk-song expert

631 [Mr Percy Grainger]
'The group of great ladies listening to Mr Percy Grainger ... is a wonderful ensemble,' Edward Marsh in 'The Blue Review', May 1913.
EXHIB L.G. 1913

THE MARCHIONESS OF GRANBY
d. 1937 Later Duchess of Rutland

632★ Lady Granby in Paris, Easter '99
OWNER Piccadilly Gallery

THE MARQUESS OF GRANBY
1852–1925 Later Eighth Duke of Rutland

633* **Lord Granby** [1896]

Full length, full face, wearing huge fur coat, top hat and monocle.

REPRO *Twenty-Five Gentlemen*, 1896

634 [**Lord Granby** 1901]

EXHIB Carfax 1901

635 **Lord Granby** [n.d.]

Walking, with top hat, umbrella and monocle.

OWNER Charles Blitzer

636 [**The Duke of Rutland**]

EXHIB L.G. 1911

THE SECOND EARL GRANVILLE
1815–91   Liberal politician

637* [**Untitled Unsigned** c. 1890]

A sheet of multiple drawings, probably done at Oxford, showing episodes in Lord G's career, with comments: 'He sat in the House of Commons when he was Mr Leveson-Gower . . . Although one of the kindliest souls he does not go into ecstasies over the gentlemen Mr Gladstone delights to honour . . . . As an after-dinner speaker no one can touch him . . . He is subject to the gout . . . He and Lord Derby did not distinguish themselves under Mr Gladstone's premiership . . . He still leads Her Majesty's Opposition in the Lords . . . Ask Lord Rosebery "who has been the best Foreign Secretary of modern times." ' Lords Derby, Salisbury and Rosebery are also recognisable.

OWNER Merton College, Oxford

638* **The 2nd Earl Granville** 1926

EXHIB L.G. 1957
OWNER Merton College, Oxford

ROBERT GRAVES
b. 1895   Poet and novelist
See 703

J. T. GREIN
1862–1935   Theatre critic and manager

639 [**Mr J. T. Grein**]

EXHIB L.G. 1911

SIR EDWARD GREY
1862–1933   Liberal politician
See also 799

640 [**Early meeting of Sir Edward Grey and Baron von Bieberstein, at the Foreign Office** 1912]

EXHIB L.G. 1952, where dated as above

641* **Sir Edward Grey wondering whether, after all, he is so wise as he looks and sounds in the House of Commons** 1913

He is being hugged by an enormous (Russian) bear wearing an imperial crown.

EXHIB L.G. 1913
REPRO *Fifty Caricatures*, 1913

J. L. GRIFFITHS

Known only from an L.G. note.

THE SECOND LORD GRIMTHORPE
1856–1917   Banker and M.P.

642* [**Untitled** 1903]

Seated alone at table in evening dress, smoking cigar.

REPRO *John Bull*, 3 Jun 1903

643* **Mr Ernest Beckett** [pre-1905]

Full length, standing, in evening dress.

OWNER Mrs Eva Reichmann

644* **Café Chose. Milor Grimthorpe qui arrive** 1907

Advancing, in evening dress, between two rows of waiters to a solitary table.

EXHIB Carfax 1907; L.G. 1945 (Guedalla) and 1957
REPRO *A Book of Caricatures*, 1907
OWNER Ashmolean Museum, Oxford

645* **V'là Milor Grimthorpe qui paie la note** 1907

At the same solitary table, smoking cigar and paying bill with a flutter of notes.

OWNER Mark Birley

GEORGE GROSSMITH, SENIOR
1847–1912   Entertainer and author

646* [**Untitled Unsigned** 1894]

Full length, leaning on piano.

REPRO *Pall Mall Budget*, 26 Jul 1894; *Max's Nineties*, 1958

647 [**Mr George Grossmith, Senr** c. 1896]
EXHIB L.G. 1928, where dated as above

648* [**Untitled** 1901]
Full length, left hand and index finger extended.
REPRO *Critic* (N.Y.), Nov 1901

649 [**Mr George Grossmith**]
EXHIB L.G. 1957

GEORGE GROSSMITH, JUNIOR
1874–1935   Actor

650* **Mr George Grossmith Junr and the Gaiety Chorus** 1910
EXHIB N.E.A.C. Summer 1910; L.G. 1911
OWNER Victoria & Albert Museum

651* [**Untitled** n.d.]
Full length, frock-coat, carrying top hat and stick.
REPRO *Fifty Caricatures*, 1913

652 [**Mr George Grossmith, Jr**]
EXHIB L.G. 1928

653* **Mr George Grossmith Jnr** [n.d.]
REPRO *Observer*, 4 Dec 1966
OWNER P.S. Bevan

SYDNEY GRUNDY
1848–1914   Playwright

654* **Mr Sydney Grundy** [n.d.]
OWNER Piccadilly Gallery

PHILIP GUEDALLA
1889–1944   Writer and Max-collector
See also 517, 1646, 1999

655* **Literature, Mr Philip Guedalla, and the Law (and all acknowledgments to Sir Joshua Reynolds)** 1921
Based on J. R.'s 'Garrick between Tragedy and Comedy'.
EXHIB L.G. May 1921 and 1945 (Guedalla)
REPRO *A Survey*, 1921
OWNER Mrs Philip Guedalla

656* **Mr Guedalla** 1929
Full length, standing with one hand on table, the other in trouser pocket.

EXHIB L.G. 1952
OWNER National Gallery of Victoria, Melbourne

657* **Mr Philip Guedalla** 1931
Full-length profile, in dinner jacket, smoking pipe.
OWNER Mrs Rau

658* [**Untitled** n.d.]
[Napoleon III:] 'Charmant et sympathique jeune homme, levez-vous Duc de Guédalla et de la rue du parc d'Hyde!'
For the Duke.
Presumably a reward for P. G.'s 'The Second Empire', 1922.
EXHIB L.G. 1945 (Guedalla)
REPRO **Plate 80**
OWNER Mrs Philip Guedalla

THE HON. IVOR GUEST
1873–1939   Later Lord Ashby St Ledgers
See also 114

659 **Mr Ivor Guest** [n.d.]
OWNER Sold at Sotheby's 14 Dec 1960

THE HON. MONTAGUE GUEST
1888–1958   Conservative M.P.

660 **Mr Montague Guest** [c. 1908]
EXHIB Carfax 1908
OWNER Sold at Sotheby's 14 Dec 1960

LUCIEN GUITRY
1860–1925   French actor-manager
See 1291

KING GUSTAV V OF SWEDEN
1858–1950
See 186

STEPHEN GWYNN
1864–1950   Irish writer and M.P.

661* **Mr Stephen Gwynn** 1914
Standing forlornly in the lobby of the House of Commons.
EXHIB L.G. May 1921
REPRO *A Survey*, 1921

H

THE REV. WILLIAM HAIG-BROWN
1823–1907   Headmaster of Charterhouse

662* **[Untitled Signed with monogram** 1890]

FLORUIT immensos schola Carthusiana per annos,
Olim Londinii pessima pernicies.
FLORET in aerio jam condita vertice montis
Quingentosque docet tristitiam pueros.
FLOREBIT nec non Plutonis regna manebunt:
Alteraque ut noscas sis memor alterius.

[Charterhouse School, once the direst pest in the City
of London, has flourished through years innumerable.
It flourishes to-day, set upon a hill-top high in air,
teaching five hundred boys to be unhappy.
Yes, and it will continue to flourish as long as the
realms of Pluto endure: if you would know what
either is like, you have but to recall the other.]

*H.-B., in gown and mortar-board, dances on a bust of
Thomas Sutton (1532–1611), the founder of Charterhouse.
In 'Mainly on the Air', 1946, Max wrote:* 'In my first
term at Oxford (A.D. 1890) I did a drawing of Thomas
Sutton . . . and under it I wrote these three elegiac
couplets . . . the verses were an unpardonable libel on
my views. I thought Charterhouse a very fine school
really. I was very glad of having been there. But – no,
I was *not* of the straitest sect. My delight in having
been at Charterhouse was far greater than had been
my delight in being there. I was well content to be
where I was: in Oxford.'

REPRO   G. F. Sims catalogue no 64, May 1966
OWNER   Fred H. Higginson

663* **Dr Haig Brown [Unsigned** n.d.]

A schoolboy drawing.

REPRO *Carthusian*, Jul 1955

664* **Some Masters of Forty Years Ago** 1928

*Shows H.-B. and thirteen of his colleagues: the Rev. J. A. A.
Tait, F. K. W. Girdlestone, the Rev. H. J. Evans, G. H.
Robinson, C. W. Moss, L. M. Stewart, Georges Petilleau,
L. Marshall, A. H. Tod, T. E. Page, the Rev. C. H.
Weekes, the Rev. G. S. Davies, and L. A. G. Becker.*

REPRO   *Greyfriar*, Dec 1928
OWNER   Charterhouse School

664A* **Some Masters of Forty Years Ago** 1928

An exact replica of 664.

EXHIB   Achenbach 1964
OWNER   U.C.L.A. (Clark)

665* **Vague random memories of some of them**
[n.d.]

For P. L. Ingpen from Max Beerbohm.

*Shows H.-B. and fifteen other masters: the first eight of
664 and seven others.*

OWNER   U.C.L.A. (Clark)

ARTHUR ELAM HAIGH
1855–1905   Oxford lecturer in classics

665A* **Mr Haigh lectures on Greek Drama [Unsigned** n.d.]

*Holding Masks of Comedy and Tragedy. A drawing done
at Oxford.*

OWNER   Robert H. Taylor

VISCOUNT HALDANE
1856–1928   Liberal politician and writer
See also 43, 44, 612, 616, 748, 1423, 1443

666* **8.30 p.m. Mr Haldane exercising a ministerial prerogative** 1907

Wearing day clothes at a fashionable dinner-party.

EXHIB   Carfax 1907; L.G. 1945 (Guedalla) and 1957
REPRO   *A Book of Caricatures*, 1907
OWNER   Ashmolean Museum, Oxford

667* **Lord Haldane**

Head and shoulders, head like cottage loaf.

EXHIB   L.G. 1911
REPRO   *Bookman*, August 1911

668* **[Untitled Unsigned** 1912]

Head and shoulders, eyes shut.

REPRO   *Bystander*, 29 May 1912
OWNER   National Portrait Gallery

669 **[Lord Haldane]**

EXHIB   L.G. 1945 (Guedalla)

THE FIRST EARL OF HALSBURY
1823–1921   Three times Lord Chancellor
See also 478, 1563

670 [**Lord Halsbury** c. 1896]
EXHIB L.G. 1928, where dated as above

671★ **Lord Halsbury** [1900]
REPRO *Idler*, Mar 1900

672★ **'The rising hope of the stern unbending Tories' (Lord Halsbury)** [**Unsigned** n.d.]
Lord Alverstone (to Mr F. E. Smith): 'Experto crede, my young friend. If you cherish – for no matter how remote a future – hopes of the Woolsack, put them from you.'
The title refers to Macaulay on Gladstone.
EXHIB L.G. 1913
REPRO *Fifty Caricatures*, 1913

ARCHIBALD HAMILTON
1876–1939   Soldier and eccentric

673 [**A reminder of a more gracious age: Mr Archibald Hamilton** 1908]
EXHIB Carfax 1908

COSMO HAMILTON
1872–1942   Writer

674★ **C. H.** [**Unsigned** 1900]
REPRO *World*, Christmas No, 1900

SIR IAN HAMILTON
1853–1947   General

675★ **Sir Ian Hamilton** [n.d.]
In mess kit, with tartan trousers and spurs. Long line of medal ribbons streaming out, hand on hip.
EXHIB L.G. 1952
REPRO Ian B. M. Hamilton, *The Happy Warrior*, 1966
OWNER Mrs Janet Leeper

676★ **Sir Ian Hamilton** 1909
Same dress, even more medal-ribbons, hand behind back.
EXHIB L.G. 1945 (Guedalla)
OWNER Mrs Philip Guedalla

HUGH HAMMERSLEY
1858–1930   Patron of the Arts

677★ **Mr Hugh Hammersley** [1909]
EXHIB N.E.A.C. Summer 1909
OWNER Lilly Library

ST JOHN HANKIN
1869–1909   Playwright

678★ **Mr St John Hankin composing the scenario of one of his witty comedies** [1907]
EXHIB Carfax 1907; L.G. 1952
REPRO *A Book of Caricatures*, 1907
OWNER Mrs Kate Mason

LANCE HANNEN
1866–1942   Senior Partner of Christie's

679★ **The Red Cross Sale at Christie's, April 1918**
Tiny in the background is L. H. on his rostrum. In front, as recorded in Max's 'Key (for Posterity – and others)' are: James Pryde, C. H. Shannon, Charles Ricketts, Conrad, W. B. Anderson, Sir Claude Phillips, Barrie, Gosse, Lord Spencer, Lord Lansdowne, Harry Higgins, Lord Ribblesdale, L. V. Harcourt, Quartermaster Walker, Sir Charles Russell, Lady Wernher, Egan Mew, Henry Tonks, Sir Frank Swettenham, Ambrose McEvoy, E. V. Lucas, Alfred Sutro, Laurence Binyon, Maurice Hewlett, Croal Thomson, P. W. Steer, Will Rothenstein, C. R. W. Nevinson, Sir Gordon Campbell, D. S. MacColl, Sir Lionel Cust, Sir Sidney Colvin, Sir Ernest Cassel, Pinero, Curzon, Gerald du Maurier, Sir Jeremiah Colman, Augustine Birrell, Sir Alfred Mond, and William Nicholson.
EXHIB L.G. 1952
REPRO H. C. Marillier, *Christie's 1766–1925*, 1926
OWNER Messrs Christie, Manson & Woods

680★ **A Supplement** [to 679] **– for Mr Lance Hannen** [1918]
An enlargement of L. H. on his rostrum.
OWNER Messrs Christie, Manson & Woods

LEWIS VERNON HARCOURT
1863–1922   Liberal politician
See also 43, 44, 335, 612, 679, 691, 692, 694, 799, 1443

681 [**Mr L. V. Harcourt** 1901]
EXHIB Carfax 1901

682 [**Mr L. V. Harcourt** 1908]
EXHIB Carfax 1908

683★ **Mr Lulu Harcourt** [n.d.]
Full length, evening dress, cloak, head hanging over high collar.
EXHIB L.G. 1911
OWNER Merton College, Oxford

684 [Mr L. V. Harcourt wishing so much to say the exactly right thing to every one of the colonies]
EXHIB L.G. 1911

685* Mr L. V. Harcourt 1912
Profile, full length, evening dress, high collar, cloak.
REPRO *Bystander,* 1 May 1912
OWNER Robert Beloe

686* Mr Lulu Harcourt [n.d.]
Head and shoulders, head looking round edge of high collar.
OWNER Piccadilly Gallery

SIR WILLIAM VERNON HARCOURT
1827–1904   Liberal politician
See also 595, 1563

687* [Untitled Unsigned 1894]
Small head and front outline of huge body.
REPRO *Pall Mall Budget,* 5 Jul 1894

688* [Untitled Unsigned 1895]
Full face, at least five chins, top hat.
REPRO *Pick-Me-Up,* 23 Feb 1895

689* [Untitled 1896]
Full-length profile, reading from paper in front of empty bench.
REPRO *Twenty-Five Gentlemen,* 1896; *Max's Nineties,* 1958

690 [Sir William Harcourt, in the New Forest, dreaming 1901]
EXHIB Carfax 1901

691* [Untitled 1901]
Shows W. H., very fat, leaning back, and in front his son L. V. H. (with high collar) leaning forward.
REPRO *Critic* (N.Y.) Nov. 1901

692* Sir William and Mr Lulu Harcourt [1902]
Very similar to 691, but L. V. H. has a much higher collar, and they are arm-in-arm.
REPRO *Pall Mall Magazine,* Feb 1902

693* The Old War-Horse [1903]
Standing, right hand inside coat, left holding paper.
REPRO *John Bull,* 6 May 1903

694* Sir William and Mr Loulou Harcourt in 1889 1926
Side by side, W. H. slightly in front.
EXHIB L.G. 1928
OWNER City of Sheffield Art Gallery

695* [Untitled n.d.]
Front view, full length, head turned to left, right hand extended, left holding paper.
EXHIB L.G. 1945 (Guedalla)

696 [Sir William Harcourt]
EXHIB L.G. 1945 (Guedalla)
OWNER Sold at Sotheby's 19 Jul 1967

SIR CECIL HARCOURT-SMITH
1859–1944   Director of Victoria & Albert Museum
See also 378

697* Sir Cecil Harcourt-Smith receives a deputation from a Northern Town that is meditating a Museum 1924
OWNER Victoria & Albert Museum

MARTIN HARDIE
1875–1952   Keeper of Paintings, Victoria & Albert Museum
See 379

WILLIAM MONEY HARDINGE
1854–1916   Poet and writer

698* Mr Willie Hardinge – a Memory 1922
OWNER Piccadilly Gallery

THE SIXTH EARL OF HARDWICKE
1867–1904   Conservative politician

699* Lord Hardwicke [c. 1902]
EXHIB L.G. 1928, where dated as above
REPRO Sotheby catalogue, 14 Dec 1960
OWNER Sold at Sotheby's 14 Dec 1960

THOMAS HARDY
1840–1928   Poet and novelist
See also 27, 529, 612, 748, 1550

700★ Mr Thomas Hardy [1902]
Large head, tiny body, hands in trouser pockets.
REPRO *Pall Mall Magazine*, Feb 1902

701★ Mr Thomas Hardy composing a lyric
EXHIB L.G. 1913 and 1952
REPRO *Fifty Caricatures*, 1913
OWNER Charterhouse School

702★ For Mrs Thomas Hardy – a recollection, not a replica, of the drawing she liked 1919
Similar to 701, but everywhere different.
OWNER Dorset County Museum, Dorchester

703★ Nicholson's Owl—revised, under flash-light from Edmund Gosse, by Max [c. 1919]
William Nicholson's cover for the first issue of the 'Owl', May 1919, consisted of a large owl in the centre, with seven smaller owls round it, facing outwards. Max redrew the owls, giving them faces of contributors to the magazine. The large one is Hardy, the others Eric Kennington, Robert Graves, Masefield, Logan Pearsall Smith, Max himself, Robert Nichols, and Galsworthy.
EXHIB L.G. 1945 (Guedalla)
OWNER Mrs Mary Roebling

704★ Thomas Hardy 1926
Standing, hands in trouser pockets, in front of a bookcase.
EXHIB L.G. 1928
REPRO Sotheby catalogue 15 Dec 1971
OWNER Sold at Sotheby's 15 Dec 1971

705 [Mr Thomas Hardy]
EXHIB L.G. 1952

706 [Hommage à Thomas . . .]
T. H. being drawn by Will Rothenstein. Known only from an L.G. note.

HENRY HARLAND
1861–1905   Editor of the *Yellow Book*
See also 1650

707★ Henry Harland Esq [1896]
REPRO *Twenty-Five Gentlemen*, 1896; *Max's Nineties*, 1958

707A★ The Yellow Dwarf [1896]
This dumpy, bearded figure, wearing a fringed black mask, carrying bow and arrows, and standing on top of a rock, has been taken to represent H. H., who is believed to be the author of three articles that had appeared over that name in the 'Yellow Book'.
REPRO *Yellow Book*, Oct 1896

708 [Editing the Yellow Book. Mr Harland and Mr Beardsley]
EXHIB L.G. 1928

709★ Henry Harland groaning at mention of Enoch Soames's name [n.d.]
As described in 'Seven Men', 1919, p. 19.
OWNER Arthur B. Spingarn

ALFRED HARMSWORTH
See Northcliffe

BRINSLEY HARPER

710★ Mr Brinsley Harper 1908
OWNER Piccadilly Gallery

FRANK HARRIS
1856–1931   Writer and editor

711★ Mr Frank Harris [1896]
Full-length profile, frock-coat and buttonhole.
EXHIB F.A.S. 1896
REPRO *Twenty-Five Gentlemen*, 1896

712★ 'My poverty, but not my will consents' [*Romeo and Juliet* V, i] Romeo – Frank Harris. Apothecary – Max [c. 1898]
M is handing F. H. a phial labelled 'Dramatic Criticism'.
REPRO Max Beerbohm, *More Theatres*, 1969
OWNER Basil Lee

713★ The Editor of the 'Saturday Review' [c. 1898]
Max to G. B. S.
F. H., oddly dressed for riding, holds a crop, while a cockaded footman holds a horse in the background. Max succeeded Shaw as dramatic critic of the 'Saturday Review' in May 1898.
OWNER University of Texas

714 [Mr Frank Harris 1901]
EXHIB Carfax 1901

715 Mr Frank Harris, lecturing [1909]
EXHIB L.G. 1952, where dated as above
OWNER Hugh Wheeler

716★ Mr Frank Harris presents. (Frontispiece for that work of brilliant and profound criticism 'The Man Shakespeare' [by F. H., 1909]) 1910

HARRIS (*continued*)

EXHIB N.E.A.C. Summer 1910; L.G. 1911 and 1952
REPRO **Plate 52**
OWNER J. I. M. Stewart

717★ [**Untitled Unsigned** c. 1910]
Rough sketch for 716, but with footlights and audience's heads in foreground.
OWNER University of Texas

718 [**Mr Frank Harris**]
EXHIB L.G. 1911

719★ **The Best Talker in London, with one of his best listeners** 1914
For my old friend Frank Harris, this scribble in record of a scene which, happily for me, has been so frequent in the past twenty years.
F. H. holding forth to Max over a table laid with bottle and glasses.
EXHIB L.G. 1957
REPRO *Modern Society*, 28 Feb 1914; Vincent Brome, *Frank Harris*, 1959
OWNER Lady Jones (Enid Bagnold)

720★ **'Had Shakespeare asked me . . . '** [**Unsigned** n.d.]
The words are said to have been F. H.'s qualification of a denial of homosexual proclivities.
REPRO **Plate 51**
OWNER S. J. Wingate

721★ **Frank Harris** [**Unsigned** n.d.]
OWNER Sold at Sotheby's Nov 1969

HENRY HARRIS
d. 1950   Art expert

722★ **Le Penseur. Mr H. Harris carefully weighing the respective merits of nine invitations for the ninth instant** 1923
EXHIB L.G. 1923
REPRO *Things New and Old*, 1923

AUSTIN HARRISON
1873–1928   Writer and journalist
See also 1043

723 **Mr Austin Harrison** [n.d.]
OWNER Sold at Sotheby's 14 Dec 1960

FREDERIC HARRISON
1831–1923   Lawyer and writer
See 748

LAWRENCE ALEXANDER HARRISON
1866–1937   Painter and patron of art
See also 1586–88

724 [**Mr L. A. Harrison**]
EXHIB L.G. 1911

MR HART

725 **Mr Hart** [n.d.]
OWNER Sold at Sotheby's 14 Dec 1960

LORD HARTINGTON
See the eighth Duke of Devonshire

MARTIN HARVEY
1863–1944   Actor

726 [**Mr Martin Harvey** c. 1897]
EXHIB L. G. 1928, where dated as above

727★ **Mr Martin Harvey** [n.d.]
REPRO *The Book of Martin Harvey*, 1928; **Plate 29**
OWNER Mrs Marie Strang

GERHART HAUPTMANN
1862–1946   German novelist and playwright

728★ **Gerhardt Hauptmann, making the most of the Riviera di Levante** 1912
EXHIB L.G. 1913 and 1945 (Guedalla)
REPRO *Fifty Caricatures*, 1913

729 [**Gerhart Hauptmann** 1931]
EXHIB L.G. 1952, where dated as above

KENNETH HAVERS

730 **Mr Kenneth Havers** [n.d.]
OWNER Mrs Eva Reichmann

CHARLES HAWTREY
1859–1923   Actor-manager

731* **Mr Hawtrey** [1895]
Illustrating a review of the first production of Oscar Wilde's 'An Ideal Husband'.
REPRO *Pick-Me-Up*, 19 Jan 1895

732* **The Messenger from Mars** [Unsigned 1900]
'A Message from Mars' by Richard Ganthony was produced by C. H. at the Avenue Theatre in Nov 1899 and ran for more than a year.
REPRO *World*, Christmas No, 1900

733 [Mr Charles Hawtrey 1901]
EXHIB Carfax 1901

734 [Mr Charles Hawtrey 1908]
EXHIB Carfax 1908

735* **Girth** 1912
Mr Hawtrey (to Mr du Maurier): 'Stick to the quiet method, and you'll be just the same presently.'
C. H. very fat, G. Du M. very thin.
EXHIB L.G. 1913 and 1952
REPRO *Fifty Caricatures*, 1913
OWNER Maxwell Halliday

736 [Mr Charles Hawtrey]
EXHIB L.G. 1945 (Guedalla)

737* **Mr Charles Hawtrey** [n.d.]
Three-quarter length, turning away, hand in trouser pocket.
EXHIB Grolier 1944
OWNER Harvard College Library

MR HAXTON

738* **Mr Haxton** [n.d.]
OWNER Mrs Eva Reichmann

E. S. P. HAYNES
1877–1949   Lawyer and writer
See also 158

738A* **Loss of Weight by E. S. P. H. owing to Our Present Discontents. See picture in Daily Mirror Aug 29 1930.** [Unsigned] 1930
OWNER Miss Celia Haynes

WALTER HEADLAM
1866–1908   Greek scholar

739* **[Untitled] Monday, February 5, 1906**
Standing by a bust of Aeschylus.
OWNER Ashmolean Museum, Oxford

WILLIAM HEINEMANN
1863–1920   Publisher
See also 27, 222

740* **Mr Heinemann** 1917
OWNER George Sassoon

ARCHIBALD HENDERSON
1877–1963   American biographer of Shaw
See 1496

W. E. HENLEY
1849–1903   Poet, critic and journalist
See also 1598

741* **It is said that [at] a supper given in farewell to Stevenson on the eve of the departure to Samoa, Mr Henley inadvertently upset the salt** 1901
See note to 1598.
REPRO **Plate 36**
OWNER Piccadilly Gallery

742* **Mr William Ernest Henley** [n.d.]
Head and shoulders.
OWNER Mrs Margaret Horrabin

FREDERICK HESS
Treasurer of Playgoers' Club

743* **Mr Frederick Hess** 1908
OWNER Mrs Eva Reichmann

744* **Mr Hess** 1910
OWNER B. P. Holt

MAURICE HEWLETT
1861–1923   Poet and novelist
See also 144, 612, 679, 1599

745* **Mr Maurice Hewlett and Heroine** [c. 1902]
M. H. as knight on horseback, with terrified girl behind.
REPRO *Artist*, Feb 1902

746* **Mr Maurice Hewlett** 1908
EXHIB Carfax 1908; L.G. 1945 (Guedalla)
REPRO **Plate 46**
OWNER Ashmolean Museum, Oxford

747 [Mr Maurice Hewlett]
EXHIB L.G. 1911

748* **Members of the Academic Committee [of the Royal Society of Literature] discussing whether at future meetings an Agenda Paper shall be provided, and (if so) what on earth to put into it** 1913
In the centre M. H. is exhorting John Morley. Round them are grouped Shaw, Austin Dobson, Hardy, Walter Raleigh, Henry James, Frederic Harrison, Gosse, Laurence Binyon, Kipling, Newbolt, Sturge Moore, Haldane, Barrie, Yeats, Galsworthy, Pinero and Anthony Hope. All are crowned with laurel wreaths.
EXHIB L.G. 1913 and 1957
REPRO *Fifty Caricatures*, 1913
OWNER J. C. Thomson

749* **Mr Maurice Hewlett being photographed** 1921
EXHIB L.G. May 1921
REPRO *A Survey*, 1921

ROBERT HICHENS
1864–1950 Novelist

750* **R. S. Hichens Esq** [1896]
Profile, standing, stirring a cup of tea.
REPRO *Twenty-Five Gentlemen*, 1896

751* **Mr Robert Hichens** [1898]
Profile, standing, in evening dress.
REPRO *Sketch*, 18 May 1898; *Max's Nineties*, 1958
OWNER Victoria & Albert Museum

752 [Mr Robert Hichens 1901]
EXHIB Carfax 1901

753* **Dawn (and Mr Robert Hichens, not less punctual) in the Desert** 1910
R. H. in cap and riding breeches is dictating to a grim female typist.
EXHIB L.G. 1911
REPRO *Bookman*, Aug 1911

754 [Mr Robert Hichens]
EXHIB L.G. 1952

SEYMOUR HICKS
1871–1949 Actor-manager

755* [Untitled 1894]
Full length, front view, hands on hips, head turned sideways.
REPRO *Pick-Me-Up*, 1 Dec 1894

756* **Mr Seymour Hicks** [1900]
Dancing in evening dress, very long nose.
REPRO *Idler*, Nov 1900
OWNER University of Texas

757 [Mr Seymour Hicks 1901]
EXHIB Carfax 1901

758 [Mr Seymour Hicks]
EXHIB L.G. 1911

SIR MICHAEL HICKS-BEACH
1837–1916 Conservative Chancellor of the Exchequer

759 [Sir Michael Hicks-Beach, guarding our interests 1901]
EXHIB Carfax 1901

HARRY HIGGINS
1855–1928 Solicitor and opera patron
See 679

SIR HUGO HIRST
1863–1943 Businessman

760* **Sir Hugo Hirst** [1930]
REPRO *Ladbroke's Racing Calendar*, 1931

THOMAS HODGKINSON
d. 1933 Contributor of light verse to *Punch*

761* **Mr Hodgkinson** 1908
OWNER University of Texas

JOHN HOLLINGSHEAD
1827–1904   Journalist and theatre manager

762★ Mr John Hollingshead [n.d.]

OWNER Piccadilly Gallery

C. J. HOLMES
1868–1936   Painter and Director of National Gallery

763★ Nocturne [1914]

Professor C. J. Holmes: 'Whistle for the police? My good men, how little you know me! The perils and adventures that attended life in the Renaissance were, as I have pointed out in *The Tarn and the Lake* (which, if you survive our impending combat, you really must read), most wholesome and stimulating to workers in the arts. You are just what I was needing, and my sole regret is that there are not more than two of you. So now, if you are ready . . .'

C. J. H. in pyjamas and holding a poker, stands between two masked and armed burglars.

EXHIB L.G. May 1921, where dated as above
REPRO *Art News*, Summer 1964
OWNER J. M. Coulson

SIR MAURICE HOLZMANN
1835–1909   Courtier

764★ The Faithful Steward. Sir Maurice Holzmann 1908

Full-length profile facing right, he stands disconsolately in front of two spiked files of documents, under portraits of Edward VII and George V.

EXHIB Carfax 1908
OWNER Lilly Library

765★ [Untitled Unsigned n.d.]

Pencil sketch for 764, but facing left.

OWNER University of Texas

HOMER
See also 589

766★ Homer, going his round [c. 1904]

EXHIB Carfax 1904; L.G. 1952
REPRO *The Poets' Corner*, 1904 and 1943

ALEXANDER NELSON HOOD
1854–1937   Courtier
See 1521

ANTHONY HOPE
1863–1933   Novelist
See 748, 976

HORACE
65–8 B.C.   Latin poet
See 590

HERBERT P. HORNE
1865–1916   Architect, writer and connoisseur
See also 1266, 1267

767★ Celestial Attributions. ? Scuola di amico di Max ?? Early venticento [c. 1905]

Virgin: 'That's a *very* doubtful Horne.'
Child: 'It seems to me rather as if it might be an early Berenson.'
Virgin (flying off at inevitable tangent): 'Pooh! Nonsense! Bah! *Everything* points to its being a particularly late Loeser.'
   (Left arguing)

The Virgin and Child are aloft among clouds and stars. H. P. H. stands below, hand in coat pocket, cigarette in mouth. Bernard Berenson and Frank Loeser were both art-experts. For explanation of signature see note to 1153.

REPRO *Burlington Magazine*, Jun 1952, where dated as above on Max's authority
OWNER Museo Horne, Florence

768★ Celestial Attributions [n.d.]

Virgin: 'That's a *very* doubtful Horne.'
Child: 'Yes. It looks rather as if it might be an early Berenson . . .'
Virgin: 'Pooh! Nonsense! *Everything* points to its being a particularly late Langton Douglas.'

A variation on 767, No stars, and H. P. H.'s cigarette is in one hand, while the other hangs by his side. Robert Langton Douglas was another art expert.

OWNER Richard Kingzett

STANLEY HOUGHTON
1881–1913   Playwright
See also 181

769★ Mr Stanley Houghton [c. 1912]

S. H.'s play 'Hindle Wakes' was a great success in 1912. Here he, the new boy, faces the established playwrights – Granville Barker, Shaw, Masefield, Galsworthy, Pinero, Sutro, Barrie and Henry Arthur Jones.

EXHIB L.G. 1913
REPRO As Christmas card by Cecily and Felix Aylmer, 1964
OWNER Sir Felix Aylmer

WALTER WYBERGH HOW
1861–1932   Fellow of Merton

769A★ The Merton Fancy Ball. Mr Howe as the 'Fat Boy' in Pickwick. [Signed with monogram n.d.]
OWNER Robert H. Taylor

FRANCIS HOWARD
1874–1945   Painter and art critic

770★ Mr Francis Howard 1911
EXHIB L.G. 1957
OWNER Peter Hughes

THE EIGHTH LORD HOWARD DE WALDEN
1880–1946   Writer and patron of the arts
See also 95, 335, 378, 612, 1049

771 [Lord Howard de Walden]
EXHIB L.G. 1911

772★ [Untitled Unsigned n.d.]
Rough sketch, full-length profile facing left, evening dress, high collar, monocle, pipe in mouth.
OWNER University of Texas

CHARLES AUGUSTUS HOWELL
1840–90   Friend and exploiter of the Pre-Raphaelites
See 369, 502

STEPHEN HUDSON
See Sydney Schiff

EDWARD BALL HUGHES
d. 1863   Regency dandy, known as 'The Golden Ball'

773 Amorous Encounters. The secret betrothal of Mr Ball Hughes to that agreeable, famous danseuse, Mlle Hullin [n.d.]
EXHIB L.G. 1945 (Guedalla)
OWNER Dr Patricia Shaw

ALBERT ALEXANDER HUMPHREY
1846–1917   Canadian pioneer and businessman

774★ [Untitled n.d.]
Head and shoulders.
OWNER Victoria & Albert Museum

775 [Untitled n.d.]
OWNER Lewis P. Renateau

WILLIAM HOLMAN HUNT
1827–1910   Painter
See also 185, 1268

776★ British and Alien Inspiration – 1849 1917

First County Member
Holman Hunt } 'Very clever, no doubt —'

Second County Member
John Millais } 'Full of wonderful ideas but —'

First County Member
Second County Member
Holman Hunt
John Millais } 'Not to be trusted for one moment.'

EXHIB L.G. Sept 1921
REPRO *Rossetti and his Circle*, 1922
OWNER Tate Gallery

THE REV. WILLIAM HUNT

777★ The Rev William Hunt [n.d.]
OWNER Mrs Eva Reichmann

W. H. HURLBERT
1827–95   American journalist

778★ [Untitled Unsigned 1951]
Shows him asleep in the witness box. Dated and identified on back by Elisabeth Jungmann.
OWNER Sir Rupert Hart-Davis

A. S. M. HUTCHINSON
1879–1971   Novelist

779★ Mr A. S. M. Hutchinson, much embarrassed 1923

Success! So this was she! In his youth he had often dreamed of her, but he had not imagined her quite like this. This was she! Success!

She is a huge, forbidding woman, holding a pineapple. H.'s most successful novel, 'If Winter Comes', appeared in 1921.

EXHIB L.G. 1923
REPRO *Things New and Old*, 1923
OWNER Savage Club

ALDOUS HUXLEY
1894–1963 Writer

780★ **Mr Aldous Huxley** 1923
EXHIB L.G. 1923
REPRO *Things New and Old*, 1923

781★ **Mr Aldous Huxley loquitur** 1932
'No, pardon me, I am *not*. To be disillusioned, one must first have suffered from illusions.'
EXHIB L.G. 1952
REPRO *Bandwagon*, Jun 1952

H. M. HYNDMAN
1842–1921 Socialist politician
See 1749, 1750

I

HENRIK IBSEN
1828–1906 Norwegian dramatist
See 22, 28

SELWYN IMAGE
1849–1930 Poet, priest and artist

782 [**S. Selwyn of Bloomsbury, preaching to the young barbarians** c. 1910]
In 1910 S. I., who had earlier given up the priesthood to become an artist, was appointed Slade Professor at Oxford. Byron's phrase 'young barbarians all at play' was applied to Oxford by Matthew Arnold in the Preface to his 'Essays in Criticism', 1865.
EXHIB L.G. 1911

W. R. INGE
1860–1954 Writer and Dean of St Paul's

783★ **Dean Inge finding, as ever, sustenance in Plotinus** 1931
REPRO *Spectator* Supplement, 14 Mar 1931
OWNER *The Spectator*

SIR HENRY IRVING
1838–1905 Actor-manager
See also 595

784★ **Untitled Unsigned** [1895]
Speaking after dinner.
REPRO *Pick-Me-Up*, 5 Jan 1895
OWNER Savage Club

785★ **Sir Henry Irving** [1900]
Full length, evening dress, stroking chin and smoking large cigar.
REPRO *Idler*, Jun 1900

786★ [**Untitled** 1900]
Full length, day clothes, wearing top hat and leaning on cane.
REPRO *World*, Christmas Supplement, 1900
OWNER Harvard College Library

787 [**Sir Henry Irving** 1901]
EXHIB Carfax 1901

788★ **Sir Henry Irving** [1901]
REPRO *Town Topics* (N.Y.), Christmas 1901; **Plate 30**
OWNER Robert H. Taylor

789★ **Sir Henry Irving** [1903]
Walking, wearing top hat and eyeglasses and using stick.
REPRO *John Bull*, 29 Apr 1903; Frances Donaldson, *The Actor-Managers*, 1970
OWNER Garrick Club

790 [**Sir Henry Irving**]
EXHIB L.G. 1911

791* **Sir Henry Irving receiving a journalist** 1922
For Alfred Sutro, affectionately.
REPRO Alfred Sutro, *Celebrities and Simple Souls*, 1933

792* **A Memory of Irving for Henry Arthur** 1926
Head and shoulders, profile.
REPRO Henry Arthur Jones, *The Shadow of Henry Irving*, 1931

793* **A Memory of Henry Irving** 1926
Sitting at table, holding glass and smoking cigar.
EXHIB L.G. 1928, 1945 (Guedalla) and 1957
REPRO *Caricatures by Max*, 1958
OWNER Ashmolean Museum, Oxford

794* **Sir Henry Irving** [n.d.]
Full length, profile, hatless, smoking cigar, hands in trouser pockets.
OWNER Lady Brunner

795 **Sir Henry Irving** [Unsigned n.d.]
OWNER Marchioness of Bath

H. B. IRVING
1870–1919   Actor and writer
See also 263, 335

796* **Overheard between the acts** [Unsigned c. 1893]

Mr H. B. Irving: 'I tell you, Sir, there *is* no drama nowadays.'
Clearly drawn when Max and H. B. I. were both Oxford undergraduates.
OWNER Piccadilly Gallery

797* **The Torch** 1908
Mr H. B. Irving (to Mr Winston Churchill): 'Going to make a speech? Why not one of your father's?'
EXHIB Carfax 1908; L.G. 1911
REPRO *Fifty Caricatures*, 1913
OWNER Mark Cory-Wright

RUFUS ISAACS
1860–1935   Lawyer, politician and Viceroy
See also 949

798* **Mr Rufus Isaacs** 1908
EXHIB Carfax 1908; L.G. 1945 (Guedalla)
OWNER Ashmolean Museum, Oxford

799* **Some Ministers of the Crown, who (monstrous though it seem) have severally some spare pounds to invest, implore Sir Rufus Isaacs to tell them if he knows of any stocks which they could buy without fear of ultimate profit** 1913
The Ministers are Winston Churchill, J. E. B. Seely, Asquith, Sir Edward Grey, Reginald McKenna, Augustine Birrell, John Burns and L. V. Harcourt. The reference is to the Marconi scandal.
EXHIB L.G. 1913
REPRO *Fifty Caricatures*, 1913

J

W. W. JACOBS
1863–1943   Writer

800* **The Member for Gravesend** 1914
Mr W. W. Jacobs [to Sir Gilbert Parker]: 'It's no sort of use talking to *them* about the Unity and Integrity of the Empire. All they want is that you should sit down on your hat and stand rum all round.'
Sir G. P. was M.P. for Gravesend, whose inhabitants provided the material for many of W. W. J.'s stories.

EXHIB L.G. May 1921 and 1945 (Guedalla)
REPRO *A Survey*, 1921

HENRY JAMES
1843–1916   Writer
See also 514, 748, 1423

801* **Mr Henry James** [1898]
Full-length profile, bearded, holding eye-glasses in front, top hat behind.
REPRO *Academy*, 26 Nov 1898; *Max's Nineties*, 1958

802★ Mr Henry James [? c. 1904]

H. J. kneels with his ear to the keyhole of a hotel bedroom, outside which are a pair of men's boots and a pair of women's shoes. Cf. H. J's essay on D'Annunzio, first published in 1904: 'it has no more dignity . . . than the boots and shoes that we see, in the corridors of promiscuous hotels, standing, often in double pairs, at the doors of rooms.'

EXHIB L.G. 1945 (Guedalla), 1952 and 1957
REPRO *Caricatures by Max*, 1958
OWNER Ashmolean Museum, Oxford

803★ Mr Henry James revisiting America [1905]

Extract from His Unspoken Thoughts.

'. . . So that, in fine, let, without further beating about the bush, me make to myself amazed acknowledgement that, but for the certificate of birth which I have – so quite indubitably – *on* me, I might, in regarding (and, as it somewhat were, overseeing) *à l'oeil de voyageur*, these dear good people, find hard to swallow, or even to take by subconscious injection, the great idea that I am – oh, ever so indigenously! – one of them' . . .

The Americans in the background are saying –
[Young girl:] 'My! Ain't he cree-ative?'
[Coloured dancer:] 'We wants yer mightly badly. Yas, we *doo*!'
[Lone ranger:] 'Guess 'e ken shoot char'cter at sight!'
[Indian squaw:] 'Hail, great white novelist! Tuniyaba – the Spinner of fine cobwebs!'
[Black mammy:] 'Why, it's Masser Henry! Come to your old nurse's arms, honey!'
[Prosperous man:] 'What's – the matter with – James?'
[Prosperous woman:] '*He's* – all – right!'
[Yankee:] '*Who's* – all – right?'
[Millionaire:] '*James!*'

In early April 1905 Max wrote to his future wife Florence: 'I have just done a rather good caricature of Henry James revisiting America. The event lends itself to comedy.'

EXHIB Baillie 1907; L.G. 1952
REPRO *A Book of Caricatures*, 1907
OWNER National Gallery of Victoria, Melbourne

804★ [London in November, and Mr Henry James in London] 1907

[. . . It was, therefore, not without something of a shock that he, in this to him so very congenial atmosphere, now perceived that a vision of the hand which he had, at a venture, held up within an inch or so of his eyes was, with an almost awful clarity being adumbrated . . .]

H. J. in thick fog. Title and legend are not on drawing, but in catalogue and book.

EXHIB Carfax 1907; L.G. 1945 (Guedalla) and 1952
REPRO *A Book of Caricatures*, 1907
OWNER Mrs Philip Guedalla

805★ A Nightmare. Mr Henry James subpoena'd, as psychological expert, in a *cause célèbre* 1908

Cross-examining Counsel: 'Come, sir, I ask you a plain question, and I expect a plain answer!'

Title and legend written on mount. The only other recognisable people in court are Sir George Lewis and his son.

EXHIB Carfax 1908
OWNER Miss Elizabeth Williamson

806★ [Untitled Unsigned c. 1908]

Rough sketch for main part of 805. Both Lewises visible.

OWNER University of Texas

807★ [Untitled Unsigned c. 1908]

Even rougher sketch for 805. Only the elder Lewis visible.

REPRO *The American Writer in England*, Charlottesville, 1969
OWNER University of Virginia

807A★ [Untitled] 1908

Say, indefatigable alchemist,
Melts not the very moral of your scene,
Curls it not off in vapour from beween
Those lips that labour with conspicuous twist?
Your fine eyes, blurred like arc-lamps in a mist,
Immensely glare; yet glimmerings intervene,
So that your May-Be and your Might-Have-Been
Leave us still plunging for your genuine gist.

How different from Sir Arthur Conan Doyle –
As clear as water, and as smooth as oil,
And no jot knowing of what Maisie knew.
Flushed with the sunset air of roseate Rye,
You stand, marmoreal darling of the few,
Lord of the troubled Speech and single Eye.

In a note to Edmund Gosse's biographer, Evan Charteris, Max explained the sonnet: 'I am not sure whether it was Walter Raleigh or I that invented the Sonnet game. I often played it – sometimes in a room, sometimes by post. In the Spring of 1908 Gosse offered to play a round with me. We played it by post – by return of post, every time. I wrote the first line, Gosse the second. The even-numbered lines are his, and the odd-numbered mine.'

The drawing, which Max gave to Gosse, shows H. J. half length, three-quarter face, with his left arm extended.

OWNER Melville E. Stone

808★ 'The Jolly Corner' [c. 1908]

H. J. descending staircase meets ghost of himself as he would have been if he had never left America. Based on H. J.'s story 'The Jolly Corner', first published Dec 1908.

EXHIB L.G. 1928
REPRO **Plate 37**
OWNER George Sassoon

809* Ideal. Mr Henry James making a match between Mona Lisa and the Man in the Iron Mask 1911

EXHIB L.G. 1911
REPRO *Bookman*, Aug 1911

810* The Old Pilgrim comes home 1913

EXHIB L.G. May 1921
REPRO *A Survey*, 1921

811* A Memory 1920

Half-length profile facing left, hands raised in front of face.
REPRO Privately by Lady Beerbohm, 1957
OWNER Mrs Eva Reichmann

812* 'And hark, what songs the Seraphim do sing!' Archbishop Benson giving Mr Henry James the idea for 'The Turn of the Screw' (See 'Letters of Henry James', vol I, p. 286) 1920

For E[dmund] G[osse] affectionately
EXHIB L.G. 1945 (Guedalla)
OWNER George Sassoon

813* The Old Diner-Out. A Memory 1926

EXHIB L.G. 1928 and 1957
OWNER University of Texas

814* A memory of Henry James and Joseph Conrad conversing at an afternoon party – circa 1904 1926

EXHIB L.G. 1928
REPRO **Plate 38**
OWNER University of Texas

815 [Mr Henry James]

EXHIB L.G. 1928

816 [Untitled Unsigned c. 1950]

Very similar to 811, dated by owner.
OWNER Thornton Wilder

817 H. J. for Elisabeth with love 1954

Again very similar to 811.
EXHIB L.G. 1957
OWNER Mrs. Eva Reichmann

818 Mr Henry James [n.d.]

Half-length profile.
EXHIB L.G. 1952
OWNER Simon Nowell-Smith

WARREN JENKINS
b. 1905   Actor and producer

819 'Oh Lily, dear Lily Dale' [c. 1930]

The title is that of a sentimental Victorian song which Max heard W. J. sing at the Gate Theatre Studio.
OWNER Warren Jenkins

SOLOMON BARNATO JOEL
1865–1931   South African millionaire

820* Mr Solly Joel fulfilling his imperial destiny 1908

Over-dressed in braided tail-coat, striped trousers and top hat, he twirls his waxed moustache.
EXHIB Carfax 1908; L.G. 1945 (Guedalla)
OWNER Ashmolean Museum, Oxford

821 Mr Solly Joel [n.d.]

EXHIB L.G. 1911
OWNER Sold at Sotheby's 14 Dec 1960

AUGUSTUS JOHN
1878–1961   Artist
See also 335, 1586-8, 1591

821A [Hommage à John 1908]

EXHIB Carfax 1908

822* Mr Augustus John 1909

REPRO *English Review*, Oct 1909

823 [Annual Meeting of Mr Stirling Stuart-Crawford, Mr Augustus John and Lord Ribblesdale, to protest against the fashions for the coming spring 1909]

All, to judge from 824, most unconventionally dressed.
EXHIB N.E.A.C. Summer 1909; L.G. 1911

824* [Untitled] 1909

Rough sketch for 823.
EXHIB Achenbach 1964
OWNER U.C.L.A. (Clark)

825* Insecurity 1909

Art-Critic (under his breath): 'How odd it seems that thirty years hence I may be desperately in love with these ladies!'
A–C (a lay figure) contemplates three John models against a rural background. A. J. stands by with folded arms.
EXHIB N.E.A.C. Summer 1909; L.G. 1952
REPRO **Plate 63**
OWNER National Gallery of Victoria, Melbourne

825A★ [Untitled Unsigned n.d.]
Pencil-sketch for 825.
OWNER Sold at Sotheby's 14 Jul 1971

826★ [Artists at the Front. No 2] 1918
Major Augustus John: 'Ah, now *there* really *is* a subject!'
A. J. in uniform of war-artist comes on three barefooted, gaily-clad women working on a farm.
EXHIB L.G. May 1921
REPRO *Reveille*, Nov 1918
OWNER The Hon Christopher Lennox-Boyd

827★ The Patron 1920
William, first Baron Leverhulme, setting out on a long, painful, and entirely unpremeditated journey adown the Ages.
A. J. is leading a headless figure by the arm. Lord L had so much disliked his portrait by A. J. that he cut the head out of it.
EXHIB L.G. May 1921 and 1957
REPRO *A Survey*, 1921
OWNER Robert Lush

828★ The Old and the Young Self 1924
Young Self: 'What are they?'
Old Self: 'Oh, applicants. Look here! Our names are the same – and the name's all they care about. Do take some of them off my hands!'
(Receives an indignant and a disappointing reply)
They face a crowd of fashionable sitters.
EXHIB L.G. 1925, 1945 (Guedalla), 1952 and 1957
REPRO *Observations*, 1925; *Caricatures by Max*, 1958
OWNER Ashmolean Museum, Oxford

829★ [Untitled Unsigned n.d.]
Full-length pencil sketch of a man in cloak and broad-brimmed hat, face mostly obscured by beard and long hair. Not certainly A. J. but very like other drawings of him.
OWNER University of Texas

KING JOHN
1167–1216
See 498

JACK JOHNSON
1878–1946   American Negro boxer

830★ Mr Jack Johnson 1915
OWNER Mrs Eva Reichmann

SAMUEL JOHNSON
1709–84   Poet, lexicographer and critic

831★ In the Shades 1915
Boswell: Are you not pleased, Sir, that your house in Gough Square is to be presented to the Nation? *Johnson*: Why, no, Sir. You are to consider that the purpose of a house is to be inhabited by some one. If a house be not fit for tenancy by Tom or Dick, let it be demolished or handed over without more ado to the rats, which, by frequentation, will have acquired a prescriptive right there. I conceive that in Gough Square a vast number of rats will have been disturbed and evicted. (Puffing, and rolling himself from side to side.) Sir, I am sorry for the rats. Sir, the rats have a just grievance. *Boswell*: Nevertheless, Sir, is it not well that the house of the great Samuel Johnson should be preserved? Will it not tend to diffuse happiness and to promote virtue? *Johnson*: Nay, Sir, let us have no more of this foppishness. The house is nought. Let us not *sublimify* lath and plaster. I know not whether I profited the world whilst I was in it. I am very sure that my mere tenement will not be profitable now that I am out of it. Alas, Sir, when 'tempus edax' has swallowed the yolk of the egg, there is no gain to be had by conservation of the egg-shell.
. . . or, (so very much was Lexiphanes a man of moods) the dialogue might run thus . . .
Boswell: Are you not pleased, Sir, that your house in Gough Square is to be presented to the Nation? *Johnson*: Why, yes, Sir. (In a solemn, faltering tone.) Nothing has pleased me half so well since the *Rambler* was translated into the Russian language and read on the banks of the Wolga.
EXHIB L.G. 1923
REPRO *Things New and Old*, 1923
OWNER Johnson House, Gough Square

HENRY ARTHUR JONES
1851–1929   Playwright
See also 95, 769

832★ [Untitled Unsigned 1894]
Full-length profile, standing on long path. Moon and stars above.
REPRO *Pick-Me-Up*, 6 Oct 1894; Doris Arthur Jones, *Life and Letters of Henry Arthur Jones*, 1930
OWNER Piccadilly Gallery

833 [Mr Henry Arthur Jones 1901]
EXHIB Carfax 1901

834★ Mr Henry Arthur Jones, England's Scourge [1907]

JONES (continued)

Full length, holding miniature American flag.
REPRO *A Book of Caricatures*, 1907

835 [**Mr Henry Arthur Jones** 1907]
EXHIB Carfax 1907

836 **Mr Henry Arthur Jones** [1931]
Full length, three-quarter face, grey frock-coat. Dated as above by Max in note to L.G.
EXHIB L.G. 1957
OWNER Mrs Hazel Holt

BENJAMIN JOWETT
1817–93   Master of Balliol and Professor of Greek

837* **The sole remark likely to have been made by Benjamin Jowett about the mural paintings at the Oxford Union** 1916
'And what were they going to do with the Grail when they found it, Mr Rossetti?'
EXHIB Grosvenor 1917; L.G. Sep 1921
REPRO *Rossetti and his Circle*, 1922
OWNER Tate Gallery

838* [**Untitled**] 1924
'Twice at least during a week's winter excursion in Cornwall, I knew, and had reason to know, what it was to feel nervous; for he would stand without any support at the end of a magnificent precipice, as though he had been a young man bred up from boyhood to the scaling of cliffs and the breasting of breakers.' (Extract from Mr Swinburne's memorial essay on Dr Jowett)
EXHIB L.G. 1925 and 1945 (Guedalla)
REPRO *Observations*, 1925
OWNER Mrs Philip Guedalla

839* [**Untitled Unsigned** n.d.]
Rough sketch for 837, on which Max noted: 'Higher louvres' and 'Widen space between windows and foot'. On the verso are a rough sketch of Rossetti's figure in the drawing, two sketches of his profile, and a first draft of title and legend.
OWNER Alan G. Thomas

SIR WILLIAM JOYNSON-HICKS
1865–1932   Conservative Home Secretary

840* **Sir W. Joynson-Hicks, still wondering that his first swift graceful gesture towards the Parks was so little applauded** 1925
In Dec 1924 W. J.-H.'s suggestion, in a 'Times' interview, that the only solution for the London traffic problem was to drive roads through the Parks had roused a storm of protest.
EXHIB L.G. 1925 and 1957
REPRO *Observations*, 1925

K

FLORENCE KAHN (later BEERBOHM)
1877–1951   Max's first wife
See 1422, 1440

THE KAISER
See Wilhelm II

EDMOND X. KAPP
b. 1890   Artist
See also 1449

841* **Kapp** 1923
OWNER Edmond X. Kapp

SIR COLERIDGE KENNARD BART
1885–1948   Diplomat

842 [**Mankind in the Making. Sir Coleridge Kennard** 1908]
EXHIB Carfax 1908

BART KENNEDY
1861–1930   Author of *A Tramp in Spain*, etc.

843 [**Mr Bart Kennedy, tramping for the Daily Mail** 1908]
EXHIB Carfax 1908

ERIC KENNINGTON
1888–1960   Painter and sculptor
See also 133, 703

844★ **Mr Eric Kennington** 1916
Full-length profile, in breeches and leggings.
OWNER Ian Struthers

845 [**Mr Eric Kennington** 1917]
EXHIB L.G. 1928, where dated as above

FRED KERR
1858–1933   Actor

846 [**Mr Fred Kerr** 1901]
EXHIB Carfax 1901

OMAR KHAYYAM
c. 1050–c. 1123   Persian poet

847★ [**Untitled** c. 1904]
Numbers indicate 1. Book of Verses, 2. Bough, 3. Loaf of Bread, 4. Jug of Wine, 5. Thou, 6. Wilderness.
EXHIB Carfax 1908
REPRO *The Poets' Corner*, 1904 and 1943

THE TWELFTH EARL OF KINNOULL
1855–1916
See also 1382

848★ **Lord Kinnoull** [n.d.]
REPRO *Cassell's Magazine*, Feb 1903

849 [**Lord Hay, afterwards 12th Earl of Kinnoull** 1926]
[A more dashing figure than is often seen nowadays].
EXHIB L.G. 1928, where dated as above

RUDYARD KIPLING
1865–1936   Poet and writer
See also 52, 514, 515, 612, 748, 1147, 1423, 1443, 1563, 1599, 1875

850★ **Mr Rudyard Kipling** [1896]
Full-length profile, huge chin, marching to left.
EXHIB L.G. 1928
REPRO *Twenty-Five Gentlemen*, 1896

851★ **Mr Rudyard Kipling** [1898]
Full face, huge eyes, hands on hips. Done to oblige young schoolboys who had been refused a contribution by R. K. and had addressed Max as 'The Whistler of Caricature'.
REPRO *Horsmonden School Budget*, 28 May 1898
OWNER Bancroft Library, U.C. (Berkeley)

852★ [**Untitled** 1900]
Alexander Pope extracts a manuscript from R. K.'s pocket.
REPRO *World*, Christmas No, 1900

853★ **Mr Rudyard Kipling** [1901]
Profile, tiny body, enormous chin, facing left.
EXHIB Carfax 1901
REPRO *Pall Mall Magazine*, Feb 1902

854★ **Scenes from the Lives of the Poets. Mr Rudyard Kipling composing 'The Absent-Minded Beggar'** [1903]
R.K. stands holding a quill pen in an empty monastic cell. On the back wall is carved: VOS PANDITE VATI PIERIDES [Reveal yourselves, ye Muses, to the bard. Claudius Claudianus, *In Rufinum*, I, 23–24].
REPRO *Things New and Old*, 1923, where dated as above
OWNER Harvard College Library

855★ **Mr Rudyard Kipling takes a bloomin' day aht, on the blasted 'eath, along with Britannia, 'is gurl** 1904
EXHIB Carfax 1904
REPRO *The Poets' Corner*, 1904 and 1943
OWNER The Hon. Christopher Lennox-Boyd

856 [**Mr Rudyard Kipling** 1907]
EXHIB Baillie 1907

857★ **The Nobel Award** 1907
'Lord God, they ha' paid in full!' [Kipling, 'The Song of the Dead']
As R. K. bears off a bag labelled £7620, Hall Caine looks on enviously, while Meredith and Swinburne recline in Olympian ease on the clouds. Above them is written:
ἀλλ' οὐδαμῶς τάδ', οἶδα, τοῖς θεοῖς μέλει
[But the gods, I know, care not at all for these things].
EXHIB Carfax 1908
REPRO **Plate 41**
OWNER Miss Jennifer Gosse

858★ [**Untitled Unsigned** n.d.]
Rough sketch for 857, with Meredith and Swinburne transposed.
OWNER Berg Collection (N.Y.P.L.)

859★ British Hempire 1907
REPRO **Plate 43**
OWNER Sold at Sotheby's 1 Nov 1967

860★ On the Shelf. Oriental brass-work (nineteenth century), very curious 1921
John Bullish figure gazing up at small model of R. K. seated.
EXHIB L.G. May 1921
OWNER Harvard College Library

861★ The Old and the Young Self 1924
Young Self: 'I *say*! Have you heard the latest about Mrs Hauksbee?'
Mrs H. was one of the leading characters in K's early stories of India.
EXHIB L.G. 1925
REPRO *Observations*, 1925
OWNER Harvard College Library

862★ Mr Rudyard Kipling [n.d.]
The usual tiny body and huge chin, this time facing right.
EXHIB L.G. 1928
REPRO *Bystander*, 5 Dec 1928

863★ Mr Kipling as political speaker; and his audience [n.d.]
Smith minor: 'Rotten low down, ain't it?'
Jones minor: 'Filthy.'
EXHIB L.G. 1945 (Guedalla)
OWNER Ashmolean Museum, Oxford

864★ Mr Kipling [n.d.]
Usual figure, facing left, hand in trouser pocket.
EXHIB L.G. 1952
REPRO *Times Ed. Sup.*, 2 May 1952

THE FIRST EARL KITCHENER
1850–1916   Soldier and politician
See also 335, 1443

865★ Lord Kitchener of Khartoum [1900]
REPRO *World*, Christmas Supplement, 1900; **Plate 17**
OWNER Piccadilly Gallery

866 [Lord Kitchener of Khartoum 1901]
EXHIB Carfax 1901

867★ Lord Kitchener of Khartoum [n.d.]
Full length, full face, in uniform, holding switch, very long legs. Known only from a photograph in Max's papers.

JOSEPH KNIGHT
1829–1907   Dramatic critic

868★ Mr Joseph Knight [1898]
Full-length profile.
REPRO *Academy*, 31 Dec 1898

869★ Mr Joseph Knight [1901]
Full length, full face.
EXHIB Carfax 1901
REPRO *Artist*, Feb 1902
OWNER Dr Sanchia Fitzmaurice

SIR FRANCIS KNOLLYS
1837–1924   Private Secretary to King Edward VII
See 491, 492

R. G. KNOWLES
1858–1919   American music-hall comedian

870★ [R. G. Knowles (There's a picture for you!) 1894]
REPRO *Pick-Me-Up*, 29 Sep 1894, where captioned as above

COLLIE KNOX
Author and journalist

871 Mr Columb Knox meditating a lyric 1920
OWNER Collie Knox

KNOX-JOHNSON

872 Knox-Johnson, "hearing the late Mr Arnold mispraised" [n.d.]
Probably a sketch for a more finished drawing. On the same sheet are six heads of K.-J. and one of Disraeli.
OWNER Mrs Eva Reichmann

M. KRATZ
Inhabitant of Dieppe

873★ M. Kratz [n.d.]
See Max Beerbohm, 'Letters to Reggie Turner', 1964, pp. 303-4.
OWNER Piccadilly Gallery

PRESIDENT KRUGER
1825–1904   Boer leader

874★ President Kruger [1900]
Full face, full length.
REPRO *Idler*, Jan 1900

875★ **[Untitled Unsigned** 1900]
Flying through stars with a bag.
REPRO *World*, Christmas No, 1900

L

HENRY LABOUCHERE
1831–1912   Journalist and Liberal M.P.
See also 931

876★ Henry Labouchere Esq [1896]
Full-length profile facing right, wearing top hat, hands in pockets, smoking cigarette.
REPRO *Twenty-Five Gentlemen*, 1896; *Max's Nineties*, 1958

877 **[Mr Henry Labouchere** 1901]
EXHIB Carfax 1901

878★ [Untitled 1901]
As 876, but bare-headed and facing left.
REPRO *Critic* (N.Y.) Nov 1901

879 **[Mr Henry Labouchere]**
EXHIB L.G. 1911

880 **[Mr Labouchere]**
EXHIB L.G. 1952

881★ [Untitled Unsigned n.d.]
As in 878, but facing right. Known only from a photograph in Max's papers.

ALFRED CHARLEMAGNE LAMBART
1861–1943   Resident in Italy

882 **Mr Alfred Lambart trying to ingenerate style among the English visitors** 1923
OWNER Mrs Molly Estridge

883 **[Mr Alfred Lambart]**
EXHIB L.G. 1952

SIR HUGH LANE
1875–1915   Irish art-collector

884★ Sir Hugh Lane producing masterpieces for Dublin 1909
EXHIB   N.E.A.C. Winter 1909
REPRO   **Plate 69**
OWNER Municipal Gallery of Modern Art, Dublin

885★ Sir Hugh Lane producing masterpieces for Dublin 1909
Identical with 884, presumably a copy made by Max, or the original of which 884 is a copy.
OWNER Johannesburg Art Gallery

886★ Bond Street v. Cheyne Walk. Sir Hugh Lane guarding a Manet 1911
H. L. shyly but firmly protecting the picture from a Jewish dealer.
EXHIB   L.G. 1911
OWNER Municipal Gallery of Modern Art, Dublin

JOHN LANE
1854–1925   Publisher
See also 1740

887★ Mr John Lane [c. 1895]
EXHIB   L.G. 1928, where dated as above
REPRO   *Without Prejudice*, ed. Cecil Woolf, 1963
OWNER Lady Lane

888 **[Mr John Lane** 1901]
EXHIB Carfax 1901

ANDREW LANG
1844–1912   Scottish poet and writer
See also 1443

888A★ **Letters to Dead Authors by Andrew Lang. [Signed with monogram** n.d.]

A. L. posting a letter in a pillar-box. Previously a Fellow of Merton and now an Honorary Fellow, his 'Letters to Dead Authors' was published in 1886. Done at Oxford.

OWNER Robert H. Taylor

889★ **Mr Andrew Lang** [1896]

Full length, full face.

REPRO *Chap-Book* (Chicago), 1 Sep 1896; *Max's Nineties,* 1958

OWNER Newberry Library, Chicago

890★ **Mr Andrew Lang** [1898]

Full length, head in profile to left.

REPRO *Academy,* 19 Nov 1898

891 [**Mr Andrew Lang** 1901]

EXHIB Carfax 1901

892★ **A Memory of Mr Andrew Lang** 1926

Three-quarter length, almost full face.

EXHIB L.G. 1928; Achenbach 1964
OWNER U.C.L.A. (Clark)

RAY LANKESTER
1847–1929   Zoologist and writer
See also 612, 614, 615, 956

893★ **Professor Ray Lankester** [1907]

EXHIB Carfax 1907
REPRO *A Book of Caricatures,* 1907
OWNER Merton College, Oxford

THE FIFTH MARQUESS OF LANSDOWNE
1845–1927   Politician and diplomat
See also 679

894 **Lord Lansdowne, in the hands of the Permanent Officials** [1901]

Lord L is shown as an articulated wooden dummy, suspended with red tape, manipulated by fingers and thumb below.

EXHIB Carfax 1901
OWNER The Marquess of Lansdowne

895★ [**Untitled** 1903]

['Owns about 143,000 acres, and can speak French.']

REPRO *John Bull,* 13 May 1903, where captioned as above

896★ **Lord Lansdowne, trying, with all the amenity of his kind, to understand just what Mr H. G. Wells means about the barrenness of official politics** 1911

EXHIB L.G. 1911
REPRO *Bookman,* Aug 1911

897★ **Lord Lansdowne** [n.d.]

Full-length profile facing left, evening dress.

REPRO *Fifty Caricatures,* 1913
OWNER J. C. Thomson

898★ **Lord Lansdowne embarrassed by the unwisdom of Lord Willoughby de Broke** 1913

Lord W. de B. is leaping out of the frame, carrying a hatchet and with feathers on his head.

OWNER Merton College, Oxford

899★ **. . . Giving Place to the New**

Lord Lansdowne (to Mr Gordon Selfridge): 'Statuary, sir? Majolica, paintings in oil, all the latest Eighteenth Century books – *this* way.'

EXHIB L.G. May 1921
REPRO *Graphic,* 21 May 1921

900 **Lord Lansdowne** [n.d.]

Full-length profile facing left.

OWNER Mrs Norah E. F. Beattie

901 [**Untitled** n.d.]

Full length, frock-coat, bow tie, buttonhole.

OWNER The Marquess of Lansdowne

VISCOUNT LASCELLES
1882–1947   Son-in-Law of King George V

902★ **Lord Lascelles (with whom his valet) inspecting the Panama hat designed and trimmed for him by Queen Mary** 1922

EXHIB L.G. 1923 and 1945 (Guedalla)
REPRO *Things New and Old,* 1923
OWNER Mrs Philip Guedalla

ANDREW BONAR LAW
1858–1923   Prime Minister
See also 47, 73, 439

903★ **Cold-Shouldered Yet** 1912

Mr Bonar Law (to Tariff Reform): 'It's a quee-er thing, laddie, but there's evidently a sor-rt of a somewhat about ye that dinna inspire confidence.'

EXHIB L.G. 1913
REPRO *Fifty Caricatures,* 1913

904 [**Untitled**]1914
Shows B. L. with the shadow of Carson behind him.
EXHIB L.G. 1928
OWNER L. J. Cadbury

905★ **'The Glasgow School'** 1923
[The shadow of Lloyd George:] 'Honest? Oh, yes, no doubt. But what price honesty without imagination? Whereas imagination . . .'
EXHIB L.G. 1923
REPRO *Things New and Old*, 1923
OWNER Columbus Gallery of Fine Arts, Ohio

906 [**Mr Bonar Law**]
EXHIB L.G. 1945 (Guedalla)

BOYLE LAWRENCE
1869–1951   Journalist and playwright

907★ **Mr Boyle Lawrence** [n.d.]
OWNER Piccadilly Gallery

EDWARD LAWSON
See Lord Burnham

W. E. H. LECKY
1838–1903   Irish historian and politician

908★ **Mr Lecky** [1899]
Full-length profile, holding top hat.
REPRO *Butterfly*, Apr 1899

909★ **Mr Lecky** [1901]
Three-quarter length, full face, arms and legs crossed.
REPRO *Critic* (N.Y.), Nov 1901

SIDNEY LEE
1859–1926   Writer and editor of the *D.N.B.*
See also 27

910 [**Mr Sidney Lee** c. 1898]
EXHIB L.G. 1928, where dated as above

911★ [**Untitled Unsigned** n.d.]
'Come on, come on!' said Hearty John;
'Lie down!' said Rose Marie;
'Be off, be off!' said Romanoff;
'I shan't' said Sidney Lee.
An arrow points to each of the four characters.
OWNER Piccadilly Gallery

RICHARD LE GALLIENNE
1866–1947   Poet and writer
See also 1650

912★ **Richard Le Gallienne** [1896]
Full length, strolling among stars, face obscured by hair.
EXHIB F.A.S. 1896
REPRO *Twenty-Five Gentlemen*, 1896

913★ [**Untitled** 1896]
A mass of hair on a tiny body.
REPRO *Chap-Book* (Chicago), 1 Dec 1896

914★ [**Untitled** 1900]
A tiny figure, with much hair, standing on a high pile of books.
EXHIB Achenbach 1964
REPRO *World*, Christmas No, 1900
OWNER U.C.L.A. (Clark)

915 [**Mr Richard Le Gallienne** 1901]
EXHIB Carfax 1901

916★ **Le Gallienne** [n.d.]
Full length, full face, two huge bunches of hair, with a top hat on each.
REPRO Richard Le Gallienne, *The Romantic 90's*, 1926

917★ [**Untitled Unsigned** n.d.]
Same hair and hats as 916, but a slighter figure, with arms crossed in front. A small cow stands in the right-hand bottom corner.
OWNER Sir John Rothenstein

918 [**Richard Le Gallienne**]
EXHIB L.G. 1952

FREDERIC LEIGHTON
1830–96   Painter
See also 595

919★ **A Man from Hymettus** 1916
Mr Frederic Leighton: 'Think not for a moment, my dear Mr Rossetti, that I am insensible to the charm of a life secluded, as yours is, from the dust of the arena, from the mire of the market-place. Ah no! – I envy you your ivory tower. How often at some council meeting of the R.A. have I echoed within me that phrase of Wordsworth's, "the world is too much with us". But alas! in all of us there is a duality of nature. You, *O felix nimium*, are singer as well as painter. I, separated from my easel, am but a citizen. And the civistic passion – yes, passion, dear Mr Rossetti – restrains the impulse of the artist in me

towards solitude and curbs the panting of the hart in me for the water-brooks. I feel that I have, in conjunction with my colleagues, a duty to the nation. To inform the taste of the Sovereign, the taste of her ever-genial first-born and his sweet and gracious consort, of the Lords Spiritual and Temporal and of the faithful Commons, of the Judicial Bench, of those who direct the Army and Navy and the Reserve forces, of our merchant princes in Threadneedle Street and of our squires in the Shires, and through all these to bring light and improvement to those toiling millions on whom ultimately the glory of Great Britain rests – all this is in me an ambition not to be stifled and an aspiration not to be forgone. You smile, Mr Rossetti, yet I am not disemboldened to say now, as I have often wished to say to you, in the words of the Apostle Paul, "Come over and help us". Our President – I grant you in confidence – is not of all men the most enlightened; but I, in virtue of what is left to me of youth and ardour, conjoined with the paltry gift of tact, have some little influence in Burlington House. Come now! – let me put your name down in our Candidates' Book.'

EXHIB Grosvenor 1917; L.G. Sept 1921
REPRO *Rossetti and his Circle*, 1922
OWNER Tate Gallery

JOSEPH LEITER
1868–1932 American tycoon

920★ **[Untitled** 1898]
REPRO *Daily Mail*, 25 Jun 1898

DAN LENO
1860–1904 Comedian

921★ **Mr Dan Leno** [1901]
On stage, full face, leaning on umbrella.
EXHIB Carfax 1901
REPRO *Pall Mall Magazine*, Feb 1902

922 **In piam memoriam**
Danielii Lenonis
Viri praecipui in scientia
cordium humanorum
non minus quam
in facetiis praeclari
[In grateful memory
of Dan Leno
Who was as remarkable
for his knowledge of the human heart

as he was famous
for the readiness of his wit]
EXHIB L.G. 1928 and 1957
OWNER Harry Sacher

923★ **The Great Commoner** [n.d.]
D. L. speaking in the House of Commons. A note on the back in Siegfried Sassoon's hand reads: 'Dan Leno. One of a series for a book which was never published, with verses by T. Mostyn Pigott'.
OWNER Glen Byam Shaw

924 **[Dan Leno]**
EXHIB L.G. 1945 (Guedalla)

POPE LEO XIII
1810–1903 Pope from 1878
See 489

KING LEOPOLD II
1835–1909
See also 186

925★ **H.M. The King of the Belgians** [n.d.]
This short stout Hebrew bears no resemblance to the tall long-bearded King, and presumably Max was recording his character rather than his features.
EXHIB Grolier 1944
OWNER Harvard College Library

THE FIRST VISCOUNT
LEVERHULME
1851–1925 Manufacturer and philanthropist
See 827

SIR GEORGE LEWIS, FIRST
BARONET
1833–1911 Solicitor
See also 805-7

926★ **Sir George Lewis** [1896]
Profile, facing right, standing on pavement, reading.
REPRO *Twenty-Five Gentlemen*, 1896; *Max's Nineties*, 1958

927★ **Sir George Lewis** [n.d.]
Almost identical with 926.
EXHIB Carfax 1901
REPRO *Pall Mall Magazine*, Feb 1902
OWNER Garrick Club

928* **One who knows** [1903]

*G. L. seated at table in front of paper and quill pen in a
round ink-pot. Forefingers each side of huge nose.*

REPRO *John Bull*, 30 Jul 1903

929* **A Keeper of Secrets** [1903]

*Almost identical with 928, but a square ink-pot and other
small differences.*

REPRO *Sketch*, 9 Dec 1903

930 **[Sir George Lewis]**

EXHIB L.G. 1911

931* **A memory of Mr George Lewis and Mr Henry
Labouchere (circa 1888)** 1926

EXHIB L.G. 1928
REPRO *Bystander*, 5 Dec 1928
OWNER Messrs Penningtons and Lewis & Lewis

932 **Sir George Lewis [Unsigned c.1940]**

Three-quarter length, carrying top hat.

OWNER Oliver R. W. W. Lodge

SIR GEORGE LEWIS, SECOND BARONET
1868–1927 Solicitor
See also 805, 806

933* **Sir George Lewis** 1916

*Full length, three-quarter face, evening dress, hands raised
in front of chin.*

OWNER Messrs Penningtons and Lewis & Lewis

934* **Sir George Lewis** 1925

Day dress with stock, full face.

OWNER D'Offay Couper Gallery

935* **Sir George Lewis** [n.d.]

A pencil sketch, probably for 933.

OWNER Mrs Eva Reichmann

SAM LEWIS

936* **Mr Sam Lewis** [1900]

REPRO *Idler*, Feb 1900

MONA LIMERICK
c. 1882–1968 Actress

937* **Miss Mona Limerick** 1909

Full-length profile.

EXHIB Achenbach 1964
REPRO Achenbach catalogue
OWNER U.C.L.A. (Clark)

938* **Miss Mona Limerick** 1909

Full face, full length, hand on hip.

REPRO *English Review*, Oct 1909

THE FIRST MARQUESS OF LINCOLNSHIRE
1843–1928 Courtier
See also 616

939* **Always Admired** [n.d.]

Two joined drawings, each titled as above, and sub-titled:
(1) Paris in the 'sixties: Lord Carrington visiting the
Foyer de l'Opéra
(2) London in the 'teens: Lord Lincolnshire visiting
the National Liberal Club

The same man in youth and age.

EXHIB L.G. 1945 (Guedalla)
OWNER Ashmolean Museum, Oxford

M. DE LINDEMANN
A Dieppe friend

940* **Monsieur de Lindemann** [n.d.]

OWNER Mrs David Karmel

SIR THOMAS LIPTON
1850–1931 Millionaire grocer and yachtsman
See also 386, 493, 494

941* **Sir Thomas Lipton** [1901]

Full face, bow tie, very long legs.

REPRO *Town Topics* (N.Y.), Christmas 1901

942* **1923 – A Forecast. Sir T. Lipton, aboard
Shamrock XIII, and almost as breezily confident
as ever** [1903]

*T. L.'s vain attempts to win the America's Cup went as far
as Shamrock V in 1930.*

REPRO *John Bull*, 23 Jul 1903

C. P. LITTLE
1856–1914 Actor and journalist

943* **Mr C. P. Little** [1901]

EXHIB Carfax 1901
OWNER The Rev R. F. Beloe

944* **Mr C. P. Little, noting zealously, for the benefit of readers of the Paris edition of the 'New York Herald', and for the delectation of Thackeray in Elysium, the fact that Lord So-and-So was among those who were out and about in the neighbourhood of Piccadilly this morning, and that he was looking the picture of health** 1908

EXHIB N.E.A.C. Summer 1909; L.G. 1911 and 1957
OWNER Victoria & Albert Museum

945 **[Title identical with that of 944]** 1908

An almost but not quite identical drawing. Either may have been a sketch for the other.
OWNER Mr and Mrs F. P. Neill

946* **[Untitled Unsigned n.d.]**

Pencil sketch of C. P. L. as in 944 and 945.
OWNER University of Texas

DAVID LLOYD GEORGE
1863–1945 Prime Minister
See also 43, 44, 261, 262, 334, 439, 905, 1804

947* **The Chancellor of the Exchequer** [c. 1908]

EXHIB L.G. 1945 (Guedalla)
REPRO **Plate 10**
OWNER National Portrait Gallery

948* **Mr Lloyd George** 1909

REPRO *English Review*, Sep 1909

949* **Mr Lloyd George and his guardians** 1913

On a bench in the House of Commons, flanked by C. F. G. Masterman and Rufus Isaacs.
EXHIB L.G. 1913
REPRO *Fifty Caricatures*, 1913
OWNER Columbus Gallery of Fine Arts, Ohio

950* **The Trick Election** 1918

Independent Liberal: 'What shall it profit a man if he gain the whole world and –'
Coalition Liberal: 'lose his own seat?'
In the background L. G. addresses voters from a tub:
I'm the Man that Won the War!
I'm the Man that's going to make Germany pay!
I'm the Man whose heart beats high on the rugged and lonely mountains of the little land that bore him!
I'm the Man that's going to hang the Kayser!
I'm the Man that, etc. etc.'
EXHIB L.G. May 1921
REPRO *A Survey*, 1921
OWNER Dr E. V. Bevan

950A **The Trick Election of 1918 [Unsigned]**

Sketch for 950 with same dialogue.
EXHIB Achenbach 1964
OWNER Mr and Mrs Joseph M. Bransten

951* **Mr Lloyd George** 1920

No longer a democrat at heart? . . . Come!
EXHIB L.G. May 1921, 1945 (Guedalla) and 1957
REPRO *A Survey*, 1921; *Caricatures by Max*, 1958
OWNER Ashmolean Museum, Oxford

952* **The Rising Hope of the Stern, Unbending Tories [Macaulay on Gladstone]** 1920

A very worried L. G. being wooed by Curzon and Carson, both on their knees.
EXHIB L.G. May 1921
OWNER Viscount Camrose

953* **The Old and the Young Self** 1924

The Old Self infuriated by chubby schoolboy. Behind them hangs a picture of a slim, ragged, barefoot boy on a mountain, labelled.
LITTLE DAVEY
watching the dawn
from the summit of
LLWCHDWRCHCHNL
EXHIB L.G. 1925
REPRO *Observations*, 1925

W. J. LOCKE
1863–1930 Novelist
See also 1443

954* **5.0 p.m. Mr W. J. Locke at the — Club** 1907

Drinking tea, surrounded by admiring ladies.
EXHIB Carfax 1907
REPRO *A Book of Caricatures*, 1907

955 **[Mr W. J. Locke]**

EXHIB L.G. 1913

SIR OLIVER LODGE
1851–1940 Physicist and spiritualist

956* **Psychic Matters** 1914

Sir Oliver Lodge: 'Strange, that a man who *looks* so very credulous —'
Sir Edwin Ray Lankester: 'Odd, that with such a brow —'
EXHIB L.G. May 1921
REPRO *A Survey*, 1921
OWNER Oliver R. W. W. Lodge

957★ **Sir Oliver Lodge** 1932
Full-length profile facing right.
OWNER National Portrait Gallery

958 **Professor Sir Oliver Lodge** [n.d.]
Similar to 957 but facing left.
EXHIB L.G. 1952
OWNER F. Brodie Lodge

OLIVER W. F. LODGE
1878–1955 Writer

959★ **Oliver** [c. 1940]
REPRO *Abinger Chronicle*, Feb 1940
OWNER Mrs Diana Kohr

CISSY LOFTUS
1876–1943 Singer and mimic

960★ **[Lines suggested by Miss Cissy Loftus** 1894]
REPRO *Sketch*, 9 May 1894, where captioned as above; Max Beerbohm, *Letters to Reggie Turner*, 1964

961★ **[Untitled Unsigned** c. 1894]
Pencil sketch for 960.
OWNER University of Texas

961A★ **Cissie Loftus** [n.d.]
A younger-looking and more idealised version of 960.
OWNER Robert H. Taylor

THE SIXTH MARQUESS OF LONDONDERRY
1852–1915 Conservative politician
See also 436

962★ **Lord Londonderry** 1911
Wearing a frock-coat and carrying a top hat, he walks past empty parliamentary benches.
EXHIB L.G. 1911 and 1952
OWNER R. A. Bevan

THE SEVENTH MARQUESS OF LONDONDERRY
1878–1949 Conservative politician
See also 297, 612, 616

963 **Lord Londonderry** 1932
OWNER Mrs M. Lincoln Schuster

964★ **Lord Londonderry** 1934
Evening dress, carrying cloak and opera hat.
EXHIB L.G. 1952 and 1957
OWNER J. C. Thomson

WALTER LONG
1854–1924 Conservative politician
See also 71

965★ **Enigma** 1920
Clio: 'But how comes it that at a time of grave stress in the story of a great old nation *you* are one of the leading men?'
Mr Walter Long: 'Well – er – really, you know – feller has a sense o' duty and all that – besides, not without plenty of official experience, quite apart from Quarter Sessions – same time – since you put it that way – come to think of it – 'pon my word – should like notice of that question!'
W. L. was First Lord of the Admiralty 1919–21. A group of puzzled admirals stand in the background.
EXHIB L.G. May 1921
REPRO *A Survey*, 1921

THE FIFTH EARL OF LONSDALE
1857–1944 Landowner and sportsman

966★ **[Untitled** 1894]
Evening dress, half length, head in profile to left.
REPRO *Pick-Me-Up*, 20 Oct 1894

967★ **[Untitled Unsigned** c. 1894]
Rough sketch for 966.
OWNER University of Texas

968 **[Lord Lonsdale** 1901]
EXHIB Carfax 1901

969★ **Lord Lonsdale** [n.d.]
Check suit, tiny hat, head in profile, smoking cigar with band on.
EXHIB L.G. 1952
OWNER Miss D. J. Hubbard

970★ **Lord Lonsdale** [n.d.]
Same check suit, hat and cigar as 969, but all in profile, and older.
OWNER Mrs David Karmel

971 **[Lord Lonsdale]**
EXHIB L.G. 1911

LONSDALE (*continued*)

972★ **Lord Lonsdale** 1912

Three-quarter-length profile facing left, top hat, buttonhole, smoking cigar.

REPRO *Bystander*, 12 June 1912

973★ **Deeply embedded in the esteem and affection of the British Public. Lord Lonsdale** 1921

For John Rothenstein an ideal to be followed.

Dressed as in 972, but with field-glasses and no cigar.

OWNER Sir John Rothenstein

974 [**Lord Lonsdale** 1932]

EXHIB L.G. 1952, where dated as above

LORD LORNE
1845–1914 Later ninth Duke of Argyll
See also 1591

975★ **Lord Lorne** [c. 1896]

EXHIB L.G. 1928, where dated as above
OWNER Keith Mackenzie

LOUIS-PHILIPPE
1773–1850 King of France

976★ **La Poire Reversée** 1912

Shade of Louis Philippe (pausing before a drawing of Mr Anthony Hope): 'Cela ne me plaît pas. Il me rappelle trop nettement la manière de l'infâme Daumier.'

L.–P.'s head is pear-shaped, big end downwards, A. H's just the reverse. It was not in fact Daumier but his master Charles Philipon (1802–62) whose caricature of L-P. as a pear caused him to be tried for lèse-majesté. He was acquitted.

EXHIB L.G. 1913 and 1952; Grolier 1944
OWNER Private (Harvard)

CLAUDE LOWTHER
1872–1929 Soldier and Conservative M.P.

977★ **A Senator** [1903]

REPRO *Sketch*, 20 May 1903

978★ **Mr Claude Lowther – dominating Paris** [1907]

EXHIB Carfax 1907; L.G. 1911
REPRO *A Book of Caricatures*, 1907

JAMES LOWTHER
1840–1904 Conservative politician

979 [**Mr James Lowther. A sportsman and statesman of those days.** c. 1896]

EXHIB L.G. 1928, where dated as above

980★ **Mr James Lowther** [1901]

EXHIB Carfax 1901
OWNER Mrs Clarissa Higginbotham

E. V. LUCAS
1868–1938 Writer and publisher
See also 679

981★ **Mr E. V. Lucas** 1923

EXHIB L.G. 1923
REPRO *Things New and Old*, 1923

982★ [**The Six-Club Man** n.d.]

For E. V. himself from Max.

Six joined drawings as follows:
E. V. at the Garrick [*wearing stock and eyeglass, talking to Squire Bancroft, similarly attired*]
E. V. at the Athenaeum [*wearing spectacles and long white beard, talking to a Bishop*]
E. V. at the Savage [*wearing neck-scarf and sombrero, talking to a decayed Savage*]
E. V. at Brooks's [*talking to Asquith, both in dinner jackets and smoking cigars*]
E. V. at the Burlington Fine Arts [*talking to Roger Fry*]
E. V. at the National Sporting Club [*wearing bowler hat and check waistcoat, talking to a prize-fighter*]

REPRO E. V. Lucas, *Reading, Writing and Remembering*, 1932, where captioned as above
OWNER Mrs Dora Man

H.W. LUCY
1845–1924 Journalist

983 [**Mr H. W. Lucy** c. 1896]

EXHIB L.G. 1928, where dated as above

984 [**Mr H. W. Lucy**]

EXHIB Carfax 1901

THE THIRD LORD LURGAN
1858–1937 Landowner

985★ **Lord Lurgan** [n.d.]

A drawing done in the 'nineties.

Full-length profile, evening dress, hand in pocket.
EXHIB Carfax 1901
OWNER Keith Mackenzie

986★ [Untitled 1901]
Almost identical with 985, but with more shading.
REPRO *Critic, (N.Y.), Nov 1901*

987★ [Untitled Unsigned n.d.]
Full-length pencil sketch, three-quarter face, wearing curved bowler hat and binoculars.
OWNER University of Texas

BOHUN LYNCH
1884–1928   Caricaturist and author
See 1449

RALPH LYNN
1882–1962   Actor

988★ Mr Ralph Lynn [1930]
REPRO *Ladbroke's Racing Calendar, 1931*

THE HON. ALFRED LYTTELTON
1857–1913   M.P. and cricketer

989★ Mr Alfred Lyttelton 1908
Sitting twisted on chair, his arm through the back.
EXHIB Carfax 1908; L.G. 1945 (Guedalla)
OWNER Ashmolean Museum, Oxford

990 [Mr Alfred Lyttelton]
EXHIB L.G. 1911

THE SECOND EARL OF LYTTON
1876–1947   Governor of Bengal

991★ Lord Lytton [1907]
EXHIB Carfax 1907
REPRO *A Book of Caricatures, 1907*
OWNER Fred Uhlman

992 [Lord Lytton]
EXHIB L.G. 1911

993 [Lord Lytton]
EXHIB L.G. 1952

M

MAARTEN MAARTENS
1858–1915   Dutch novelist

994★ [Mr Maarten Maartens at home]
EXHIB L.G. 1913

D. S. MacCOLL
1859–1948   Art Critic and Keeper of the Tate Gallery
See also 679, 1533, 1586–8

995★ A quiet morning in the Tate Gallery 1907
The Curator trying to expound to one of the Trustees [Alfred de Rothschild] the spiritual fineness of Mr William Rothenstein's 'Jews Mourning in a Synagogue'.
EXHIB Carfax 1907

REPRO *A Record of Ten Years, 1917–1927*, Tate Gallery, 1927
OWNER Tate Gallery

RAMSAY MacDONALD
1866–1937   Prime Minister
See also 439

996★ Sweet Fancies and Hard Facts, or, The Tragedy of Holding Office 1924
Mr Ramsay MacDonald: 'Somehow I never noticed these things [a cliff of rocks] at the end of my garden'
EXHIB L.G. 1925
REPRO *Observations, 1925*
OWNER City Art Gallery, Manchester

MacDonald (*continued*)

997* Mr Ramsay MacDonald listening to a supporter 1931
EXHIB L.G. 1952
OWNER Columbus Gallery of Fine Arts, Ohio

998 Mr Ramsay MacDonald listening to a speech by a supporter 1931
A sketch for 997.
OWNER Frank Hardie

998A* Mr Ramsay MacDonald listening to a speech by a supporter 1931
Another (pencil) sketch for 997.
EXHIB L.G. 1952
OWNER National Portrait Gallery

AMBROSE MCEVOY
1878–1927 Painter
See 679

REGINALD MCKENNA
1863–1943 Liberal politician
See also 799

999* Mr Reginald McKenna 1912
EXHIB L.G. 1928 and 1957
REPRO *Fifty Caricatures*, 1913
OWNER David McKenna

1000* [Mr Reginald McKenna impulsively uncovers, showing us how Men of not very Obvious Abilities may yet Rise to Highest Posts in the Public Service]
Unveiling a statue of himself.
EXHIB L.G. 1913
REPRO *Daily Sketch*, 11 Apr 1913

SIR ALEXANDER MACKENZIE
1847–1935 Scottish conductor and composer

1001 [Sir Alexander Mackenzie c. 1900]
EXHIB L.G. 1928, where dated as above

1002* An English Musician. Sir Alexander Mackenzie [c. 1903]
REPRO *Cassell's Magazine*, Feb 1903

1003* A Born Knight [1903]
Conducting with a tasselled walking-stick.
REPRO *John Bull*, 29 Oct 1903

1004* Sir Alexander Mackenzie [1907]
Conducting with an umbrella.
EXHIB Carfax 1907
REPRO *A Book of Caricatures*, 1907

MAURICE MAETERLINCK
1862–1949 Belgian poet and dramatist
See also 146

1005* ['The Belgian Poet' 1908]
Three-quarter-length profile, in knee-breeches, holding cigar.
REPRO *Vanity Fair*, 22 Jul 1908, where captioned as above

MAJOR HUBERT MAGNIAC
1858–1909 Soldier

1006* [Untitled n.d.]
OWNER Ashmolean Museum, Oxford

HARRINGTON MANN
1864–1937 Painter

1007 [Mr Harrington Mann]
EXHIB L.G. 1913

FREDERIC MANNING
c.1880–1935 Writer

1008* Mr Frederic Manning 1913
F. M. as ventriloquist, a dummy Pope on one knee, a dummy soldier on the other. A reference to F. M.'s 'Scenes and Portraits', 1909.
EXHIB L.G. 1923
REPRO *Things New and Old*, 1923

MARCHESE GUGLIELMO MARCONI
1874–1937 Italian inventor of radio

1009* S. E. Marchese Marconi 1931
EXHIB L.G. 1952
OWNER Marconi Co Ltd

MARIE ANTOINETTE
1755–93 Queen of France

1010★ [Untitled] 1921

'And surely never lighted on this orb a more delightful vision. I saw her just above the horizon, decorating and elevating the exalted sphere she just began to move in – glittering like the morning star, full of life, and splendour, and joy' . . . [From Burke's *Reflections on the French Revolution*, slightly misquoted]

The haughty queen, nose in air, fills the picture. Burke a small timid figure in the top corner.

EXHIB L.G. 1952

HARRY HANANEL MARKS
1855–1916   M.P. and Editor of the *Financial News*

1011★ **Mr Harry Marks** [1895]

REPRO *Pick-Me-Up*, 19 Jan 1895
OWNER Sold at Sotheby's 14 Dec 1960

THE NINTH DUKE OF MARLBOROUGH
1871–1934   Conservative politician
See also 332

1012★ **A Prince of the Holy Roman Empire** [1899]

REPRO *Sketch*, 8 Feb 1899

1013 [**The Duke of Marlborough** 1901]

EXHIB Carfax 1901

1014★ [**Untitled** 1901]

REPRO *Critic* (N.Y.), Nov 1901

1015 [**The Duke of Marlborough**]

EXHIB L.G. 1911

THOMAS MARLOWE
1868–1935   Journalist
See 564

EDWARD MARSH
1872–1953   Civil servant and writer
See 329, 337, 616

L. MARSHALL
Charterhouse master
See 664, 665

CYRIL MARTINEAU
1871–1918   Stockbroker

1016★ **Mr Cyril Martineau** [n.d.]

Wearing straw hat and carrying umbrella.
OWNER Mrs Eva Reichmann

1017★ **Mr Cyril Martineau** [n.d.]

Wearing bowler hat and carrying stick.
OWNER Piccadilly Gallery

EDWARD MARTYN
1859–1923   Irish playwright
See 1825

QUEEN MARY
1867–1953   Consort of King George V
See 577, 1570

JOHN MASEFIELD
1878–1967   Poet Laureate
See also 95, 144, 181, 614, 615, 703, 769

1018★ **A swear-word in a rustic slum
A simple swear-word is to some,
To Masefield something more.** 1913

Refers to the expletives in J. M.'s 'The Everlasting Mercy', 1911, and is a skit on:

> *A primrose by a river's brim*
> *A yellow primrose was to him,*
> *And it was nothing more.*
> *(Wordsworth, 'Peter Bell')*

EXHIB L.G. 1913
REPRO *Fifty Caricatures*, 1913

1019★ **Mr Masefield cultivating his garden** 1913

He is gravely watering a single lily in a pot, with rolling country in background.
EXHIB L.G. May 1921
REPRO *Sketch*, 25 May 1921
OWNER John H. Whitney

1020★ **Mr John Masefield** 1931

REPRO *Spectator* Supplement, 4 Apr 1931
OWNER *The Spectator*

A. E. W. MASON
1865–1948   Novelist
See also 335

1021★ [**'Four Feathers'** 1908]

MASON (continued)

A. E. W. M.'s most successful novel was 'The Four Feathers', 1902.

REPRO *Vanity Fair*, 10 Jun 1908, where captioned as above; R. L. Green, *A. E. W. Mason*, 1952

C. F. G. MASTERMAN
1873–1927   Liberal M.P. and writer
See also 949

1022★ **Mr C. F. Masterman preserving his ideals** 1911

EXHIB   L.G. 1911 and 1945 (Guedalla)
REPRO   *Bookman*, Aug 1911
OWNER   Ashmolean Museum, Oxford

AYLMER MAUDE
1858–1938   Translator of Tolstoy
See 1484

CYRIL MAUDE
1862–1951   Actor-manager

1023★ **Mr Cyril Maude** [c. 1899]

EXHIB   L.G. 1928, where dated as above
OWNER   Judge John Maude

PHIL MAY
1864–1903   Caricaturist

1024★ **[Untitled ?Unsigned** 1894]

REPRO   *Pall Mall Budget*, 7 Jun 1894; *Max's Nineties*, 1958

1025 **[Mr Phil May** 1901]

EXHIB   Carfax 1901

HARRY MELVILL
1861–1936   Dandy and raconteur

1026★ **Mr Harry Melvill** [c. 1901]

EXHIB   L.G. 1928, where dated as above; Achenbach 1964
REPRO   **Plate 78**
OWNER   U.C.L.A. (Clark)

MORTIMER MENPES
1859–1938   Australian artist

1027 **[Mr Mortimer Menpes, closeted with Mr Raymond Blathwayt, for whose benefit he evaluates an almond blossom** 1908]

EXHIB   Carfax 1908; L.G. 1957

COUNT ALBERT MENSDORFF
1861–1945   Austrian Ambassador in London
1904–14
See also 1567, 1568

1028 **Count Albert Mensdorff** 1930

EXHIB   L.G. 1952
OWNER   Sold at Sotheby's 14 Dec 1960

1029★ **Count Mensdorff** [n.d.]

OWNER   Patrick Baldwin

1030★ **[Untitled Unsigned** n.d.]

Full-length pencil sketch, profile facing left. In front some measurements such as: From collar to waistline measured down back 18 inches.

OWNER   University of Texas

GAETANO MEO
1850–1925   Italian painter and mosaic artist

1031 **Signor Gaetano Meo** 1922

OWNER   Sold at Sotheby's 14 Dec 1960

GEORGE MEREDITH
1828–1909   Poet and novelist
See also 857, 858, 1268, 1274

1032★ **['Our First Novelist'** 1896]

EXHIB   F.A.S. 1896; L.G. 1945 (Guedalla) and 1957
REPRO   *Vanity Fair*, 24 Sep 1896, where captioned as above; *Max's Nineties*, 1958
OWNER   Ashmolean Museum, Oxford

1033★ **Box Hill – a memory** 1926

EXHIB   Achenbach 1964
OWNER   Bender Room, Stanford University

1034 **George Meredith, Recollection of the drawing done in 1896. For Ralph Wood chez lui** 1943

R. W. was living in G. M.'s cottage on Box Hill.

OWNER   Mrs Marguerite Ruffer

GEORGE METAXA
1899–1950   Actor and singer

1035* **Mr Metaxa as Carl Linden** [c. 1931]
REPRO *Heroes and Heroines of Bitter Sweet, 1931*
OWNER Lilly Library

EGAN MEW
1862–1945 Writer and expert on old china
See also 679, 1701

1036 **[Untitled]** 1913
One of Elbert's Enemies (Be it clearly understood that this is no attempt to portray an actually most charming, debonair and juvenile personage. It seeks but to show the light in which perhaps he appears to local naughty-boyhood embittered at knowing itself disapproved, distrusted and constantly decried).
Shows E. M. on Hampstead Heath, looking down at urchins playing on a road.
OWNER Douglas Cleverdon

CARL MEYER
1851–1922 Businessman

1037 **Mr Carl Meyer** [n.d.]
OWNER Sold at Sotheby's 14 Dec 1960

1038 **[Sir Carl Meyer and another, awaiting with no impatience the foundation of the National Shakespeare Memorial Theatre]**
EXHIB L.G. 1911

JOHN STUART MILL
1806–73 Philosopher
See 1280, 1280A

J. E. MILLAIS
1829–96 Painter
See also 776

1039* **A momentary Vision that once befell young Millais** 1917
EXHIB L.G. Sept 1921
REPRO *Rossetti and his Circle, 1922*
OWNER Tate Gallery

VISCOUNT MILNER
1854–1925 Statesman and proconsul

1040* **Lord Milner awaiting the fulfilment of his worst fears about the South African Constitution** 1913
He stands on a cliff-edge, looking distastefully across to South Africa, where John Bull and an Afrikaner loll back to back.
EXHIB L.G. 1913
REPRO *Daily Sketch,* 11 Apr 1913
OWNER New College, Oxford

1041* **Viscount Milner** 1924
Four joined half-length drawings, in which Lord M is pondering as follows:
1. 'I was mainly instrumental in bringing about the South African War – that adventure in which, as every one now admits, we covered ourselves with glory.'
2. 'I opposed, with all the weight of my authority, the granting of a constitution to our late enemies – that step of which the consequences have been so disastrous.'
3. 'With unwonted passion I urged the Lords to throw out Lloyd George's Budget, and thereby paved the way for that Parliament Act which has so lightened for them the awful load of their legislative responsibilities.'
4. 'I presided over the Committee that drew up an exquisitely full scheme of Tariffs for Great Britain in view of Amery's General Election; and quite a number of Tories were returned to Parliament. And yet – in spite of all these things – somehow – somewhere deep down in my heart . . .'
This drawing was reproduced for inclusion in 'Observations', 1925, but was omitted because of Lord M's recent death. A proof was among Max's papers.
EXHIB L.G. 1925

SIR ALFRED MOND
1868–1930 Industrialist
See also 69, 679

1042 **[Sir Alfred Mond c. 1908]**
EXHIB L.G. 1928, where dated as above

1043 **[Sir Alfred Mond congratulating Mr Austin Harrison on the current issue of 'The English Review' 1910]**
A. M. was the proprietor, and A. H. the editor, of the paper.
EXHIB L.G. 1911 and 1957, where dated as above

GEORGE MOORE
1852–1933 Irish writer
See also 24, 27, 95, 281, 335, 514, 515, 612, 613, 1307, 1423, 1443, 1650, 1827

1044* Mr George Moore [1896]

Full length, looking at his own hand.

EXHIB F.A.S. 1896
REPRO *Twenty-Five Gentlemen*, 1896; *Max's Nineties*, 1958

1045* Mr George Moore [1898]

Full length, full face, carrying top hat and stick.

REPRO *Sketch*, 6 Jul 1898

1046* [Untitled 1900]

G. M. and W. B. Yeats clutching a harp and perched on a steeple.

EXHIB Achenbach 1964
REPRO *World*, Christmas No, 1900
OWNER U.C.L.A. (Clark)

1047* Mr George Moore [1901]

Full length, large bow tie, top hat and stick in left hand.

EXHIB Carfax 1901
OWNER University of Texas

1048 Nil

1049* Mr George Moore, preacher to Lord Howard de Walden 1907

EXHIB Carfax 1907
REPRO *A Book of Caricatures*, 1907

1050* Reappearance of Mr George Moore in Chelsea 1909

Artist's Model: 'Ought to be ashamed o' yerself – coming an' taking the bread out o' us pore girls' mouths . . .'

EXHIB N.E.A.C. Summer 1909; L.G. 1952
REPRO *Fifty Caricatures*, 1913
OWNER J. C. Thomson

1051 [Mr George Moore]

EXHIB L.G. 1911

1052 [Mr George Moore]

EXHIB L.G. 1911

1053 [Mr George Moore]

EXHIB L.G. 1911

1054* An illustration for 'Hail and Farewell'. Mr Moore under the influence of the Boer War 1911

G. M., disconsolate on a chair, is being cherished by Steer, Sickert and Tonks.

EXHIB N.E.A.C Winter 1911; L.G. 1945 (Guedalla)
REPRO L.G. Catalogue, 1945
OWNER Ashmolean Museum, Oxford

1055* Elegy on *Any* Lady by G. M. [c. 1916]

> That she adored me as the most
>   Adorable of males
> I think I may securely boast.
>   Dead women tell no tales

G. M. in deep mourning stands by a tombstone, which reads:

HIC JACET
MULIER QUAEVIS
OBIIT
1876–1916

REPRO **Plate 39**
OWNER Miss Jennifer Gosse

1055A* Elegy on *Any* Lady by George Moore. [Unsigned n.d.]

A sketch for 1055, with G. M. on left instead of right. Verse identical, tombstone reading only HIC JACET/ANY LADY.

OWNER Robert H. Taylor

1056* The Old and the Young Self 1924

Young Self: 'And have there been any painters since Manet?'
Old Self: 'None'
Young Self: 'Have there been any composers since Wagner?'
Old Self: 'None'
Young Self: 'Any novelists since Balzac?'
Old Self: 'One'

EXHIB L.G. 1925 and 1957
REPRO *Observations*, 1925
OWNER Gluck

1057* George Moore 1955

With love to Elisabeth [Jungmann]
A pencil sketch, believed to be Max's last drawing.

EXHIB L.G. 1957
OWNER Mrs Eva Reichmann

1058* [Untitled n.d.]

Standing, left hand raised, between two pictures.

EXHIB L.G. 1945 (Guedalla)
REPRO *Caricatures by Max*, 1958
OWNER Ashmolean Museum, Oxford

1059 [Mr George Moore]

EXHIB L.G. 1945 (Guedalla)

1060* [Untitled n.d.]

Head and shoulders of G. M. and an elegant and beautiful woman face to face.

EXHIB L.G. 1952
OWNER John Brett-Smith

1061* **A Survivor of the Nouvelle Athènes – Mr George Moore** [Unsigned n.d.]

Half-length profile facing left. The N. A. was a Parisian café frequented by artists and writers in the 1880s.

OWNER University of Texas

1062* **Mr George Moore** [n.d.]

Full length, wearing astrakhan coat, carrying bowler hat.

OWNER University of Texas

MARY MOORE
1862–1931 Actress
See 1815

T. STURGE MOORE
1870–1944 Poet and engraver
See 144, 748

JOHN MORLEY
1838–1923 Radical politician and writer
See also 612, 748, 1280, 1280A

1063* **Mr John Morley** [1900]

Full-length profile, facing left, wearing top hat.

REPRO *Idler*, Oct 1900

1064 **Morley, monumental mason** 1901

J. M. is placing a halo on a statue of Gladstone, the base of which is inscribed 'KHARTOUM. MAJUBA'.

OWNER Lord Hylton

1065 [**Mr John Morley, trundling his own hoop** 1901]

EXHIB Carfax 1901

1066* **The Great Biography** [?c. 1901]

Lord Rowton to Mr Morley: 'My *dear* Sir, why spend three years in writing a Life, when you can spend twenty in *not* writing it? Come! Build a Model Lodging-House!'

J. M.'s Life of Gladstone appeared in 1903, in which year Lord R died. He had been private secretary to Disraeli, whose papers he inherited. Instead of writing D's Life he was responsible for the building of six Rowton Houses – lodging-houses for the poor.

EXHIB N.Y. 1912; L.G. 1945 (Guedalla)
REPRO *Caricatures by Max*, 1958
OWNER Ashmolean Museum, Oxford

1067* **Lord Morley of Blackburn** 1911

Perched on a portcullis.

EXHIB N.E.A.C. Winter 1911; L.G. 1945 (Guedalla)
OWNER Ashmolean Museum, Oxford

1068* **[Untitled]** 1913

Lord Morley of Blackburn: 'I often think, old friend, that there's one thing for which we ought to be very thankful. And that is –'
Lord Courtney of Penwith: 'That George Eliot was not spared to see us here, John?'
Lord Morley of Blackburn: 'Yes, Leonard.'

Both perched on a portcullis.

EXHIB L.G. 1913
OWNER Fitzwilliam Museum, Cambridge

1069 [**Lord Morley** 1923]

EXHIB L.G. 1928, where dated as above

1070 [**Mr John Morley. 'In Memoriam G. O. M.'**]

EXHIB L.G. 1957

SIR LEWIS MORRIS
1833–1907 Welsh poet
See also 1875

1071 **Sir Lewis Morris** [n.d.]

EXHIB L.G. 1928
OWNER Harold Matthews

WILLIAM MORRIS
1834–96 Poet, craftsman and Socialist
See also 1268, 1276

1072* **Topsy [W. M.] and Ned [Burne-] Jones, settled on the settle in Red Lion Square** 1916

In 'The Poets' Corner', 1943, Max added this note:
In this plate Morris has dark hair. In Plate 23 [here 1268] his hair is pale gold. It may be mentioned that I had noticed this dreadful discrepancy, and had been sorry that in my young days I supposed that Morris (never set eyes on by me) was as blond as a Viking; but that I wished the error to stand, as an awful warning against guesswork by the young.

EXHIB Grosvenor 1917; L.G. Sept 1921
REPRO *Rossetti and his Circle*, 1922; *The Poets' Corner*, 1943
OWNER Tate Gallery

R. BOYD MORRISON
Stage designer
See also 382, 383

1073 [Mr Boyd Morrison and Mr Gordon Craig
1926]
EXHIB L.G. 1952, where dated as above

EDWARD MORTON
d. 1922   Dramatic critic and playwright

1074 [Mr Edward Morton 1901]
EXHIB Carfax 1901

1075★ The Palmy Days of Dramatic Criticism 1935
REPRO   G. F. Sims catalogue no 64, May 1966
OWNER Mark Birley

1076★ Mr Edward Morton [n.d.]
Wearing straw hat.
OWNER Piccadilly Gallery

1077★ [Untitled n.d.]
Half-length rough sketch, bare-headed. Known only from a photograph in Max's papers.

SIR OSWALD MOSLEY BART
b. 1896   Politician

1078★ A Self-Made Man. Sir Oswald Mosley 1931
REPRO   *Spectator* Supplement, 28 Feb 1931
OWNER *The Spectator*

C. W. MOSS
Charterhouse master
See 664, 665

BENITO MUSSOLINI
1883–1945   Italian dictator

1079★ The Beneficent Despot 1923
One Constitutional Monarch [King Victor Emanuel III of Italy] to another [King George V]: 'He has worked wonders for my people. If you'd like me to lend him to you . . .'
EXHIB   L.G. 1923 and 1945 (Guedalla)
REPRO   *Things New and Old*, 1923
OWNER Ashmolean Museum, Oxford

1080 Ménage à Trois 1924
B. M., King Victor Emanuel III and a figure representing Italy, all sitting on a sofa.
EXHIB   L.G. 1925
OWNER Lord Hylton

N

NAPOLEON I
1769–1821   Emperor of France
See also 1112, 1113, 1371

1081★ St Helena [1899]
Arms folded, face obscured by hat, on a tiny labelled rock in the ocean.
EXHIB L.G. 1945 (Guedalla)
REPRO *Butterfly*, Dec 1899; *Max's Nineties*, 1958

1082★ [Untitled 1900]
Crossing the Alps in a motor-car.
EXHIB Achenbach 1964
REPRO   *World*, Christmas No, 1900
OWNER U.C.L.A. (Clark)

1083★ [Untitled] 1913
Yea, though thy child shall childless die,
Time will provide fair progeny
To call thee forebear.
                    Ben Jonson
Behind N., who is riding disconsolate on a horse, stand with folded arms five contemporary Napoleons – Lord Northcliffe, Sir Edgar Speyer, Edmund Davis, John Redmond, and one still unidentified.
OWNER The Marquess of Anglesey

1084★ St Helena [Unsigned 1951]
A pencil variant of 1081, dated on back by Elisabeth Jungmann.
OWNER Sir Rupert Hart-Davis

1085★ [**Untitled** n.d.]

Same attitude as 1081 and 1084, but no island or sea.

EXHIB Cincinnati 1965
OWNER Lilly Library

NAPOLEON III
1808–73 Emperor of France
See also 658

1086★ **What Had She Expected?** 1924

'He is excessively kind in private, and so very quiet'
(Extract from letter written by Queen Victoria in
Paris, September 1, 1855, to Baron Stockmar).

EXHIB L.G. 1945 (Guedalla) and 1957
REPRO **Plate 20**
OWNER Mrs Philip Guedalla

JULIA NEILSON
1868–1957 Actress

1087★ [**Untitled Unsigned** 1895]

*Outline head, illustrating review of 'An Ideal Husband' by
Oscar Wilde.*

REPRO *Pick-Me-Up*, 19 Jan 1895; *Max's Nineties*, 1958

1088★ **Miss Neilson** [n.d.]

Outline head (very similar to 1087) and shoulders.

OWNER Victoria & Albert Museum

OSCAR NEMON
b. 1906 Yugoslav sculptor
See also 1386

1088A★ [**Untitled**] 1939

For Monsieur Nemon from Max
Full-length profile facing left.

OWNER Oscar Nemon

1088B★ **Némon** 1940

Full-length, head in profile to left.

OWNER Oscar Nemon

J. T. NETTLESHIP
1841–1902 Painter

1089★ **Mr Nettleship** [n.d.]

OWNER Piccadilly Gallery

CHARLES NEUMANN

1090 [**Mr Charles Neumann** 1901]

EXHIB Carfax 1901

SIGMUND NEUMANN
1857–1916 Banker

1091 [**Mr Sigismund Neumann**]

EXHIB L.G. 1911

RALPH NEVILL
1865–1930 Writer

1092★ **Mr Ralph Nevill pointing out to members
of the Young Men's Christian Association the
temptations to which they are no longer exposed**
1913

Showing a slide of a gaming table.

EXHIB L.G. May 1921 and 1957
REPRO *A Survey*, 1921
OWNER St James's Club

LORD WILLIAM NEVILL
1860–1939 Son of first Marquess of Abergavenny

1093★ **Lord William Nevill** [1896]

REPRO *Twenty-Five Gentlemen*, 1896
OWNER George F. Benson

C. R. W. NEVINSON
1889–1946 Painter
See 679

HENRY NEWBOLT
1862–1938 Poet
See also 144, 748

1094★ [**Untitled**] 1914

6 April 1914
My dear Newbolt, Here is that transcription of the
Newbolt Plan of features, without Hewlett to inter-
rupt the view. Yours ever Max Beerbohm.

*Three-quarter-length profile facing right, hand on chin.
H. N. had just propounded in 'The Times' a Plan to
solve the Irish Question.*

REPRO *Later Life and Letters of Sir Henry Newbolt*, 1942
OWNER Messrs Chas J. Sawyer

1095* Mr Henry Newbolt [pre-1915]

Full-length profile, holding Union Jack.

EXHIB L.G. 1952
REPRO *Times Ed. Sup.*, 2 May 1952

NATHANIEL NEWNHAM-DAVIS
1854–1917 Soldier, author and gourmet

1096* Colonel Newnham Davis 1907

EXHIB Carfax 1908
OWNER Lilly Library

A. E. NEWTON
1863–1940 American book-collector

1097* Mr Arthur [should be Alfred] Newton on the Riviera di Levante 1923

Lovely sky, yes. But where are the books?

EXHIB L. G. 1952; American Academy 1952
OWNER Harvard College Library

THE SECOND LORD NEWTON
1857–1942 Conservative politician

1098 In an age of advertisement – Lord Newton conjured to introduce some more of those little bills 1913

Lord N introduced into the House of Lords bills on betting, smoke-abatement, the 24-hour clock, and reform of the Lords themselves.

OWNER G. H. Chipperfield

NICHOLAS II
1868–1918 Tsar of all the Russias
See 186, 1629, 1727

ROBERT NICHOLS
1893–1944 Poet
See 703

BEN NICHOLSON
b. 1894 Painter

1099 [Mr Benjamin Nicholson 1918]

EXHIB L.G. 1952, where dated as above

WILLIAM NICHOLSON
1872–1949 Painter
See also 382, 383, 614, 615, 679, 703, 1198, 1656

1100 [Mr William Nicholson 1901]

EXHIB Carfax 1901

1101 [Mr William Nicholson 1903]

EXHIB L.G. 1957, where dated as above

1102* Mr William Nicholson 1907

Full length, full face, very high collar, wasp waist, holding stick.

EXHIB Carfax 1907
REPRO *A Book of Caricatures*, 1907

1103 [Mr William Nicholson, painting a forget-me-not in a thimble 1910]

EXHIB N.E.A.C. Summer 1910

1104* Mr William Nicholson (last century)

Three-quarter length, full face, yellow waistcoat, high collar, broad-brimmed hat. The words 'last century' were clearly written in later.

REPRO *Winter Owl*, 1923

1105* [Untitled n.d.]

Full length, bare head in profile, black hair with broad grey streak, high collar, heavily buttoned greatcoat, bowler hat in hand.

EXHIB L.G. 1957
OWNER Charles Bravington

SIR WILLIAM ROBERTSON NICOLL
1851–1923 Scottish journalist and writer
See 119

HAROLD NICOLSON
1886–1968 Diplomat and writer

1106 [Mr Harold Nicolson 1929]

EXHIB L.G. 1952, where dated as above

1107* [Untitled Unsigned n.d.]

Three-quarter-length profile, drawn on a sheet of Great Western Royal Hotel paper.

OWNER Mrs Eva Reichmann

THE FIFTEENTH DUKE OF NORFOLK
1847–1917 Earl Marshal of England

1108★ [The Duke of Norfolk 1913]

Bristling hair and a shaggy beard.

EXHIB L.G. 1928 and 1957, where dated as above
REPRO *Bystander,* 5 Dec 1928

COLONEL J. T. NORTH
1841–96   Financier and racehorse-owner

1109★ [Untitled 1895]

REPRO *Pick-Me-Up,* 6 Apr 1895

LORD NORTHCLIFFE
1865–1922   Newspaper proprietor
See also 493, 494, 1083, 1423, 1875

1110★ Alfred Harmsworth [c. 1897]

Full-length profile facing left, striped suit, smoking cigarette, holding sheet of paper.

EXHIB L.G. 1928, where dated as above
OWNER Viscount Rothermere

1111★ Mr Alfred Harmsworth [1901]

Full-length profile facing right, the smoke from his cigarette repeating the outline of his face.

EXHIB Carfax 1901
REPRO *English Illustrated Review,* Jul 1923
OWNER Viscount Rothermere

1112★ Napoleon, the Later but not Lesser [1903]

Standing, arms folded, top hat on sideways, in front of a framed drawing of Napoleon (a variant of 1081).

REPRO *John Bull,* 22 Apr 1903

1113★ Mr Alfred Harmsworth [?c. 1903]

A more finished version of 1112, with the framed drawing titled Napoleon Bonaparte *and signed* Max.

REPRO **Plate 71**
OWNER Viscount Rothermere

1114★ Mr Alfred Harmsworth [n.d.]

An outline drawing, full-length profile facing left, cigarette in mouth, hands in pockets.

OWNER Viscount Rothermere

1115★ [Untitled n.d.]

Again the Napoleonic stance, but older and a little weary, before a background of skyscrapers and tall chimneys.

EXHIB L.G. 1957
OWNER Cecil King

1116★ Lord Northcliffe suggesting a head-line to Mr Edmund Gosse 1907

In 1907 Gosse was in charge of 'Books', a literary supplement to N's 'Daily Mail'.

EXHIB Carfax 1907; L.G. 1945 (Guedalla)
REPRO *A Book of Caricatures,* 1907
OWNER Mrs Philip Guedalla

1117 [Lord Northcliffe 1907]

EXHIB Baillie 1907

1118★ Evenings in Printing House Square 1911

Lord Northcliffe: 'Help! Again I feel the demons of Sensationalism rising in me. Hold me fast! Curb me, if you love me!'

N had become proprietor of 'The Times' in 1908.

EXHIB N.E.A.C. Winter 1911; L.G. 1913
REPRO *Fifty Caricatures,* 1913
OWNER *The Times*

1119★ 'The Times' [1914]

N as ringmaster training an elephant with 'Id' on its head. N reduced the price of 'The Times' to one penny in 1914.

REPRO *History of The Times,* vol IV (1), 1952
OWNER L. J. Cadbury

1120★ 'The Times' 1914

Almost identical with 1119, cancelled with Sketch Sp[oilt].

OWNER Lilly Library

1121★ Lord Northcliffe 1920

Full length, three-quarter face, hands in pockets, against a rural background.

EXHIB L. G.1928
OWNER Viscount Rothermere

1122★ A Memory of Alfred Harmsworth 1955

Outline drawing, full-length profile facing left, similar to 1114, but older and without cigarette.

REPRO *Stampa Estera,* date unknown

1123★ [Untitled Unsigned 1955]

Rough pencil sketch for 1122, very similar but with cigarette in mouth. Dated on back by Elisabeth Jungmann.

OWNER Sir Rupert Hart-Davis

CLAUDE NUGENT
Composer

1124★ Mr Claude Nugent [n.d.]

Full-length profile facing left, morning dress, walking with top hat held in front.

OWNER Private (Yale)

1125★ Mr Claude Nugent [n.d.]

Full-length profile facing left, standing, wearing fur-collared overcoat and holding top hat in front.

OWNER Robert Beloe

O

COLONEL OCHILTREE

1126* **Colonel Ochiltree** [n.d.]
OWNER Piccadilly Gallery

T. P. O'CONNOR
1848–1929 Irish journalist and M.P.

1127 **[Faithful Yet]**
[Mr T. P. O'Connor: 'Whisht, whisht, Oireland dear, 'tis with yourself my heart is always. As for these members of the Saxon nobility – brave though all the men are, and beautiful all the women, and ivry one of them wittier and more elegant than ivry other one, and more popular, bedad, and more given to good works – 'tis but the eye of pity and scorn I cast on them, mavourneen!']
EXHIB L.G. 1911

STUART OGILVIE
1858–1932 Playwright

1128* **Mr Stuart Ogilvie** [n.d.]
OWNER Mrs Eva Reichmann

SIR LAURENCE OLIPHANT
1846–1914 Soldier

1129 **[General Sir Laurence Oliphant** 1908]
EXHIB Carfax 1908

WILLIAM ORPEN
1878–1931 Painter
See also 1586-8

1130* **Mr William Orpen executing, in his own way, a commission for a portrait** 1909
REPRO **Plate 70**
OWNER Sir John Rothenstein

1131 **Mr William Orpen painting,** *more suo,* **a portrait of one of our merchant princes** [c. 1909]
A rough sketch for 1130.
OWNER L. J. Cadbury

1132* **Bravura. Mr Orpen trying whether it wouldn't be possible to paint, for the Uffizi, one mirror's reflection of another's reflection of a soap-bubble's reflection of himself** 1914
EXHIB L.G. May 1921
OWNER Tate Gallery

1133 **[Mr William Orpen]**
EXHIB L.G. 1952

1134* **British Artists at the Front. No 1. Sir William Orpen** 1918
A German Prisoner: 'Let us right-well-lengthily discuss how is it that this so cultured artist does not the never-sufficiently-to-be-praised Cubismus adopt'
REPRO *Reveille,* Aug 1918

P

IGNACE JAN PADEREWSKI
1860–1941 Polish pianist and President
See also 401

1135* **[Untitled** 1895]

Tiny figure, hands by sides, face obscured by two huge bunches of hair.
REPRO *Pick-Me-Up,* 30 Mar 1895; *Max's Nineties,* 1958
OWNER Victoria & Albert Museum

1136* **Paderewski** [1896]

Similar figure, but face showing beneath a single fuzz of hair.
REPRO *Twenty-Five Gentlemen*, 1896

1137★ **M. Paderewski** [n.d.]
All hair, with the back view of a tiny figure below.
OWNER Benjamin Sonnenberg

T. E. PAGE
1850–1936   Charterhouse master and Loeb editor
See 664, 664A

JOHN PALMER
1885–1944   Dramatic critic and writer

1138 **Restoration dramatists thanking Mr John Palmer for all his kindness** 1914
J. P.'s book 'The Comedy of Manners' appeared in 1913.
EXHIB L.G. May 1921 and 1957
OWNER Ronald Searle

CHRISTABEL PANKHURST
1880–1958   Suffragette

1139★ **'Not so much difference after all!' Miss Rosie Mackenzie and Miss Christabel Pankhurst** [1909]
R. M., from Thackeray's 'The Newcomes', clutches a rose to her bosom, C. P. a placard saying VOTES FOR WOMEN.
EXHIB N.E.A.C. Summer 1909; L.G. 1911
REPRO *Daily Mail*, 22 May 1909

1140★ **Not so much difference after all** [Unsigned n.d.]
Pencil sketch for 1139.
OWNER University of Texas

SIR GILBERT PARKER
1862–1932   Canadian novelist and playwright
See also 800

1141★ **'Climbing, climbing, climbing'** [1903]
On a ladder through the stars.
REPRO *John Bull*, 11 Jun 1903
OWNER Lilly Library

1142 **[Sir Gilbert Parker]**
EXHIB L.G. 1911

LOUIS N. PARKER
1852–1944   Playwright and composer

1143★ **Mr Louis N. Parker** [1901]
EXHIB Carfax 1901
OWNER The Rev R. F. Beloe

CHARLES STEWART PARNELL
1846–91   Irish politician
See 591

VIRGINIA PARSONS
b. 1917   Max's great-niece
See also 2035

1144★ **Virginia** 1935
OWNER Dottore Cesare Pio

LORD PASSFIELD
See Sidney Webb

WALTER PASSMORE
1867–1946   Actor and vocalist

1145★ **Mr Walter Passmore** [1895]
REPRO *Pick-Me-Up*, 5 Jan 1895

WALTER PATER
1839–94   Writer and Oxford don
See also 1276, 1829

1146 **[Oxford, 1891. Mr Walter Pater taking his walk through the meadows** 1926]
EXHIB L.G. 1928, where dated as above

COVENTRY PATMORE
1823–96   Poet
See 1279

KINSEY PEILE
1862–1934   Actor and playwright

1147★ **[Mr Kinsey Peile, adaptor of 'The Man Who Was', and Mr Rudyard Kipling, the author of the little tale** 1903]

PEILE (continued)

K. P., elegant in evening dress, patronisingly lays his hand on a bust of R. K.

REPRO *Sketch*, 10 Jun 1903 and Christmas No, 1958

1148 **Mr Kinsey Peile** [n.d.]

OWNER Sold at Sotheby's 14 Dec 1960

JOSEPH PENNELL
1860–1926 American etcher and biographer of Whistler
See also 1772

1149* **Mr Joseph Pennell thinking of the old 'un** 1913

Sitting as did the subjects of Whistler's portraits of his mother and of Carlyle.

EXHIB L.G. 1913 and 1957
REPRO *Fifty Caricatures*, 1913

MR PERIPETOS

1150* **The sun vainly trying to produce a highlight on the head of Mr Peripetos** [Unsigned n.d.]

OWNER Mrs Eva Reichmann

SAINT PETER
d. A.D. 65
See 584, 593

GEORGES PETILLEAU
d. 1913 French master at Charterhouse
See also 664, 665

1151* **M. George Petilleau. Dieppe** 1904

OWNER Mrs Eva Reichmann

SIR CLAUDE PHILLIPS
1846–1924 Art critic and Keeper of the Wallace Collection
See also 679, 1266, 1267

1152* **Sir Claude Phillips endeavouring, under the auspices of Mr Ernest Brown, not to think my caricatures are in the worst possible taste** [n.d.]

EXHIB L.G. 1913 and 1952
REPRO Oliver Brown, *Exhibition*, 1968
OWNER Mrs Oliver F. Brown

1153* **Sir Claude Phillips 'going on'. ? Scuola d'Amico di Cugino di Max** [1914]

The signature is a skit on Berenson's invention of 'Amico di Sandro [Botticelli]'. Cf. 767.

EXHIB L.G. May 1921, where dated as above
REPRO *A Survey*, 1921

1154* **[Untitled Unsigned n.d.]**

Three-quarter-length pencil sketch, profile facing left, in evening dress, holding lorgnette in right hand.

OWNER University of Texas

1155* **[Untitled Unsigned n.d.]**

As in 1154 but full face, head on one side, no lorgnette.

OWNER University of Texas

STEPHEN PHILLIPS
1868–1915 Poet and playwright
See also 27

1156* **Mr Stephen Phillips** [1900]

Full-length profile facing right.

REPRO *World*, Christmas Supplement, 1900

1157* **[Untitled Unsigned ?c. 1900]**

Very similar to 1156.

OWNER Princeton University Library

1158* **Mr Stephen Phillips** [1901]

Half-length profile facing left.

EXHIB Carfax 1901
REPRO *Pall Mall Magazine*, Feb 1902

MOSTYN T. PIGOTT
1865–1927 Author and journalist
See also 923

1159* **M.T.P.** [1900]

REPRO *World*, Christmas No, 1900

1160 **Mr Mostyn Pigott** [n.d.]

EXHIB L.G. 1911
OWNER J. F. McCrindle

ARTHUR WING PINERO
1855–1934 Playwright
See also 26, 27, 335, 514, 515, 612, 616, 679, 748, 769, 1307, 1423, 1443

1161* **[Untitled 1895]**

Full-length profile facing right, striped trousers, cigarette in mouth.
REPRO *Pick-Me-Up*, 9 Feb 1895; *The Poets' Corner*, 1943

1162★ **A. W. Pinero Esq** [1896]
Full length, full face, holding quill to mouth.
REPRO *Twenty-Five Gentlemen*, 1896

1163★ **[Untitled** 1898]
Full-length profile facing left, check trousers, hands in pockets.
REPRO *Daily Mail*, 21 Jan 1898

1164★ **Mr Arthur Wing Pinero** [1903]
Full length, all eyebrows and fur coat, repeated to infinity in a series of mirrors.
REPRO *Sketch*, 28 Oct 1903; S. N. Behrman, *Conversation with Max*, 1960
OWNER Garrick Club

1165★ **Mr Arthur Wing Pinero** [?c. 1903]
Same figure as in 1164, but no mirrors.
OWNER Sold at Parke-Bernet Galleries, N.Y., in 1966

1166 **[Mr A. W. Pinero** 1904]
EXHIB Carfax 1904

1167★ **Mr A. W. Pinero** [n.d.]
Head and shoulders profile, facing left.
OWNER Princeton University Library

1168★ **[Untitled** *Signed* **Bilbo** 1906]
['Though it is an arguable point whether I be, as I was once reputed, and as I still venture to deem myself, the most intellectual, I remain, beyond dispute, the dressiest, of contemporary British dramatists']
A. W. P., smartly dressed, passes Shaw in his utility Jaeger suit. For explanation of signature, see note to 1485.
REPRO *Vanity Fair*, 1 Feb 1906, where captioned as above
OWNER University of Texas

1169 **[Mr A. W. Pinero, wistfully: 'Perhaps I shall get an European reputation now'** 1907]
EXHIB Carfax 1907

1170 **[Sir A. W. Pinero]**
EXHIB L.G. 1911

1171★ **Sir Arthur Pinero** 1912
Full length, three-quarter face, wearing riding breeches and cloth cap.
EXHIB L.G. 1945 (Guedalla)
REPRO *Bystander*, 26 Jun 1912; *Theatre Notebook*, Spring 1967
OWNER Ashmolean Museum, Oxford

1172★ **Diffidence** November 1922
Sir Arthur Pinero: 'Oh, by the way, Mr Conrad, I was going to ask you: if I apply at Trinity House for a Master Mariner's certificate, d'you think they – er ——'
Conrad's dramatisation of his own 'Secret Agent' was produced in London on 2 Nov 1922.
EXHIB L.G. 1923
REPRO *Things New and Old*, 1923
OWNER Mrs John D. Gordan

1173 **[Le Sourciliste** 1926]
His eyebrows (sourcils), bushier than ever, are tied with a blue bow behind his head.
EXHIB L.G. 1928, where dated as above

1174 **[Mr Arthur Wing Pinero]**
EXHIB L.G. 1952

1175★ **A. W. Pinero** [n.d.]
Black and white, full-length profile, black face and top hat, overcoat, holding stick.
EXHIB Cincinnati 1965
OWNER Lilly Library

1176★ **[Untitled Unsigned** n.d.]
Pencil sketch, full-length profile facing left, in overcoat, bowler hat in hand, enormous eyebrow jutting forward over huge nose.
OWNER Berg Collection (N.Y.P.L.)

1177 **[A. W. Pinero]**
OWNER Mrs Previté

CAMILLE PISSARRO
1830–1903   French painter

1178 **[M. Camille Pissarro** 1901]
EXHIB L.G. 1928, where dated as above

PRINCE LOUIS PONIATOWSKY
1864–1954

1179★ **Prince Poniatowsky** [1907]
Full-length profile, check suit, cap, smoking cigar.
EXHIB Carfax 1907
OWNER Patrick Baldwin

1180★ **Prince Poniatowsky** [n.d.]
Three-quarter length profile, check suit, cigar, bare-headed.
OWNER Mrs Rut Chaim

ARTHUR PONSONBY
1871–1946   Writer and Socialist politician

1181* The Old and the Young Self 1924

Old Self: 'Pause, child! Reflect! What would Tchitcherin say? What would Zanovieff's view be? Consider the feelings of Rykoff and Stalin and Lansbury and Manuilsky!'

The Young Self is bearing an ermine train as royal page. A. P. had been page to Queen Victoria, but was now a leading Socialist.

EXHIB L.G. 1925
REPRO *Observations*, 1925

ALEXANDER POPE
1688–1744   Poet
See 852

THE SIXTH DUKE OF PORTLAND
1857–1943   Master of the Horse

1182 [The Duke of Portland 1901]

EXHIB Carfax 1901

THE SIXTH EARL OF PORTSMOUTH
1856–1917   Liberal politician

1183* Lord Portsmouth suggesting (more or less unconsciously) a design for the Shakespeare memorial 1908

Full face, stout, tight-waisted, hands on hips, head turned to right.

EXHIB   Carfax 1908
REPRO   *Art News*, Summer 1964
OWNER Alan Evans

1184 [Lord Portsmouth]

EXHIB L.G. 1911

1185* [Untitled n.d.]

Same position as 1183, but head turned to left.

OWNER Frank Launder

1186* [Untitled Unsigned n.d.]

Probably a sketch for 1183.

REPRO   G. F. Sims catalogue no 55, Jan 1963
OWNER Miss Julia K. Williams

BERNARD POSNO

1187* Mr Bernard Posno [n.d.]

Framed alongside drawing of Helen Forsyth (554), presumably by Philip Guedalla, to whom Max wrote from 12 Well Walk, Hampstead, on 22 Mar 1919:

Dear Mr Guedalla, I never thought the name of Bernard Posno would be a name to conjure with. But, as I had quite forgotten it, you, by your sudden use of it, have wafted me back across a wide gulf of years; and I see clearly Bernard Posno seated at that particular table which was reserved for him every night at supper time by the manager of the Savoy Restaurant – a table for two, a table for him and Miss Helen Forsyth, a pretty though too plump actress whose protector he was. I wish I could tell you all about him, but I know so little. I wasn't personally acquainted with him – only with this and that acquaintance of his, who seemed to have nothing to say about him except that Miss Forsyth really adored him. This adoration seemed to me, having regard to his age and appearance, odd. I doubt whether it existed. I saw in her no sign of a broken heart, or even of a bruised one, when presently (in '96, I think) I went to stay in the country with Frank Lawson and found her living under *his* protection. A year or two later, Bernard Posno, it would seem, decided that the time had come for him to marry and settle down. He induced (by what means I know not: I should think she and her family must have been starving) a respectable young woman to marry him. He settled down further than he had intended: into the grave. Miss Forsyth, too, has been dead this many a year. Perhaps she and he are once more united.
 I cudgel my brains to remember more about him. Nothing recurs except that he was a member of the Orleans Club. And this fact you could, I am sure, deduce from the drawing. At least, I hope so. I remember the drawing only dimly. If it doesn't proclaim 'Orleans Club' it is a failure, and you had better throw it away! Yours sincerely, Max Beerbohm.

The Orleans Club was primarily famous for its food and drink.

EXHIB   L.G. 1945 (Guedalla)
REPRO   **Plate 79**
OWNER Mrs Philip Guedalla

EZRA POUND
b. 1885   American poet

1188* [Untitled] 1914

'Dante and I are come to learn of thee,
Ser Guido of Florence, master of us all,
Love, who hath set his hand upon us three,
Bidding us twain upon thy glory call' . . .
          'To Guido Cavalcanti' by Ezra Pound
                          [*Canzoni*, 1911]

E. P. drags a scowling Dante towards a magisterial, laurel-crowned Cavalcanti.

EXHIB L.G. May 1921, 1945 (Guedalla) and 1952
OWNER Mrs Derek Schreiber

1189 Il Pound. Rapallo 1932

Walking on the shore.

EXHIB L.G. 1952; American Academy 1952
OWNER Donald Wing

1190★ Mr Ezra Pound. Rapallo 1934

REPRO **Plate 49**
OWNER C. Waller Barrett

COURTICE POUNDS
1862–1927   Actor and vocalist

1191★ Mr Courtice Pounds [1895]

REPRO *Pick-Me-Up*, 5 Jan 1895

F. YORK POWELL
1850–1904   Professor of Modern History at Oxford

1192★ [Untitled 1895]

Seated at table, wearing tiny mortar-board.

REPRO Cover of Sette of Odd Volumes menu, 5 Jul 1895

1193★ Professor Yorke Powell [n.d.]

Full length, full face, walking on pavement with umbrella.

OWNER Merton College, Oxford

FRANK PREVITÉ
1870–1929   Oxford friend of Max

1194★ Design for a fresco to be placed upon the walls of the VII Quad in memory of S. Pita of Aces [Unsigned n.d.]

An undergraduate drawing, showing F.P., whose nickname was Pita, full length in profile facing left. His hat is decorated with the four aces, and he carries another ace up his sleeve. An I.O.U. protrudes from his pocket, and

with both hands he holds a long cigarette-holder in his mouth.

OWNER Miss Mary Parker

CAMILLE PRÉVOST
Inhabitant of Dieppe.   Fencing master to Maupassant

1195★ Souvenir de Dieppe [n.d.]

Three-quarter length in fencing kit.

OWNER Sold at Sotheby's 19 Jul 1967

T. H. PRITCHARD
Schoolmaster and painter

1196★ Mr T. H. Pritchard [n.d.]

Holding paintbrush and palette.

OWNER Mrs D. E. Barker

JAMES PRYDE
1866–1941   Painter
See also 679

1197★ Mr James Pryde 1911

He stands posed on stage. Behind him voluminous curtains are open enough to show a vast piazza and cathedral-entrance.

EXHIB N.E.A.C. Winter 1911
OWNER Sir John Rothenstein

1198★ The Old and the Young Selves 1924

[William Nicholson:] 'Who were that?'
[James Pryde:] 'Who was those?'

The Old Selves contemplate the Siamese-twin figure of the Young Selves, each holding a stick labelled BEGGAR-STAFF. The two had won fame as poster-artists called The Beggarstaff Brothers.

EXHIB L.G. 1925
REPRO *Observations*, 1925

1199 James Pryde Esq [n.d.]

Full length, face to right, eyeglass in right eye.

EXHIB L.G. 1957
OWNER William B. Harris

Q

THE EIGHTH MARQUESS OF QUEENSBERRY
1844–1900 Patron of boxing

1200★ **Lord Queensberry** [1894]
Full-length profile, evening dress, smoking cigar.
REPRO *Pick-Me-Up*, 17 Nov 1894
OWNER Arents Collection (N.Y.P.L.)

1201 **Lord Queensberry** [c. 1895]
EXHIB L.G. 1928, where dated as above

1202★ **[Untitled** 1896]
Full length, full face, riding crop under arms behind back.

REPRO *Twenty-Five Gentlemen*, 1896

1203 **[Lord Queensberry]**
EXHIB L.G. 1945 (Guedalla)

1204 **The Most Noble the Marquis of Queensberry**
[n.d.]
OWNER D. W. L. Earl

'QUIZ' (POWYS EVANS)
Caricaturist
See 384, 1449

R

PRINCE CONSTANTIN RADZIWILL
1850–1920 Polish-French original of Proust's
Prince de Guermantes

1205 **Prince Constantine Radziwill** 1910
OWNER Denys Parsons

ANDRÉ RAFFALOVICH
1864–1934 Writer

1206★ **[Untitled** n.d.]
Holding opera-glasses and looking up to the stars.
OWNER Michael Maclagan

PROFESSOR WALTER RALEIGH
1861–1922 English don and critic
See 748, 807A, 1820, 1821

PRINCE RANJITSINHJI
1872–1933 Cricketer

1207 **Ranji** [n.d.]
OWNER Sold at Parke-Bernet Galleries, N.Y., 2 Nov 1966

LEONARD RAVEN-HILL
1867–1942 *Punch* cartoonist

1208★ **[Untitled** 1894]
REPRO *Pick-Me-Up*, 3 Nov 1894; *Idler*, May 1899

THE FIRST MARQUESS OF READING
See Rufus Isaacs

JOHN REDMOND
1856–1918 Irish politician
See also 1083

1209 **[Mr John Redmond** 1901]
EXHIB Carfax 1901

1210* Mr John Redmond 1912

'Nec facundia deseret hunc nec lucidus ordo' [His flow of lucid, ordered speech will never fail him. Horace, *Ars Poetica*, 41]

REPRO *Bystander*, 31 Jul 1912
OWNER Sold at Sotheby's 14 Dec 1960

1211 [Mr John Redmond]

EXHIB L.G. 1928

HARRY REECE

1212* Harry Reece [n.d.]

EXHIB Cincinnati 1965
OWNER Lilly Library

ADA REEVE
1874–1966   Actress

1213* [Untitled 1894]

REPRO *Pick-Me-Up*, 24 Nov 1894; *Max's Nineties*, 1958
OWNER D'Offay Couper Gallery

WILLIAM PEMBER REEVES
1857–1932   New Zealand politician and writer

1214* Mr W. P. Reeves [n.d.]

REPRO Keith Sinclair, *William Pember Reeves*, 1965
OWNER Keith Mackenzie

SIR JOHN REITH
1889–1971   First Director-General of the B.B.C.

1215* [Untitled] 1938

Here, dear Sibyl [Colefax], is what I meant about Sir John Reith's appearance – his essentially poetic (and queerly *Preraphaelite*) appearance. This I have caught, I think. But I seem to have missed the steely, practical look that is there too.

REPRO Asa Briggs, *The Golden Age of Wireless*, 1965
OWNER British Broadcasting Corporation

CHARLES A'COURT REPINGTON
1858–1925   Military correspondent and diarist

1216 Colonel Repington 1918

Full-length profile facing left, in khaki, smoking cigar.

EXHIB L.G. 1957
OWNER Sir Edward Maufe R.A.

1217* 'A Chiel' (1914–1918) 1920

Eminent Lady: 'I wonder what dear sweet Colonel Repington always carries that funny little note-book with him for.'
Cf. Burns's 'A chiel's amang ye takin' notes'

EXHIB L.G. May 1921
REPRO *A Survey*, 1921
OWNER City Art Gallery, Manchester

CECIL RHODES
1853–1902   Empire-builder
See 164

THE FOURTH LORD RIBBLESDALE
1854–1925   Soldier and courtier
See also 679, 823, 824, 1443

1218* Lord Ribblesdale 1907

EXHIB Carfax 1907
REPRO *A Book of Caricatures*, 1907

1219* Lord Ribblesdale [Unsigned n.d.]

For Kils[een Conover, to whom Max was engaged]
Almost identical with 1218

OWNER Harvard College Library

1220 [Lord Ribblesdale]

EXHIB L.G. 1911

1221 The Last of the Whigs — the late Lord Ribblesdale 1926

OWNER Brinsley Ford

FRANK RICHARDSON
1870–1917   Barrister and writer
See also 1698

1222* Mr Frank Richardson 1908

REPRO Frank Richardson, *More Bunkum*, 1909
OWNER Keith Mackenzie

JEAN RICHEPIN
1849–1926   French poet and dramatist

1223* M. Richepin [1898]

Full length, full face, evening dress, stick in left hand.

REPRO *Sketch*, 20 Jul 1898
OWNER Victoria & Albert Museum

RICHEPIN (continued)

1224* **Monsieur Richepin** [c. 1903]
Back view of 1223.
REPRO *Cassell's Magazine*, Feb 1903
OWNER Dr A. Herxheimer

1225 **M. Jean Richepin** [Unsigned n.d.]
Pencil sketch, front view.
EXHIB L.G. 1952
OWNER Dr A. Herxheimer

THE EIGHTH DUKE OF RICHMOND
1870–1935   Soldier and landowner

1226* **The Duke of Richmond** [1930]
REPRO *Ladbroke's Racing Calendar*, 1931

CHARLES RICKETTS
1866–1931   Artist and writer
See also 382, 383, 679, 1309

1227* **Mr Ricketts and Mr Shannon, in the enjoyment of popular success** 1907
John Bull appraising a picture in their studio.
EXHIB Carfax 1907; L.G. 1952
OWNER Fitzwilliam Museum, Cambridge

1228* **'Found' (with all acknowledgments to Rossetti)** 1911
'Yet I had planted thee a noble vine, wholly a right seed: how then art thou turned into the degenerate plant of a strange vine unto me?' Jeremiah, II, 21.
The scene is exactly as in Rossetti's picture, with a calf under a net in a cart, but instead of the drover rescuing his old love in the street, Ricketts is trying to rescue Shannon from Burlington House. Shannon was elected A.R.A. in 1911. Rossetti used another quotation from the same chapter of Jeremiah.
EXHIB L.G. 1911
REPRO **Plate 62**
OWNER Johannesburg Art Gallery

THE SECOND MARQUESS OF RIPON
See Lord de Grey

M. RIVARDE
Inhabitant of Dieppe

1229* **M. Rivarde** [n.d.]
OWNER Piccadilly Gallery

1230* **[Untitled** n.d.]
Almost identical with 1229.
OWNER Sold at Sotheby's 19 Jul 1967, where wrongly described as Reginald Turner

ARTHUR ROBERTS
1852–1933   Comedian

1231* **[Untitled** 1894]
On the boards, in evening dress, top hat, big buttonhole.
REPRO *Pall Mall Budget*, 4 Oct 1894

1232* **Mr Arthur Roberts** [c. 1895]
Morning dress, top hat, high collar, right arm raised.
EXHIB L.G. 1928, where dated as above
OWNER J. C. Thomson

1233* **Mr Arthur Roberts** [1896]
Check suit, straw hat, stick.
REPRO *Savoy*, Jul 1896; *Max's Nineties*, 1958

1234 **[Mr Arthur Roberts]**
EXHIB L.G. 1952

R. ELLIS ROBERTS
1879–1953   Journalist and author
See also 2051

1235* **Ellis Roberts** [n.d.]
OWNER University of Texas

GEORGE ROBEY
1869–1954   Comedian
See 47

G. H. ROBINSON
Music master at Charterhouse
See also 664, 665

1236* **[Untitled Unsigned** n.d.]
A drawing done at Charterhouse, showing G. H. R. playing the piano and saying: 'I assure you it's a gem'.
REPRO *Times*, 12 Mar 1968
OWNER University of Texas

HENRI ROCHEFORT
1832–1913   French journalist and politician

1237★ [Untitled Unsigned 1894]

REPRO *Pall Mall Budget*, 4 Oct 1894

AUGUSTE RODIN
1840–1917   French sculptor

1238★ [Untitled] 1907
For Albert [Rutherston]

Shows R, very tiny, his enormous hands touching the ground, being received by a fashionable lady and gentleman. In 1930 Max wrote to the editor of 'Farrago': 'Don't leave your public in the dark. Well-informed undergraduates know perfectly well that Pheidias existed and that Epstein exists. But of Rodin they have probably never heard – and certainly won't know that the old gentleman (who wasn't a gentleman) did in the first decade of the present century (i.e. in the Dark Ages) appear for a brief space in fashionable society (a thing now extinct) and was received with rapture (a now discarded emotion). Therefore . . . I implore you to write a rather elaborate editorial "gloss." Else will your publication founder in the darkness shed by that old drawing.'

EXHIB   Baillie 1907; L.G. 1952 and 1957
REPRO   *Farrago*, Oxford, Feb 1930
OWNER   David Rutherston

1239★ Rodin [1912]
Head and shoulders, facing right.

REPRO *Bystander*, 19 Jun 1912

1240★ Rodin [1912]
Full-length profile facing left, holding knife. Bust on pedestal in background. For dating, see note to 400.

EXHIB   L.G. 1913
REPRO   *Fifty Caricatures*, 1913

1241★ Simple Lessons in the art of drawing M. Rodin – offered to Miss Ailsa [Tweed] by Max Beerbohm 1914

REPRO   Plate 67
OWNER   Merton College, Oxford

1241A★ Rodin dans le beau monde. [Unsigned 1939]
Almost identical with the final drawing in 1241. Annotated in another hand: 'Abinger Dec 15, '39, after looking at V's drawing' (i.e. 1241, which then belonged to Violet Schiff).

OWNER   Merton College, Oxford

1242★ [Untitled Unsigned n.d.]
Rough sketches for 1241, four drawings only.

OWNER   Mrs Eva Reichmann

THEODORE ROOSEVELT
1858–1919   President of the United States

1243★ Mr Rooseveldt's visit to Europe–a Souvenir 1910

[T. R. to robed and spectacled Europa:] '2 plus 2 makes 4 ! ! !'

EXHIB   L.G. 1911
OWNER   W. P. G. Collet

1244★ Theodore Roosevelt, Past President of the United States and Permanent Prince of Bores [1912]

EXHIB   L.G. 1945 (Guedalla)
REPRO   *Bystander*, 14 Aug 1912
OWNER   Ashmolean Museum, Oxford

EDWARD ROSE
1849–1904   Playwright

1245★ Mr Edward Rose [n.d.]

OWNER   Mrs Eva Reichmann

THE FIFTH EARL OF ROSEBERY
1847–1929   Prime Minister
See also 439, 493, 494, 514, 515, 637, 1307, 1443, 1746

1246★ Lord Rosebery [1896]
Full length, full face, evening dress, wearing sash and star

REPRO *Twenty-Five Gentlemen*, 1896

1247 [Lord Rosebery c. 1897]

EXHIB L.G. 1928, where dated as above

1248★ Lord Rosebery ploughing his own furrow – in his own sofa [1901]

EXHIB   Carfax 1901
REPRO   *Candid Friend*, 14 Dec 1901

1249★ The 'Vossische Zeitung' regards Lord Rosebery as the Coming Man in British politics – December 15, 1901

Lord R.: 'The colour of the hair is right enough now, François. But Parker, you really must have another pull at the waist-belt.'

EXHIB   L.G. 1945 (Guedalla) and 1957
OWNER   Ashmolean Museum, Oxford

1250* **The Durdans** [1903]

Full length, quarter face, toy horses in foreground. The Durdans was Lord R's house at Epsom.

REPRO *John Bull*, 27 May 1903
OWNER Victoria & Albert Museum

1251 [**Lord Rosebery** 1904]

EXHIB Carfax 1904

1252* **Lord Rosebery** [1905]

Walking down red carpet, wearing order of the Garter. For dating see note to 65.

EXHIB L.G. 1945 (Guedalla) and 1957
REPRO *Pearson's Magazine*, Feb 1906; **Plate 8**
OWNER Ashmolean Museum, Oxford

1253 **Lord** ~~Rosebery~~ **Roseberry** 1908

Talking, with arms folded, on terrace.

EXHIB Carfax 1908
OWNER Maxwell Halliday

1254 [**Lord Rosebery**]

EXHIB L.G. 1911

1255* **Lord Rosebery, beset by the Spectre of the End of All Things** 1911

EXHIB L.G. 1911
REPRO *Tatler*, 26 Apr 1911
OWNER Lord Hylton

1256 [**Lord Rosebery**]

EXHIB L.G. 1911

1257* **Lord Rosebery** 1912

Full length, three-quarter face, arms folded, morning dress, bare-headed.

EXHIB L.G. 1928 and 1952
OWNER Lilly Library

1258* **Lord Rosebery** [n.d.]

Full length, arms folded, wearing straw hat.

REPRO *Fifty Caricatures*, 1913

1259 [**Lord Rosebery in 1885** 1926]

EXHIB L.G. 1928, where dated as above

1260* **Lord Rosebery** [n.d.]

Full length, full face, on pavement, holding umbrella, wearing huge collar and tiny top hat.

OWNER Sir John Rothenstein

1261* **Rosebery – that's for Remembrance** [n.d.]

Head only. Cf. 'There's rosemary, that's for remembrance' ('Hamlet', IV. 5).

EXHIB L.G. 1952
REPRO *Britain To-day*, Jul 1952

1262* [**Untitled Unsigned** n.d.]

Full-length profile facing left, arms folded.

OWNER University of Texas

ROBERT ROSS
1869–1918   Art-critic and author
See also 1598, 1671A, 1726

1263* **English Journalism** [Signed with monogram n.d.]

Full-length back view, top hat, long hair, cloak. A very early drawing.

REPRO *Robert Ross, Friend of Friends*, 1952
OWNER James Robertson

1264* [**Untitled Unsigned** n.d.]

Rough sketch for 1263.

OWNER Giles Robertson

1265* **Mr Robert Ross counting his various titles to fame** 1909

EXHIB N.E.A.C. Winter 1909; L.G. 1957
OWNER King's College, Cambridge

1266* *Resolved*, **more or less unanimously, after a disputation lasting for five hours and a half, that the panel – by whomsoever, or by whosesoever friend, or brother, or pupil, or pupils, it may have been painted; and by whatsoever person, or persons, at what date soever, it may have been restored – is 'amusing'** 1909

R with fellow art-critics, Laurence Binyon, Roger Fry, Herbert Horne and Claude Phillips.

OWNER Art Institute of Chicago

1267* [**Title exactly as for** *1266* **Unsigned** c. 1909]

Rough sketch for 1266, with the names of the characters added in another hand.

EXHIB Cincinnati 1965
OWNER Lilly Library

CHRISTINA ROSSETTI
1830–94   Poet
See 1278

DANTE GABRIEL ROSSETTI
1828–82   Poet and painter
See also 502, 595, 837, 839, 919, 1358, 1784, 1829

1268* [**Dante Gabriel Rossetti, in his back garden**
c. 1904]

Also present, besides a tortoise, a kangaroo, a pelican, a snake, and a red-haired model, are Swinburne, Watts-Dunton, Meredith, Hall Caine, Whistler, Burne-Jones, William Morris, Holman Hunt, and Ruskin.

EXHIB Carfax 1904
REPRO *The Poets' Corner*, 1904 and 1943, where captioned as above

1269* **D. G. Rossetti, precociously manifesting, among the exiled patriots who frequented his father's house in Charlotte Street, that queer indifference to politics which marked him in his prime and his decline** [c. 1916]

As a little boy D. G. R. lies happily drawing under the table while the exiles argue and vociferate all over the room.

EXHIB L.G. Sept 1921
REPRO *Rossetti and his Circle*, 1922
OWNER Tate Gallery

1270* **Rossetti's Courtship – Chatham Place, 1850–1860** 1916

EXHIB Grosvenor 1917; L. G. Sept 1921
REPRO *Rossetti and his Circle*, 1922
OWNER Tate Gallery

1271 [**Untitled Unsigned** c. 1916]

Pencil sketch for 1270.

OWNER William W. Appleton

1272* [**An Introduction**] 1916

Miss Cornforth: 'Oh, very pleased to meet Mr Ruskin, I'm sure.'

EXHIB Grosvenor 1917; L.G. Sept 1921
REPRO *Rossetti and his Circle*, 1922, where captioned as above
OWNER Tate Gallery

1273* **Mr Browning brings a lady of rank and fashion to see Mr Rossetti** 1916

EXHIB Grosvenor, 1917; L.G. Sept 1921
REPRO *Rossetti and his Circle*, 1922
OWNER Tate Gallery

1274* **Rossetti insistently exhorted by George Meredith to come forth into the glorious sun and wind for a walk to Hendon and beyond, Autumn 1862** 1916

EXHIB Grosvenor 1917; L.G. Sept 1921
REPRO *Rossetti and his Circle*, 1922
OWNER Tate Gallery

1275* **The small hours in the 'sixties at 16 Cheyne Walk – Algernon [Swinburne] reading 'Anactoria' to Gabriel and William [Rossetti]** 1916

EXHIB Grosvenor 1917; L.G. Sept 1921
REPRO *Rossetti and his Circle*, 1922; *The Poets' Corner*, 1943
OWNER Tate Gallery

1276* **Mr William Bell Scott wondering what it is those fellows see in Gabriel** 1916

Around D. G. R. in his garden are grouped Ford Madox Brown, Burne-Jones, Swinburne, Walter Pater, William Morris and an unidentified young man, also two animals from the menagerie.

EXHIB Grosvenor 1917; L.G. Sept 1921
REPRO *Rossetti and his Circle*, 1922
OWNER Tate Gallery

1277* **Quis Custodiet Ipsum Custodem?** [**Who will guard the guard himself? Juvenal, VI, 347-8**] 1916

Theodore Watts: 'Mr Caine, a word with you! Shields and I have been talking matters over, and we are agreed that this evening and henceforth you *must* not and *shall* not read any more of your literary efforts to our friend. They are too – what shall I say? – too luridly arresting and are the allies of insomnia.'

EXHIB Grosvenor 1917; L.G. Sept 1921
REPRO *Rossetti and his Circle*, 1922
OWNER Tate Gallery

1278* **Rossetti, having just had a fresh consignment of 'stunning' fabrics from that new shop in Regent Street, tries hard to prevail on his younger sister to accept at any rate one of these and have a dress made of it from designs to be furnished by himself** 1917

D. G. R. 'What *is* the use, Christina, of having a heart like a singing bird and a water-shoot and all the rest of it, if you insist on getting yourself up like a pew-opener?'
C. R. 'Well, Gabriel, I don't know. I'm sure you yourself always dress very simply.'

EXHIB L.G. Sept 1921
REPRO *Rossetti and his Circle*, 1922
OWNER Tate Gallery

1279* **Spring Cottage, Hampstead, 1860** 1917

Coventry Patmore comes round from Elm Cottage yonder, and very vehemently preaches to the Rossettis that a tea-pot is not worshipful for its form and colour, but rather as one of the sublime symbols of Domesticity.

EXHIB L.G. Sept 1921
REPRO *Rossetti and his Circle*, 1922
OWNER Tate Gallery

1280* **Mr Morley of Blackburn, on an afternoon in the spring of '69, introduces Mr John Stuart Mill** 1917

'It has recently,' he says, 'occurred to Mr Mill that in his life-long endeavour to catch and keep the ear of the nation he has been hampered by a certain deficiency in – well, in warmth, in colour, in rich charm. I have told him that this deficiency (I do not regard it as a defect) might possibly be remedied by *you*. Mr Mill has in the press at this moment a new work, entitled 'The Subjection of Women.' From my slight acquaintance with you, and from all that I have seen and heard of your work, I gather that women greatly interest you, and I have no doubt that you are incensed by their subjection. Mr Mill has brought his proof-sheets with him. He will read them to you. I believe, and he takes my word for it, that a series of illustrative paintings by you would' etc., etc.

EXHIB L.G. Sept 1921
REPRO *Rossetti and his Circle*, 1922
OWNER Tate Gallery

1280A [**Title as in 1280. Unsigned** n.d.]
Sketch for 1280, marked SPOILT *by Max. Only first sentence of speech included.*
EXHIB Achenbach 1964
OWNER Dr and Mrs James D. Hart

1281★ [**Untitled Unsigned** n.d.]
A round-topped fresco, depicting D. G. R., Swinburne and a Pre-Raphaelite lady. For Max's three other frescoes, see 514, 515, 614, 615, 1282, 1283, 1837 and 1838.
REPRO **Plate 55**
OWNER Merton College, Oxford

1282★ [**Untitled Unsigned** n.d.]
Finished sketch for 1281. Against the lady Max wrote: Brow wider ?nose shorter.
OWNER Mrs Virginia Surtees

1283★ **Sketch for Fresco!** [n.d.]
A rougher sketch for 1281.
EXHIB Achenbach 1964
OWNER U.C.L.A. (Clark)

1284★ [**S. H. vainly endeavouring to enlist D. G. R's interest in some singularly interesting experiment. Unsigned** n.d.]
This title, taken from an L.G. list of Max drawings, exactly fits this drawing, which shows an earnest youth pestering D. G. R. as they walk on the Embankment. S. H. is clearly the Sylvester Hethway of 'Hethway Speaking'. See 'Mainly on the Air', 1957.
EXHIB L.G. 1957, where wrongly titled 'Rossetti and the young Swinburne'
REPRO **Plate 56**
OWNER A. N. L. Munby

GABRIELE ROSSETTI
1783–1854 Italian poet and writer
See 1269

WILLIAM MICHAEL ROSSETTI
1829–1919 Civil servant and writer
See 1275

THE FIFTH EARL OF ROSSLYN
1869–1939 Soldier, actor and writer
See also 1382

1285★ **Lord Rosslyn in 'Trelawny of the Wells'** [1898]
As James Erskine Lord R played a small part in the original production of Pinero's play in Jan 1898.
REPRO *Sketch*, 8 Jun 1898

1286 [**Lord Rosslyn** c. 1899]
EXHIB L.G. 1928, where dated as above

1287 [**Lord Rosslyn** 1901]
EXHIB Carfax 1901

1288 [**Lord Rosslyn**]
EXHIB L.G. 1928

1289 **The Fifth Lord Rosslyn** [n.d.]
EXHIB L.G. 1957
OWNER The Earl of Rosslyn

EDMOND ROSTAND
1868–1918 French poet and playwright
See also 399, 1563

1290 [**One Thing Accomplished** 1910]
[M. Rostand: '*Au moins, maintenant*, grâce à moi, on ne dira plus que l'acteur est vaniteux']
EXHIB N.E.A.C. Summer 1910

1291★ [**Untitled**] 1910
Five drawings of the same subject, one fully coloured and signed, two partially coloured, and two sketches. They show E. R. reclining, elegantly dressed, on a Directoire couch, while to one side stand his three most famous characters as first presented: Coquelin as Cyrano, Sarah Bernhardt as L'Aiglon, and Lucien Guitry as Chantecler.
REPRO **Plate 31**
OWNER D. Coombs

1292 [**Edmond Rostand** c. 1911]
EXHIB L.G. 1928, where dated as above

1293 [? **Untitled** c. 1912]
[M. Rostand (rehearsing 'Cyrano de Bergerac'):

Mais avec tout, mon cher, et surtout, il faudra être
fièrement et sincèrement romantique.'
M. Coquelin (rather tartly): 'Parfaitement.']
EXHIB New York 1912; L.G. 1945 (Guedalla)

1294★ Rostand [?**Unsigned** n.d.]
Half-length profile facing left.
REPRO *Fifty Caricatures*, 1913

1295★ [**Untitled Unsigned** n.d.]
*Three-quarter length, full face, a very willowy figure,
right hand raised, left in trouser pocket. A pencil sketch.*
OWNER Ellis M. Pryce-Jones

ALBERT ROTHENSTEIN
See Albert Rutherston

ALICE ROTHENSTEIN
1867–1957 Wife of Will Rothenstein
See 1328, 1834

JOHN ROTHENSTEIN
b. 1901 Art historian and Director of the Tate Gallery
See also 973, 1838

**1296★ On the Threshold of Life. Mr John Rothen-
stein** 1923
EXHIB L.G. 1952 and 1957
REPRO John Rothenstein, *Summer's Lease*, 1965
OWNER Sir John Rothenstein

1297 Mr John Rothenstein 1924
OWNER Miss Joan Wilson

WILLIAM ROTHENSTEIN
1872–1945 Artist
*See also 378, 514, 515, 679, 706, 995, 1349, 1423, 1443, 1586-8,
1650, 1834, 1842, 1844, 1879*

1298★ Will Rothenstein The Creative Artist *au lit*
[**Signed**] **H. M. B.** [n.d.]
*The signature places this very early, probably in 1893,
when Max first met W. R.*
OWNER Lilly Library

1299★ Will R in Faubourg and in Quartier [**Unsigned** c. 1893]
*Two drawings on one sheet, showing W. R. elegantly
and artistically dressed.*
OWNER Sir John Rothenstein

**1300 Will Rothenstein taking the Apple of
Discord for the world** [**Unsigned** c. 1893]
*A tiny figure holding huge apple on his shoulders, in front
of seven stars. Max in profile, very young, in foreground.*
OWNER Lady Dynevor

**1301★ Where there's a Will (Rothenstein) there's a
Way** [**Unsigned** c. 1893]
In mortar-board and gown, holding pipe.
OWNER Lilly Library

1302 Where there's a Will there's a way [**Unsigned**
c. 1893]
Back view.
OWNER Lady Dynevor

1303 [**Professor Rothenstein** c. 1893]
EXHIB L.G. 1928, where dated as above

1304★ Will Rothenstein 1894
*Standing on pavement in frock coat and top hat with a
tasselled walking stick much taller than himself.*
REPRO David Cecil, *Max*, 1964
OWNER Merton College, Oxford

1305 [**Untitled** n.d.]
Very similar to 1304.
OWNER Mrs Rachel Ward

1306★ [**Untitled Unsigned** n.d.]
Similar to 1304 and 1305 but hatless, and a shorter stick.
OWNER Lilly Library

1307★ [**Will Rothenstein laying down the law**
c. 1895]
*Ten interlocking drawings showing W. R. laying down
the law:*
    To Oscar [Wilde] on Deportment
    To Arthur Pinero on Playwriting
    To Lord Coleridge on Law
    To the Prince [of Wales] on Dress
    To Aubrey [Beardsley] on Decadence
    To Mr [Charles] Furse on Folly
    To Lord Rosebery on La Haute Politique
    To George Moore on Caution
    To Mr [Eugene] Stratton on Art
    To Himself on Modesty
EXHIB L.G. 1952, where titled and dated as above
OWNER Mrs Christopher Powell

1308★ Will Rothenstein [1899]
*Back view, hatless, head turned to left, hands clasped
behind back.*
REPRO *Page*, 20 Sep 1899
OWNER Art Gallery of New South Wales, Sydney

1309* 'Mr Rothenstein heads for Italy' 1905

Pasted on is a cutting from the 'Daily News' of 5 Oct 1905, part of which reads: 'His labours in this connection over, Mr Rothenstein heads for Italy, in quest of recreation and refreshment, not least from sight of great things by Giotto and Fra Angelico, by Piero della Francesca and Masaccio. By the way, the honest but unenlightened comments of some members of the public on so-called unfinished pictures are often amusing. A case in point is the correspondence which has appeared as to the portrait of Mr Rothenstein presented this summer to the public gallery at Liverpool.'

In the drawing W. R. is hurtling towards an outline-map of Italy divided into four sections named after the four painters. Around him is written:
'An Honest but Unenlightened Comment'
To your tents, oh Israel!
The New Aestheticism
Whaur's Charlie Ricketts the noo?

OWNER Patrick Baldwin

1310 **Sudden and Belated Recognition of Mr Will Rothenstein as the Messiah** February 1906

OWNER Sir Anthony Hooper Bart

1311* **Mr William Rothenstein warns Mr Tagore against being spoilt by occidental success** 1912

EXHIB L.G. 1913
REPRO *Imperfect Encounter,* ed. Mary M. Lago, 1972
OWNER Richard Spiegelberg

1312* **Frontispiece for W. R.'s Pamphlet – an attempt to realise the Author's Beautiful Dream of the Interfering Patron** [?Unsigned c. 1916]

Patron: 'Your work yesterday wasn't hup to sample. Your Hattitude towards Life haint noble enough for *me* – not 'arf. Your Vision of the World lacks hintensity. You've got ter pull yerself together. Understand? Read Ecclesiastes III-VII, and Job V-XI, and a bit o' the Koran and Talmud, and W. Wordsworth's "Excursion", and then get to yer canvas and put some spiritual helbow-grease into it, young man.'
W. R.: 'Yessir. Thankyousir. I'll do my best to give satisfaction.'
Patron: 'Nah then, none of your hargufying and theoryfying! Silent 'ard work – that's what I pays you for! Hoff with you!'
W. R. 'Yessir' (Exit quickly and respectfully)
W. R.'s pamphlet was 'A Plea for the Wider Use of Artists and Craftsmen', 1916.

REPRO William Rothenstein, *Since Fifty,* 1939

1313 **The Connoisseur** 1916

OWNER Mrs Rachel Ward

1314 [**Untitled**]1916

Full-length profile.

OWNER Phillip N. Davis

1315 **Will, as he might, and should, be** 1916

Heavily bearded against a Cotswold background.

OWNER Malcolm Borthwick

1316 **Mr W. Rothenstein and Mankind** 1916

Standing tiptoe on a little hill and turning away in disgust.

OWNER Lilly Library

1317* **Audi Alteram Partem [Hear the other side. St Augustine]** 1916

W. R. at his easel is painting a picture of a tree. On the left a clergyman has thrown down palette and brushes and is saying: 'Not a *good* painter. A very difficult man to work with.'

OWNER Samuel Hessa

1318 **The Trials of the Devil. No. XXXVII. Being drawn by Mr Rothenstein** [?c. 1916]

The Devil, with red tie and long waxed moustache, sits infuriated while W. R. holds up a huge set-square to get perspective.

OWNER The Hon Christopher Lennox-Boyd

1319* **If the Age-Limit is Raised to Forty-Five** [Unsigned c. 1917]

Colonel: 'Complaints again? Well?'
Pte. Rothenstein: 'Our drill during the past week has averaged no more than eleven hours daily. The regiment is being demoralised. Yesterday I saw Private Beerbohm buying a packet of cigarettes. The Sergeant, to whom I had been talking for some minutes after Parade, said "Oh, blow them Ajanta Frescoes". I must press the question I put to you yesterday: Is this Salisbury Plain or is it Capua?'

REPRO William Rothenstein, *Men and Memories,* vol. 2, 1932
OWNER Sir John Rothenstein

1320* **Professor Rothenstein lecturing on the need for closer and closer co-operation between the artist as citizen and the citizen as artist** 1924

OWNER Victoria & Albert Museum

1321* **The Old and the Young Self (Royal School of Art, South Kensington)** 1924

Old Self: 'Take off your hat, Sir! – and leave the room!'

EXHIB L.G. 1925, 1952 and 1957
REPRO *Observations,* 1925
OWNER Sir John Rothenstein

1322★ Is *this* what you would imply, Will? 1929

Pasted on is a cutting of some words by W. R.: 'I was often called upon for sympathy when Conder was in difficulties. Sober men are, alas, poor comforters and sorry companions for men crowned with vine leaves."Will, don't look so sensible," said Oscar Wilde one evening as I sat with him and Conder and Max at the Café Royal.'

In the drawing the other three are tipsy, while W. R. sits primly upright, his bowler hat under his chair.

REPRO William Rothenstein, *Men and Memories*, 1931
OWNER John Arlott

1323★ Professor Sir William Rothenstein. Ever ready – and able – to assist us all 1931

EXHIB L.G. 1952
REPRO *Yorkshire Observer*, 1 May 1952
OWNER Royal College of Art, London

1324★ Will Himself [c. 1940]

Head and shoulders in pencil.

REPRO *Abinger Chronicle*, Jul 1940

1325★ William and his English Garden [n.d.]

In shirt-sleeves and braces beside garden fence.

OWNER Lilly Library

1326★ [Untitled Unsigned n.d.]

Full-length profile facing right, carrying butterfly net over left shoulder.

OWNER Private (Yale)

1327★ Will Rothenstein [Unsigned n.d.]

Standing on pavement in striped suit, holding bowler hat and umbrella. An early drawing.

EXHIB Cincinnati 1965
OWNER Lilly Library

1328 Love in a Pembroke Cottage [n.d.]

W. R. with his wife Alice. From 1898 to 1902 they lived at 1 Pembroke Cottages, Edwardes Square, Kensington.

OWNER Mrs Rachel Ward

OTTO ROTHFIELD

1329★ [Untitled n.d.]

A gay undergraduate 'Blood' (O. R.) in cap and gown, flying through the stars holding a bottle of champagne, while below a glum scholar ('Smug') digs with a spade. An undergraduate drawing. Cf. 1945.

OWNER Louis M. Rothfield

ALFRED DE ROTHSCHILD

1842–1918   Banker and patron of the arts
See also 198, 995

1330★ [Untitled 1895]

Peering out of a box at the opera.

REPRO *Pick-Me-Up*, 20 Apr 1895
OWNER Victoria & Albert Museum

1331★ Mr Alfred Rothschild [1900]

Full-length profile facing left, evening dress, holding closed opera-hat behind his back.

REPRO *Idler*, May 1900

1332 [Mr Alfred Rothschild 1901]

EXHIB Carfax 1901

1333★ Mr Alfred Rothschild [1904]

Alone in a box at the opera, with programme, glasses and a packet of sweets.

EXHIB Carfax 1904; Edwardian Exhibition, Eastbourne, 1951
REPRO Eastbourne catalogue, 1951
OWNER Maxwell Halliday

1334 [Roughing it at Halton ?1905]

Halton was A. R.'s house in Buckinghamshire. On 27 Jan 1905 Max wrote to his future wife Florence: 'All this week I have been doing a large and elaborate caricature-composition: Alfred Rothschild at Home: a sort of commission from the Wertheimer family.' Presumably either this or 1337.

EXHIB New York 1912, where wrongly described as of Lord Rothschild; L.G. 1945 (Guedalla)

1335★ A Quiet Evening in Seamore Place [?1905]

Doctors consulting whether Mr Alfred may, or may not, take a second praline before bed-time.

EXHIB New York 1912, where wrongly described as of Lord Rothschild; L.G. 1952
REPRO **Plate 73**
OWNER David Rutherston

1336 [Mr Alfred de Rothschild]

EXHIB L.G. 1911

1337★ Rothschilds at Play [1926]

A. R. in a box with his brother Leopold.

EXHIB L.G. 1928, where dated as above

1338 [Mr Alfred de Rothschild]

EXHIB L.G. 1952

1339★ Mr Alfred de Rothschild [n.d.]

Full length in long overcoat, top hat in right hand, stick in left.

EXHIB L.G. 1957
OWNER University of Texas

BARON HENRI DE ROTHSCHILD
1872–1944 Doctor and writer

1340★ One of Fortune's Favourites. Baron Henri de Rothschild 1925
EXHIB L.G. 1925 and 1957
REPRO *Observations*, 1925
OWNER Mark Birley

JAMES DE ROTHSCHILD
1878–1957 Liberal M.P.

1341★ Mr James de Rothschild [1930]
REPRO *Ladbroke's Racing Calendar*, 1931

LEOPOLD DE ROTHSCHILD
1845–1917 Banker
See 198, 1337

LORD ROWTON
1838–1903 Politician and philanthropist
See also 1066

1342 [Lord Rowton 1901]
EXHIB Carfax 1901

1343 [Lord Rowton]
EXHIB L.G. 1957

RAYMOND RÔZE
1875–1920 Composer and conductor

1344★ Mr Raymond Rôze 1914
Conducting with a Union Jack in his buttonhole.

PAUL RUBENS
1875–1917 Composer and playwright

1345 [Mr Paul Rubens 1908]
EXHIB Carfax 1908

JOHN RUSKIN
1819–1900 Writer
See 595, 1268, 1272, 1829

BERTRAND RUSSELL
1872–1970 Philosopher and writer

1346★ Logic and Mathematics reconciled through the bitterness of beholding the passionate advances now made by Mr Bertrand Russell to Physics 1924
Logic: 'How unlike dear Mr Mill!'
Mathematics: 'Odiously incontinual and fluxional!'
Politics: 'He even had the impertinence to flirt with *me* once. And no man ever understood me less well.'
The four Sciences are sexless creatures in white robes, three of them spectacled.
EXHIB L.G. 1925
REPRO *Observations*, 1925

SIR CHARLES RUSSELL
1863–1928 Solicitor
See 679

WALTER RUSSELL
1867–1949 Painter
See also 1586–8, 1591

1347★ Mr Walter Russell [n.d.]
Full-length profile facing left. Marked Amended Version *by Max in pencil.*
OWNER John S. Russell

1348★ W. W. Russell [n.d.]
Three-quarter length, full face.
OWNER Armand G. Erpf

ALBERT RUTHERSTON
(né Rothenstein)
1881–1953 Artist
See also 382, 383, 484, 1525, 1586–1588

1349★ Will and Albert 1906
For the former from Max.
REPRO **Plate 68**
OWNER Herbert D. Schimmel

1350★ Mr Albert Rothenstein [? c. 1906]
Full-length profile facing left, wearing bowler hat and carrying portfolio under arm. The shape and design of the figure are so like those of 1349 as to suggest a similar date.
OWNER David Rutherston

1351★ Mr Albert Rothenstein 1909
OWNER David Rutherston

1352★ Landed Gentry. No. 1. Mr Albert Rothenstein 1913
EXHIB L.G. 1913 and 1952
OWNER David Rutherston

THE SEVENTH DUKE OF RUTLAND
1818–1906   Conservative politician

1353★ **The 7th Duke of Rutland – sole survivor of a young England that never was. Memory by Max** 1926

In the 1840s R, then Lord John Manners, was one of the leaders of the 'Young England' party, with Disraeli and others.

EXHIB L.G. 1928
OWNER City of Sheffield Art Gallery

THE EIGHTH DUKE OF RUTLAND
See Marquess of Granby

HERBERT EDWARD RYLE
1856–1925   Dean of Westminster
See 211

MR RYMAN
See 612

S

PHILIP SAINSBURY
1899–1937   Printer, publisher and hotelier

1354★ **Mr Philip Sainsbury** 1923
OWNER Piccadilly Gallery

1355 **Mr Philip Sainsbury in Rapallo** 1923
OWNER Geoffrey Sainsbury

IVY ST HELIER
d. 1971   Actress

1356★ **Miss Ivy St Helier as Manon** [c. 1931]
REPRO *Heroes and Heroines of Bitter Sweet*, 1931
OWNER Lilly Library

FLORENCE ST JOHN
1855–1912   Actress and singer

1357★ **Miss St John** [n.d.]
An early drawing.
REPRO *Theatre Notebook*, Winter 1966–67
OWNER Victoria & Albert Museum

GEORGE AUGUSTUS SALA
1828–95   Journalist and author

1358★ **Rossetti in his worldlier days (circa 1866–**

1868) leaving the Arundel Club with George Augustus Sala 1916

Mr Sala: 'You and I, Rossetti, we like and we understand each other. Bohemians, both of us, to the core, we take the world as we find it; and as for our work, I give Mr Levy what *he* wants, and *you* give Mr Rae and Mr Leyland what *they* want, and glad we are to pocket the cash and foregather at the Arundel.' (The monologue is apocryphal, but not so the acquaintance. M.B.)

J. M. Levy was the proprietor of the 'Daily Telegraph', for which Sala wrote. George Rae and F. R. Leyland were two of Rossetti's chief patrons.

EXHIB Grosvenor 1917; L.G. Sept 1921
REPRO *Rossetti and his Circle*, 1922
OWNER Tate Gallery

THE THIRD MARQUESS OF SALISBURY
1830–1903   Prime Minister
See also 439, 637, 1739

1359★ **Lord Salisbury leading the nation** [1901]
EXHIB Carfax 1901; L.G. 1957
REPRO **Plate 7**

1360★ **A memory of Lord Salisbury** 1927
Full-length profile facing right, carrying official bag.
EXHIB L.G. 1928
REPRO Simona Pakenham, *Sixty Miles from England*, 1967
OWNER Glen Byam Shaw

THE FOURTH MARQUESS
OF SALISBURY
1861–1947 Conservative politician
See 260

MARIO SAMMARCO
1873–1930 Italian baritone
See also 1664, 1666

1361* **[Untitled Unsigned n.d.]**
Three-quarter-length full-face pencil sketch for his figure in 1664 and 1666.
OWNER University of Texas

EUGENE SANDOW
1867–1925 German 'strong man'
See 386

JOHN SINGER SARGENT
1856–1925 American painter
See also 614, 615, 1423, 1443, 1587

1362* **Mr Sargent** [1900]
REPRO *World*, Christmas Supplement, 1900; **Plate 65**
OWNER Mrs M. E. Yates

1363* **[Untitled Unsigned c. 1900]**
Rough sketch for 1362, on two joined pieces of paper.
OWNER Tate Gallery

1364* **[Untitled** 1903]
Back view, quarter face, arms folded.
REPRO *John Bull*, 20 Aug 1903

1365* **Mr Sargent at Work** 1907
On 29 March 1907 Max wrote to his future wife Florence: 'I have just done a rather good "Mr Sargent at Work" – more or less suggested by a musical party he gave some nights ago. Two fiddlers and a 'cellist in the foreground, and a duchess on a platform in the background, and he in between, dashing at a canvas, with a big and swilling brush in either hand. I wish I could make my living by drawing.'
EXHIB Carfax 1907
REPRO *A Book of Caricatures*, 1907
OWNER Patrick Baldwin

1366* **The Queue outside Mr Sargent's** 1908
Six ladies of fashion and four messenger boys queue outside 31 Tite Street, observed by J. S. from a window. According to Evan Charteris, two of the ladies are the Duchess of Sutherland and Lady Faudel-Phillips, of both of whom J. S. painted portraits. A very rough sketch in the University of Texas shows that Max also contemplated a male queue.
EXHIB Carfax 1908
REPRO Evan Charteris, *John Sargent*, 1927

1367* **['A Great Realist'** 1909]
Three-quarter length, evening dress, cigarette in hand.
REPRO *Vanity Fair*, 24 Feb 1909, where captioned as above

1368* **Cashmere – and again the queue!** 1909
Mr Sargent (to Cook's interpreter): 'What is it they want? What? . . . No! confound it: really, this is too bad! Don't they know that I've made up my mind, absolutely and irrevocably, not to accept any more commissions?'
EXHIB N.E.A.C. Summer 1909
REPRO *Fifty Caricatures*, 1913
OWNER Miss Elizabeth Williamson

1369* **Mr Sargent in Cashmere [Unsigned** n.d.]
Mr Sargent (to Cook's interpreter): 'What is it they want? What? No! confound it: really this is too bad. I've made up my mind, absolutely and irrevocably, not to accept any more commissions!'
Pencil sketch for 1368.
OWNER Robert Bird

1370 **[Mr J. S. Sargent R.A.]**
EXHIB L.G. 1911

1371* **Mr Sargent in Venice** 1911
Lion of S. Mark: 'Ecco ancora quest' Americano!' [Shade of Napoleon:] 'Bon! Il n'a pas plus peur de Venise que moi!'
EXHIB L.G. 1911
REPRO *Bookman*, Aug 1911
OWNER Johannesburg Art Gallery

1372 **Mr John Sargent** 1912
Three-quarter-length back view, head to left, holding cigar.
EXHIB L.G. 1957
OWNER Mrs Dilys Sullivan

1373* **The Strong Man of the Royal Academy** [c. 1912]
J. S. in frilled shorts and singlet marked J. S. outside a fair-booth called Royal Academy.
EXHIB New York 1912; L.G. 1945 (Guedalla)
REPRO *Caricatures by Max*, 1958
OWNER Ashmolean Museum, Oxford

1374 **Artists who were at the Front. Mr John Sargent** 1918

'That strain again; it had a dying fall;
O, it came o'er my ears like the sweet south
That breathes upon a bank of violets,
Stealing and giving odour.'
                              [*Twelfth Night*, I, i]
Rapture, enchantment, of Mr Sargent, at hearing again, after all those starved days, a little music

J. S. in British warm, fur collar, swagger cane and cigar, his painting gear carried by a staff officer, comes on an other rank playing an accordion.

REPRO *Reveille*, Feb 1919

1375 [A Sketch of John Sargent]
EXHIB L.G. 1928

1376★ Sargent, Mr John S., some attributes of [n.d.]
Three-quarter length, tiny head to left, tight-waisted frock-coat.
OWNER Rodney Armstrong

1377★ Mr John Sargent [n.d.]
Half length, full face.
OWNER William S. Lieberman

1378★ Mr John Sargent [n.d.]
Full-length profile facing left, tight-waisted frock-coat.
OWNER Victoria & Albert Museum

ARTHUR SASSOON
1840–1912   Merchant and banker
See 198

SIR PHILIP SASSOON
1888–1939   Conservative politician

1379★ Sir Philip Sassoon in the House of Commons 1913
EXHIB L.G. May 1921
REPRO *A Survey*, 1921
OWNER Yale University Library

SIEGFRIED SASSOON
1886–1967   Poet and writer
See also 2036

1380★ Mr Siegfried Sassoon 1931
REPRO *Spectator* Supplement, 21 Mar 1931; Stanley Jackson, *The Sassoons*, 1965
OWNER *The Spectator*

THE SECOND LORD SAVILE
1853–1931   Diplomat

1381 [Lord Savile taking a walk 1907]
EXHIB Carfax 1907

1382 [Arbitrium Olympi [The Decision of Olympus] 1909]
Besides Lord S, shows Lords de Grey, Alington, Rosslyn, Kinnoull, Craven, and the Duke of Westminster.
EXHIB N.E.A.C. Winter 1909, where subtitled 'The Budget in the Balance'; L.G. 1911

1383 [Lord Savile]
EXHIB L.G. 1911

1384 Lord Savile [n.d.]
Full-length profile facing left.
OWNER Ludovic Kennedy

SYDNEY SCHIFF
('STEPHEN HUDSON')
1868–1944   Novelist
See also 1455

1385★ 'Stephen Hudson' 1925
EXHIB L.G. 1925 and 1952
REPRO *Observations*, 1925
OWNER Lady Beddington-Behrens

1386★ Sydney Schiff 1939
For Monsieur [Oscar] Nemon.
OWNER Ashmolean Museum, Oxford

FRANK SCHUSTER
1840–1927   Music lover

1387 Mr Frank Schuster, discovering a pianist 1909
EXHIB N.E.A.C. Summer 1909
OWNER David McKibbin

1388★ 'Frankie Schu' 1923
Full-length profile facing left.
OWNER George Sassoon

1389★ 'Frankie Schu' 1923
Full length, three-quarter face, hands extended.
OWNER The Rev. R. F. Beloe

CLEMENT SCOTT
1841–1904   Dramatic critic

1390 [Mr Clement Scott c. 1897]
EXHIB L.G. 1928, where dated as above

1391* Mr Clement Scott [1901]
EXHIB Carfax 1901; L.G. 1952
REPRO *Candid Friend*, 26 Oct 1901; **Plate 27**
OWNER Robert Aickman

1392 [The late Clement Scott]
EXHIB L.G. 1911

1393* Untitled Unsigned [n.d.]
Head and shoulders profile facing left, holding stick. Known only from a photograph in Max's papers.

WILLIAM BELL SCOTT
1811–90 Painter and poet
See 1276

ANTONIO SCOTTI
1866–1936 Italian baritone
See 1664-66

OWEN SEAMAN
1861–1936 Parodist and editor of *Punch*
See also 144

1394* Mr Owen Seaman [c.1903]
Full-length profile facing left, smoking pipe.
REPRO *Cassell's Magazine*, Feb 1903

1395 [Sir Owen Seaman c. 1905]
EXHIB L.G. 1928, where dated as above

1396* The Resident Physician
Mr Owen Seaman wondering whether any one who has not actually lived with Punch, year in, year out, can realise the horror of that existence.
O. S. sits on one side of the fire, opposite Punch, who has a bandaged foot, and a medicine-bottle beside him.
EXHIB L.G. 1911
REPRO *Bookman*, Aug 1911

1397* [Untitled n.d.]
Full length facing left, three-quarter face, pipe in hand, straw hat on ground.
OWNER Keith Mackenzie

J. E. B. SEELY
1868–1947 Soldier and Liberal politician
See also 799

1398* Colonel Seely overhears, in the Reading-room of the Cavalry Club, talk about the Territorials 1913
EXHIB L.G. 1913 and 1945 (Guedalla)
REPRO *Fifty Caricatures*, 1913
OWNER Piccadilly Gallery

SELF-CARICATURES
See also 34, 208, 384, 440, 703, 712, 719, 1300, 1322, 1484, 1487, 1499, 1605, 1612, 1618, 1620, 1623, 1645, 1650, 1679, 1730, 1843, 1847-51, 2031

1399* [Untitled Unsigned c. 1890]
Half-length profile facing left, Eton collar, hand in jacket pocket. Done at Charterhouse.
OWNER University of Texas

1400* [Untitled Signed with monogram c. 1890]
A central head, profile facing left, in high collar. Around it five smaller drawings showing Max: At the Bar, At Oxford, Drawing, Walking, and At the Haymarket. Done at Charterhouse.
REPRO Bohun Lynch, *Max Beerbohm in Perspective*, 1921

1400A* [Untitled Unsigned n.d.]
Walking tipsily, cigarette in mouth, wearing straw hat and carrying stick. Done at Oxford.
OWNER Robert H. Taylor

1401* [Untitled c. 1893]
Full-length near-profile facing left. Check trousers, frock-coat, very curved top hat, high collar, stick held behind back.
REPRO *Max's Nineties*, 1958 (frontispiece)
OWNER Merton College, Oxford

1402* [Untitled Unsigned c. 1893]
REPRO **Plate I (frontispiece)**
OWNER Merton College, Oxford

1403* Mr Max Beerbohm [1896]
Full length, full face, evening dress, high collar, top hat, smoking cigarette, stick in left hand.
REPRO *Chap-Book* (Chicago), 15 Oct 1896
OWNER Newberry Library, Chicago

1404* [Untitled Unsigned 1896]
Max as pierrot, holding huge quill with quasi-human head and feet.
REPRO Binding-case of *Twenty-Five Gentlemen*, 1896; *Max's Nineties*, 1958 (dust-jacket)
OWNER Robert H. Taylor

1405* **[Untitled** 1897]
Full-length profile, facing left. As schoolboy in Eton collar and jacket, top hat, cane in left hand.
REPRO *Figaro*, 4 Feb 1897

1406* **[Untitled** c. 1897]
Almost identical with 1405, perhaps a sketch for it.
OWNER Sir Rupert Hart-Davis

1407* **[Untitled** 1898]
Max as stout rubicund veteran, crowned with a laurel wreath, sitting in an arm-chair wearing slippers and holding a stick.
REPRO *London Life*, 17 Sep 1898

1408* **[Untitled]** October 1899
Dear Mr Denselow, I have much pleasure in sending you my autograph: also a faithful portrait of myself, as a warning to you not to become a caricaturist when you grow up. Yours very truly, Max Beer-bohm.
Full length, full face, very tall top hat, frock-coat, buttonhole, right hand on cane, left on hip.
EXHIB L.G. 1945 (Guedalla)
REPRO *Bookman Annual*, Dec 1959; Ellen Moers, *The Dandy*, 1960
OWNER Ashmolean Museum, Oxford

1409* **[Untitled** 1899]
Full-length back view, top hat and tails, hair coming to a point, cane in left hand, right on hip, legs apart.
REPRO *Academy*, 10 Dec 1899; *Max's Nineties*, 1958 (tailpiece)

1410* **[Untitled Unsigned** n.d.]
Very similar to 1409, but body in outline only, cane in right hand, feet together.
REPRO *The Poets' Corner*, 1943
OWNER Sir John Rothenstein

1411* **The Debutant [Unsigned** n.d.]
Back view of a figure very much like 1409 and 1410, being led down to the footlights by a much taller woman.
OWNER Piccadilly Gallery

1412* **Mr Max Beerbohm** [1901]
Max as youthful cricketer, with bat and ball.
EXHIB Carfax 1901
REPRO *Pall Mall Magazine*, Feb 1902

1413* **[Untitled]** Dec:5:'01
Regretting that I live in this self-advertising age, I respond to the invitation to portray myself. Max Beerbohm [*all printed below the drawing*]
Full length, three-quarter face, huge head, facing left,

morning (if not mourning) clothes, top hat in right hand, stick in left.
REPRO *Daily Mail*, 27 Dec 1901

1414* **Max** [?c. 1901]
Similar to 1413 in stance and proportions, but in evening dress.
OWNER John S. Russell

1415* **[Untitled Unsigned]** 1902
Sandringham House, Norfolk – November 10, 1902.
Mr Max Beerbohm is in receipt of Mr Norreys Connell's interesting design. He has submitted it to H.I.M. William II, who has been graciously pleased to be disgusted by its sordid realism and to forbid Mr Beerbohm to bestow on Mr Connell the tin medal which had been prepared. In accordance to his custom, the Imperial Idealist has with His own hand roughed out the accompanying picture, to be developed (in mosaic: 60 feet x 40 feet) at Mr Connell's leisure.
Max as Apollo, driving the Chariot of the Sun. Norreys Connell was the early pen-name of the Irish writer Conal O'Riordan (1874–1948). The Kaiser visited Sandringham for the King's birthday on 9 Nov, but the point of this drawing is obscure.
OWNER H. A. Cahn

1416* **Portrait of the Artist** [*signed*] **Max Beerbohm** 1903
Half-length back view, as in 1409, but with more hair.
REPRO *Sketch*, 11 Mar 1908

1417* **Mr Max Beerbohm** 29 August 1903
With compliments to Mr H. Lester Grant
Half-length profile, facing left. Drawn on a sheet of paper of the Maison A. Lefèvre, Dieppe.
OWNER Ashmolean Museum, Oxford

1418* **London: Dieppe** [n.d.]
Plus ça change: plus c'est la même chose.
Two joined drawings: in London Max is slim, wearing morning dress and holding a lighted cigarette: in Dieppe he is plump.
REPRO Jacques-Emile Blanche, *Portraits of a Lifetime*, 1937
OWNER Robert Beloe

1419* **[Untitled Unsigned]** 1904
Max as Early Victorian beau, with tiny chin-beard, top hat and fur-collared short coat.
REPRO *Daily Mail*, 15 Jan 1904, where captioned 'Mr Max Beerbohm in the reformed dress he would like to wear'; J. A. Hammerton, *Humorists of the Pencil*, 1905

1420* [Untitled Unsigned 1904]

Max shining torch on statue-bust in Poets' Corner

EXHIB Achenbach 1964
REPRO Binding-case of *The Poets' Corner*, 1904 and 1943
OWNER U.C.L.A. (Clark)

1421* For my Proof-Reader – this picture of Mr Max Beerbohm seeing Job XXXIX, 25

Mostly obscured by the huge Bible in which he is reading.

EXHIB Cincinnati 1965
REPRO Cincinnati catalogue, 1965
OWNER Lilly Library

1422* [Untitled Unsigned n.d.]

Head and shoulders facing left, with a blob of red sealing-wax as a buttonhole. Pasted on beside it is another drawing entitled: Miss F[lorence] K[ahn] recovering from boredom at Hampstead 1907. *She sits dejectedly on a stool.*

OWNER Robert H. Taylor

1423* Mr Max Beerbohm receives an influential, though biassed, deputation, urging him, in the cause of our common humanity, and of good taste, to give over 1908

The deputation consists of Soveral (as spokesman), Lord Burnham, Hall Caine, Carson, Chesterton, Haldane, Henry James, Kipling, George Moore, Northcliffe, Pinero, Will Rothenstein, Sargent, Shaw, Steer, Tosti and Zangwill.

EXHIB Carfax 1908
REPRO **Plate 6**
OWNER Art Institute of Chicago

1424* My Craving for Knighthood [?1908]

Myself (to Sir F. C. Gould): 'Tell me frankly, is one born, or can one *become*, amiable?'

EXHIB Carfax 1908; L.G. 1952, where wrongly dated 1904, since Gould was knighted in 1906
OWNER J. C. Thomson

1425* Homage to Praxiteles paid by Max [n.d.]

Shows Praxiteles's statue of Hermes bearing the infant Dionysus, and in front Max, in morning clothes, in the same attitude, with one arm missing and a doll on the other.

REPRO **Plate 100**
OWNER Phillip N. Davis

1426* Mr Max Beerbohm [n.d.]

Full length, three-quarter face, morning dress, stick in right hand, top hat in left.

OWNER Peter Hughes

1427 For Marjorie [Battine] from Max – who has tried not to flatter himself, but simply couldn't help it [n.d.]

Full-length profile, hands in trouser pockets.

OWNER Dr I. O. Macaulay

1428* Max [n.d.]

Full-length profile, facing left, evening dress, stick in left hand, large top hat with curling brim on the floor in front of him.

OWNER Private (Maine & N.Y.)

1429* Max Beerbohm. Portrait of the artist – to the greater artist, Mr Clarkson [n.d.]

Full-length profile facing left, evening dress, hand on hip, smoking cigarette. William Clarkson (1865–1934) was the best known costumier and wig-maker in London.

EXHIB American Academy 1952
OWNER Harvard College Library

1430* Moi-même [n.d.]

Full-length profile, facing left, in pencil.

OWNER Huntington Library

1431* [Untitled n.d.]

Half-length full face in pencil, wearing top hat.

REPRO *U.C.L.A. Librarian*, Sep 1969
OWNER U.C.L.A. (Clark)

1432* [Untitled n.d.]

Three-quarter-length profile facing left, day clothes, stick in right hand, left on hip.

OWNER University of Texas

1433* Mr Max Beerbohm [n.d.]

Back view, quarter face, wearing straw hat, holding stout stick and smoking a cigarette.

EXHIB L.G. 1945 (Guedalla)
REPRO *Caricatures, by Max* 1958 (cover); Lord David Cecil, *Max*, 1964
OWNER Ashmolean Museum, Oxford

1434* Sudden Appearance of Mr Beerbohm in the New English Art Club [1909]

Max, exquisitely dressed, stands among a shabby crowd of lay-figure artists. A bust of Wilson Steer over the door. This is the earliest known drawing in which Max has a moustache.

EXHIB N.E.A.C. Summer 1909
REPRO *Daily Mail*, 22 May 1909
OWNER Sir Anthony Hooper Bart

1435* Un Revers [1909]

Essayist: 'They call me the inimitable, and the incomparable, and the sprightly and whimsical . . . I wonder if I *am*.'

EXHIB N.E.A.C. Winter 1909; L.G. 1945 (Guedalla), 1952 and 1957

REPRO *Daily Mail*, 20 Nov 1909; L.G. 1945 catalogue
OWNER Mrs Philip Guedalla

1436★ [Untitled c. 1909]
'They call me the inimitable, and the incomparable, and the sprightly and whimsical . . . I wonder if I *am*?'
Very like 1435. Probably a sketch for it.
REPRO Lord David Cecil, *Max*, 1964
OWNER Charterhouse School

1437★ Three things adjudged perfect. 1 Beerbohm 2 Pachmann 3 Genée [n.d.]
Max, moustached, as a ballet-dancer (Adeline Genée) playing the fiddle. Presumably Max believed that the famous Russian pianist Vladimir de Pachmann (1848–1933) was a violinist.
EXHIB Achenbach 1964
OWNER U.C.L.A. (Clark)

1438★ [Untitled Unsigned n.d.]
For E[rnest] B[rown] from M. B.
Full-length, three-quarter face, moustached, very elegant, holding top hat and stick, fishtail legs.
REPRO Cover of L.G. catalogue 1957
OWNER Roland Brown

1439★ [Untitled Unsigned n.d.]
Pencil head and shoulders of Max, moustached, in a grand foreign uniform, with a decoration on his chest, in the style of Bismarck, whom he curiously resembled.
EXHIB Achenbach 1964
OWNER U.C.L.A. (Clark)

1440★ [Untitled n.d.]
Shows Max in straw hat and voluminous flannels on a cliff-top with his wife Florence.
OWNER John Buxton

1441★ Inglese Italianato [1911]
Max in a large black sombrero, standing among Italian castles, mountains and lakes.
EXHIB L.G. 1911
REPRO *Daily Mirror*, 22 Apr 1911
OWNER J. G. Milner

1442★ [Untitled Unsigned 1911]
Black silhouette, full length facing left, arm extended.
REPRO Cover of L.G. 1911 catalogue; **Plate 2 (title-page)**

1443★ One fine morning, or, How they might undo me 1911
Max starts back appalled from a procession of his victims, each of whom has adopted a new style of hair or clothing. They are L. V. Harcourt, Chesterton, Kitchener, W. J. Locke, W. L. Courtney, Balfour, Curzon, Zangwill,

Steer, Tonks, F. E. Smith, Lord Ribblesdale, Andrew Lang, Sargent, Walkley, Lord Burnham, Lord Spencer, Pinero, Sutro, George Moore, Arnold Bennett, Kipling, Will Rothenstein, Hall Caine, Haldane, The Rev. R. J. Campbell, Lord Rosebery, Soveral, Shaw, and Asquith.
EXHIB N.E.A.C. Winter 1911; L.G. 1913; American Academy 1952
REPRO *Colophon* (N.Y.), Part 10, 1932
OWNER Robert Montgomery

1444★ [Untitled Unsigned 1913]
Full-length profile facing left, drawing on a piece of paper.
REPRO Cover of L.G. 1913 catalogue

1445★ [Untitled c. 1917]
Full-length profile facing left, cigarette in right hand.
REPRO *Hampstead and Highgate Express*, 25 May 1958

1446★ The Theft — 1894. The Restitution — 1920 [?1920]
Two drawings framed together. In one Max the undergraduate is surreptitiously removing a book from the College Library: in the other, an aged man with spectacles, long white beard and stick, he returns it.
EXHIB L.G. 1957
REPRO *Postmaster*, Oxford, Dec 1960
OWNER Merton College, Oxford

1447★ [Untitled] 1921
For my friend C. S. Evans.
Half-length profile facing left.
EXHIB American Academy 1952
REPRO *The Windmill*, ed. L. Callender, 1921; cover of American Academy catalogue 1952 (without inscription)

1448 [Untitled Unsigned 1921]
From the top of an outline map of Italy emerge Max's head and shoulders. He is holding a pencil and paper.
REPRO *A Survey*, limited edition, 1921 (title-page)

1449★ Bohun Lynch, Edmond Kapp, and 'Quiz', wondering how long the veteran exile will go doddering on 1923
Max, immensely old, with a skull-cap and long beard, sits drawing at a desk on the terrace at Rapallo, while the other three caricaturists stand watching.
EXHIB L.G. 1923, 1945 (Guedalla) and 1957
REPRO *Things New and Old*, 1923

1450 The splendid influence of Russian literature upon ours 1924
A. (a feeble but inquisitive old connoisseur): 'What are you writing to-day?'
B. (a young Englishman of genius): 'Short story.'

A.: 'Wouldn't you be more comfortable if you wrote at a writing-table?'
B.: 'Writing-table? Bah! "Carpentry"! Not me!'
A.: 'But – how about the – er – window-frame? – and the floor?'
B.: 'I'm having them removed to-morrow.'

A is a diffident, bald-headed Max. B is a young red-headed tough, who stands engrossed in what he is writing and doesn't look at Max. In the 1925 catalogue Max added: To any not literary person it should be explained that 'carpentry' is a term which the best critics apply to any piece of work that has been carefully thought out and constructed with low cunning.

EXHIB L.G. 1925
OWNER Maxwell Halliday

1451* **School for those about to become Cartoonists** 1924

Self-appointed Professor: 'It will all be perfectly plain sailing for you, boys. You never will have to think for yourselves. All you need do is to say publicly what the best and sanest people think but don't publicly say.'

A row of boys in Eton collars face Max in mortar-board and gown. He stands on a rostrum and points to a blackboard, on which is written:

A is an Ass
B is a Scoundrel
C means well no doubt
D's ideas are all wrong
Heaven defend us from E

REPRO *Observations*, 1925 (extra plate in limited edition)
OWNER Adrian Evans

1452 **'The Stricken Deer'. Mr Max Beerbohm trying to think of a suitable wedding present** Oct 1932

Half of this drawing is for Rachel, the other half for David Cecil.

Max is standing on the terrace at Rapallo, clutching his brow. Lord D. C.'s 'The Stricken Deer' appeared in 1929.
OWNER Lord David Cecil

1453* **M.B., L.L.D. (Edin.)** 1935

For A[lbert] B[ernard] B[urney] affectionately
Three-quarter-length profile, facing left, in academic cap and gown. Max received his honorary degree on 3 Jul 1935. A. B. B. was a Merton friend.
OWNER Sir Rupert Hart-Davis

1454* **[Untitled]** 1938

Two half-length drawings, side by side. In the first Max

appears long-haired, whiskered and elegantly dressed, in the other in a drab modern suit. They are captioned:

[1] As Miss Jungmann would have seen me in the good old days of Octavius Hill; and I think Miss Jungmann would have been impressed and interested.

[2] I don't blame Miss Jungmann for being uninterested and unimpressed by me as I am; nor do I wholly blame myself: I blame partly the tailor and the hairdresser and the dismal standardisation of all mankind.

The Scottish painter David Octavius Hill (1802–70) was the first artist to take portrait photographs (c. 1845).
OWNER Mrs Eva Reichmann

1455* **[Untitled]** Christmas 1939

Good Heavens! You still here? Poor Violet! Poor Sydney!

Max in summer clothes meets himself in a winter overcoat. He and his wife had been staying with Violet and Sydney Schiff at Abinger in Surrey since February.
REPRO Edward Beddington-Behrens, *Look Back Look Forward*, 1963
OWNER Merton College, Oxford

1456* **I. M. THE XIX CENTURY** 1943

Max, old and disillusioned, leans on a pedestal, inscribed as above, which bears a funeral urn.
OWNER Stephen Greene

1457* **Self Portrait Uffizi Style** 1945

For my dear A. C. R. C[arter]
Half-length, standing at easel, with palette and brush.
REPRO *The Year's Art*, 1942–44, ed. A. C. R. Carter, 1945

1458 **['Max']**

EXHIB L.G. 1945 (Guedalla)

1459 **Me as I more or less am nowadays. Certainly an older and possibly a wiser man** 1946

OWNER W. R. M. Maxwell

1460* **M. B. Anno Domini, 1949 – or (to anticipate the chronology of future ages), Anno Atomico, 4.** 1949

EXHIB L.G. 1957
REPRO L.G. 1957 catalogue; *The Times*, 30 May 1957
OWNER Merton College, Oxford

1461* **[Untitled Unsigned** 1952]

Head and shoulders silhouette facing left.
REPRO Private view card of L.G. exhibition, 1952

1462* **'MAX' IN RETROSPECT** [1952]

Rough sketch for 1461 on envelope.
OWNER Sir Rupert Hart-Davis

1463★ Max A.D. 1952

Full-length profile facing left, cigarette in hand.

REPRO Lord David Cecil, *Max*, 1964
OWNER Mrs Eva Reichmann

1464★ [Untitled Unsigned 1952]

Pencil sketch for 1463, but with cigarette in mouth. Dated on back by Elisabeth Jungmann.

OWNER Sir Rupert Hart-Davis

1465★ [Untitled n.d.]

Although this depicts Max in the 1890s, in evening dress, holding hat and stick, it looks much more like a drawing done at the end of his life.

REPRO J. G. Riewald, *Sir Max Beerbohm*, 1953
OWNER J. G. Riewald

1466★ [Untitled Unsigned n.d.]

Pencil sketch for 1465. Two other self-caricatures on verso.

OWNER Sir Rupert Hart-Davis

1467★ [Untitled n.d.]

Full length, full face, morning dress, holding top hat. A late drawing.

OWNER David Tree Parsons

GORDON SELFRIDGE
1858–1947 Store proprietor
See 899

A. SELIGMANN

1468★ A. Seligmann [c. 1895]

EXHIB L.G. 1928, where dated as above
OWNER Dr A. Herxheimer

'SEM' (GEORGE GOURSAT)
1863–1934 French Caricaturist

1469★ 'Sem' [1907]

Full length, three-quarter face, wearing straw hat.

REPRO *A Book of Caricatures*, 1907

1470★ 'Sem' 1907

Full-length profile, carrying straw hat.

EXHIB Baillie 1907
OWNER University of Texas

SIR FELIX SEMON
1849–1921 Laryngologist

1471★ Felix qui potuit regum cognoscere fauces. Sir Felix Semon 1908

A play on Virgil, Georgics, ii, 490, in which, by altering 'rerum' to 'regum', and 'causas' to 'fauces', Max has changed the meaning from 'Happy is he who can know the causes of things' to 'Happy is he who can know the throats of kings'.

EXHIB Carfax 1908
OWNER Malcolm Borthwick

WILLIAM SHAKESPEARE
1564–1616 Poet and playwright
See also 716, 717, 720, 1816, 1875

1472★ William Shakespeare, his method of work [c. 1904]

Being furtively handed the manuscript of 'Hamlet' by Francis Bacon.

EXHIB Carfax 1904
REPRO *The Poets' Corner*, 1904 and 1943
OWNER Mrs Mary Hyde

1473★ William Shakespeare writing a sonnet 1907

EXHIB Carfax 1907; N.Y. 1912; L.G. 1945 (Guedalla), where wrongly dated 1905, and L.G. 1952
REPRO **Plate 53**
OWNER Mrs Alice Shalvi

EDWARD SHANKS
1892–1953 Poet and writer
See 616, 1556

C. H. SHANNON
1863–1937 Artist
See 679, 1227, 1228

GEORGE BERNARD SHAW
1856–1950 Irish playwright and writer
See also 35, 95, 181, 335, 614, 615, 748, 769, 1168, 1423, 1443, 1599, 1652, 1731, 1732, 1749, 1750, 1761

1474★ Mr Bernard Shaw (a very early impression) [1896]

The words in brackets were added later. Shows G. B. S. standing in profile, his head full face, holding a folded sheet of paper.

REPRO *Chap-Book* (Chicago), 1 Nov 1896
OWNER Mark Birley

1475* **George Bernard Shaw Esq** [1896]

Full-length profile facing left, in overcoat, holding umbrella.

REPRO *Twenty-Five Gentlemen*, 1896

1476 **Popular version of Bernard Shaw since marriage** [1900]

Max to A. B. W[alkley]

G. B. S. very fat: mentioned in a 'World' interview with Max on 5 Dec 1900.

OWNER Sold at Sotheby's 13 May 1959

1477* **Mr George Bernard Shaw – Capitalist** [1901]

Very fat, in evening dress and fur coat, smoking cigar. On 17 Dec 1901 G. B. S. wrote to Max: 'I went to Carfax yesterday, and, to my horror, found my wife there . . . on the point of buying the capitalist G. B. S. with the object of concealing or destroying it as a libel on her husband's charm'.

EXHIB Carfax 1901
OWNER Arents Collection (N.Y.P.L.)

1478* **Frontispiece to 'Three Plays for Puritans' (second edition)** [1901]

Miss Tolty Drama: 'Garn! 'Ow should I earn my livin'?'

A girl of the streets with DRAMA on her hat is being called to redemption by G. B. S. in Salvation Army uniform, with a copy of 'The Shaw Cry' (Max's variant of the S.A.'s 'War Cry') sticking out of his pocket.

EXHIB Carfax 1901
OWNER Yale University Library

1479* **Light-headed from want of food. From a photograph – showing how cruelly they wrong him** 1901

Max to A. B. W[alkley]

Very shabby, with gap between waistcoat and trousers.

OWNER University of Texas

1480* **Mr George Bernard Shaw in his library** [1903]

Before impressive rows of books G. B. S. sits in an armchair reading a press-cutting.

EXHIB N.Y. 1912
REPRO *Sketch*, 18 Nov 1903

1481* **Frontispiece for 'Man and Superman'** [1903]

'Woman *projecting herself* dramatically by my hands' (See Preface). Man undramatically withdrawing himself

A grim woman in pince-nez and a décolleté ballet-dress.

Only a foot of the escaping man visible. Accompanied by a letter from Max to G. B. S. dated 21 Sep 1903, in which he says: 'I send you a picture no framer would touch.'

OWNER British Museum (Add. MSS. 50529, f. 31)

1482* **Historic scene at 10 Adelphi Terrace** [Unsigned] December 10, 1903

[James Timewell:] 'But here I stay till I find something that he *is* sound on!'

The air round J. T. is full of queries and exclamation-marks.

REPRO *Bookman*, Jul 1905
OWNER University of Texas

1483* **[Untitled** 1904]

G. B. S.: 'Ecoutez! Moi aussi je suis homme de génie!'

Anatole [France]: 'Ici, monsieur, je cherche en vain la réponse. Ça doit être bien commode, l'esprit du dôme . . . Mais voilà, en bas, des escaliers infinis . . . Peut-être, en route . . .'

For A. B. W[alkley]

On 30 May 1904 A. B. W. wrote to Max: 'I have had a wonderful letter from G. B. S., who is at Rome, describing a meeting with Anatole France. They go together up scaffolding and ladders to a sort of trapeze at the top of the Sistine Chapel, and up there G. B. S. (France obviously wondering who the d . . . l he was) bursts out "We're two of a trade; I'm a man of genius". France replies: "Ah, yes, me, too. When one is a whore, one calls oneself a merchant of pleasure." Now I want you to do me a sketch (GRATIS) of that tremendous incident. Will you?'

EXHIB Achenbach 1964
OWNER U.C.L.A. (Clark)

1484* **[Untitled]** 1905

[*A few bogus musical notes*] To G. B. S. from Max. Saturday, January 14, 1905

A modern version of the fight in Act IV of Gounod's 'Faust'.

Valentine Max, angry brother of Marguerite Tolstoy [*attacks*] Aylmer Faust, betrayer of Marguerite Tolstoy, [*with*] Mephisto Bernard, influential friend of Aylmer Faust [*as referee and*] Marguerite Tolstoy [*in background*].

On 31 Dec 1904 in the 'Saturday Review' Max attacked Aylmer Maude's translation of Tolstoy's play 'The Power of Darkness'. G. B. S. defended it in a letter on 7 Jan, and Max returned to the attack on 14 Jan.

REPRO *Bookman*, Jul 1905
OWNER University of Texas

1485* **[Untitled** signed **RUTH** 1905]

['Magnetic, he has the power to infect almost everyone with the delight that he takes in himself']

Standing with legs crossed, right hand on beard, left on hip. On 9 Mar 1906 Max wrote to his future wife Florence: 'The reason for the pseudonym was simply that Harmsworth thought it would be commercially better that people should wonder who the cartoonist was who drew so like me. Presently I shall, of course, have my own signature.' Three more drawings (565, 1168 and 1566) were signed pseudonymously, and thereafter Max reverted to his usual signature.

REPRO *Vanity Fair*, 28 Dec 1905, where captioned as above

1486★ [Untitled 1907]

G. B. S. as devil, his tail wound over his arm, flames rising round him.

REPRO *A Book of Caricatures*, 1907

1487★ A Counsel of Perfection 1907

G. B. S. (to myself): 'Now why can't you do me like *that*?'

They stand before a romantic portrait of G. B. S. by Bertha Newcombe, dated 1893.

EXHIB Carfax 1907; American Academy, 1952
REPRO *Saturday Review of Literature* (N.Y.), 22 Jul 1944
OWNER Mrs John Mason Brown

1488★ [Untitled] 1907

Pasted on is a cutting from 'The Times' of 15 Oct 1907, which Max has identified as by A. B. W[alkley]: 'Mr Shaw found it amusing to work up this sketch of himself disguised in a wig and an old-world courtliness of manner, and that settled it.' This refers to the character of General Burgoyne in 'The Devil's Disciple', which had opened the previous night. The drawing shows G. B. S. bowing in wig and eighteenth-century dress.

OWNER University of Texas

1489 [Bernard Shaw 1908]

EXHIB L.G. 1952, where dated as above

1490★ Mr Shaw's Sortie [Unsigned 1909]

'But this shall be written of our time: that when the Spirit who Denies besieged the last citadel, blaspheming life itself, there were some – there was one especially – whose voice was heard, and whose spear was not broken.' Concluding words of Mr Chesterton's biography of Mr Shaw.

Chesterton stands stoutly calling for help behind the battlements while G. B. S., dressed as Pantaloon, with a red-hot poker in his hands and a megaphone in his mouth, threatens another G. B. S. dressed as Mephistopheles, who warms his hands on the poker.

EXHIB N.E.A.C. Winter 1909
REPRO **Plate 32**
OWNER Fitzwilliam Museum, Cambridge

1491★ Mr Shaw's Sortie 1909

Sketch for 1490, identical legend and drawing, except for

the legs of Mephistopheles, which are wide apart instead of together.

EXHIB Achenbach 1964
REPRO Achenbach catalogue 1964
OWNER Mr and Mrs Joseph M. Bransten

1492★ Leaders of Thought. Mr Shaw and Mr Chesterton [1909]

They face each other, G. B. S. very thin, G. K. C. very fat.

REPRO Drury Lane charity matinée souvenir and programme, 11 May 1909

1493 The Fabian Society

G. B. S. addressing the Society from platform.

EXHIB L.G. 1911
OWNER Mrs M. Lincoln Schuster

1494★ Mr George Bernard Shaw [n.d.]

Full length, three-quarter face, braces showing between jersey and trousers, legs astride.

EXHIB L.G. 1911, where subtitled '(years ago)'
OWNER Mr and Mrs J. S. Frieze

1495 [? Before the Publication 1911]

See next entry

1496★ After the Publication [1911]

G. B. S.: 'What name? . . . Ah, to be sure; and let me tell you, Mr Henderson, I've just been writing to the press to point out some of your inaccuracies, and to say I can't wade through your pages, and have no further use for you.'

Pencil sketch on much-folded paper, showing G. B. S. in wide-brimmed hat, and an appalled Archibald Henderson, whose monumental life of G. B. S. appeared in 1911. The drawing is numbered 2, and assuredly accompanied some such drawing as 1495. On 6 Nov 1911 Max wrote to G. B. S.: 'I have . . . found these two vague skeletons for two caricatures. They were done a few months ago, and "left at that" because I couldn't remember Henderson's features well enough to make further operations worth while.'

OWNER University of Texas

1497 [Untitled] 1912

Head and shoulders, eyes shut.

EXHIB L.G. 1928 and 1957
OWNER Lady Marks

1498★ [Untitled] 1912

For Holbrook Jackson

Head and shoulders, similar to 1497.

REPRO Sotheby catalogue, 26 Nov 1969; *Art at Auction*, ed. Philip Wilson, 1970
OWNER Sold at Sotheby's 26 Nov 1969

1499* **Mr Bernard Shaw. Mild surprise of one who, revisiting England after long absence, finds that the dear fellow has not moved** 1913

Max contemplates G. B. S. who is standing on his head.

EXHIB L.G. 1913 and 1952
REPRO *Fifty Caricatures*, 1913

1500* **Life-Force, Woman-Set-Free, Superman, etc** 1914

Georg Brandes ('chand d'Idées): 'What'll you take for the lot?'
George Bernard Shaw: 'Immortality.'
Georg Brandes: 'Come, I've handled these same goods before! Coat, Mr Schopenhauer's; waistcoat, Mr Ibsen's; trousers, Mr Nietzsche's –
George Bernard Shaw: 'Ah, but look at the patches!'

EXHIB L.G. May 1921
REPRO *A Survey*, 1921
OWNER J-P. B. Ross

1501* **George Bernard Shaw** 1915

For Mr Shujiro Onodo with best regards from Max Beerbohm

Head and shoulders profile facing left, wearing spectacles. Known only from a photograph in the Witt Library, Courtauld Institute.

1502* **Mrs [Patrick] Campbell and Mr Shaw as they respectively appeared to themselves.** July 1922

Handsome and starry-eyed teenagers. This drawing and the next five were occasioned by the publication in 1922 of Mrs C's 'My Life and some Letters', which included some of G. B. S.'s letters to her.

REPRO Alan Dent, *Mrs Patrick Campbell*, 1961
OWNER Messrs S. H. Benson Ltd

1503* **Mrs Campbell and Mr Shaw as they respectively appeared to each other** July 1922

She enormous, he shrunken, old and spectacled.

REPRO Alan Dent, *Mrs Patrick Campbell*, 1961
OWNER Messrs S. H. Benson Ltd

1504* **Berny and Stell, Revue Artistes** July 1922

Dancing on stage, G. B. S. as red-nosed comedian, Mrs Campbell as ingénue.

OWNER Messrs S. H. Benson Ltd

1505* **The Babes in the Wood (G. B. Shaw's version of that tale)** July 1922

Mrs Campbell huge in a nightgown, G. B. S. thin and spectacled.

OWNER Messrs S. H. Benson Ltd

1506* **The Campbell Tartan and the Cockney Fling (if fling it can be called)** July 1922

G. B. S. in kilt and glengarry doing a Scottish dance.

OWNER Messrs S. H. Benson Ltd

1507* **G. B. S. (to Mrs Campbell): 'But why do you call me "Joey"? I'm only the pantaloon.'** 10 July 1992 [*sic*]

On stage. Mrs C. as plump Columbine, G. B. S. as lean and slippered pantaloon.

OWNER Messrs S. H. Benson Ltd

1508* **'Who mashed Stella?' (See Collected Poems of G. B. Shaw)** July 1922

'Morning, Miss. Small soda, please. How's things? You look pretty bobbish. (Etc, etc)'
G. B. S., dashing in sombrero, leans on bar. Mrs Campbell, a stout barmaid, polishes a glass. On 28 Feb 1913 G. B. S. sent Mrs C a long parody of a nursery rhyme, beginning:
> 'Who mashed Stella?
> I, that rejoice
> In a nice Irish voice,
> I mashed Stella.'
To mash meant to flirt with.

OWNER Messrs S. H. Benson Ltd

1509* **'Mr Shaw's apotheosis is one of the wonders of the age' A. B. W[alkey] in** *The Times*, **July 9 1924**

A large half-length profile of G. B. S. leaning on his elbows on the floor. In front of him five tiny worshippers burn incense, and A. B. W., in evening dress, says: 'And calls himself a non-smoker!'

EXHIB L.G. 1925
REPRO *Observations*, 1925
OWNER University of Texas

1510* **The Old and the Young Self** 1924

Old Self: 'Strange! You strike me as frivolous, irreligious, and pert; full of a ludicrous faith in mankind and in the efficacy of political propaganda; squalidly needy in circumstances, and abominably ill-dressed . . . And I used to think you quite perfect!'

EXHIB L.G. 1925, 1952 and 1957
REPRO *Observations*, 1925

1511* **Publicity** 1929

Mr Shaw, to the Laureate: 'Bravo! Without any blarney. Bravo! But look here: you'll never cut me out unless you broadcast.'

Half-length profiles, face to face. Refers to the success of Robert Bridges's 'Testament of Beauty', 1929. R. B. and G. B. S. were both members of the B.B.C. Advisory Committee on Spoken English, but G. B. S. was also a successful broadcaster.

EXHIB L.G. 1952
REPRO *Manchester Guardian*, 23 Nov 1929

1512 Nil

1513 [G. B. S. unstricken with years 1931]
EXHIB L.G. 1952, where dated as above

1514 [G. B. S. illustrating (on the morning after the production of a play, or the publication of a book or pamphlet, or the delivery of a speech or lecture) the haughty motto of his mantelpiece]
['They say' – 'Quhat say thay?' – 'Lat tham say!']
These words, the motto of the Earl Marischal, were engraved over a mantelpiece in G. B. S.'s flat in Adelphi Terrace.
EXHIB L.G. 1952

1515 [A Perfect Fit]
EXHIB American Academy 1952
OWNER Robert Montgomery

1516★ The Iconoclast's One Friend [n.d.]
A Member of Mrs Warren's Profession: 'Mr Shaw, I have long wished to meet you, and grasp you by the hand . . . God bless you! . . . I understand that the Army and Navy, the Church, the Stage, the Bar, the Faculty, the Fancy, the Literary Gents, the Nobility and Gentry, and all the Royal Family, will have nothing more to do with you. Never mind! *My* house will always be open to you.' (Exit, dashing away a tear)
OWNER Cornell University Library

1517★ Mr George Bernard Shaw [n.d.]
Full length, full face, hands in trouser pockets
REPRO Christie's catalogue, 19 Mar 1971
OWNER Messrs Chas J. Sawyer

R. H. SHERARD
1861–1943 Journalist and author
See 224

FREDERIC SHIELDS
1833–1911 Artist
See 1277

CLEMENT SHORTER
1858–1926 Journalist and author

1518 [The Centenary of Edward FitzGerald 1909]
[Mr Clement Shorter: 'Here! Don't be stand-offish, FitzGerald! We literary men ought to stand shoulder to shoulder.']
The horrified shade of E. F. G. retreats before the rapacious advance of C. S.
EXHIB N.E.A.C. Summer 1909; L.G. 1911

1519★ The Centenary of Edward FitzGerald [1909]
Mr Clement Shorter: 'Here! Don't be stand-offish, FitzGerald! We men of letters ought to stand shoulder to shoulder.'
Rough sketch for 1518.
OWNER University of Texas

1520★ Mr Clement Shorter [n.d.]
Full-length profile, facing left, sheet of paper under arm.
OWNER Piccadilly Gallery

1521★ Let Justice Be Done [n.d.]
Mr Clement Shorter (to Mr Alexander Nelson Hood): 'And so you're the Duke of Brontë! Now do, like a good fellow, go and pull a wire or two at Court, and get Lottie and Em and Annie made Duchesses in retrospect!'
Picture of the Brontë sisters on wall behind. C. S. wrote much about them and edited their works. A. N. H. was descended from Nelson, who was Duke of Bronte in Sicily.
EXHIB L.G. 1925
REPRO *Observations*, 1925

WALTER SICHEL
1855–1933 Author and journalist

1522★ Mr Walter Sichel 1913
OWNER Mrs Clarissa Higginbotham

WALTER RICHARD SICKERT
1860–1942 Artist
See also 151, 1054, 1586-8, 1591, 1650, 1772

1523 [Mr Walter Sickert 1901]
EXHIB Carfax 1901

1524★ Mr Walter Sickert explaining away the Piazza San Marco 1907
EXHIB Carfax 1907; L.G. 1952
REPRO *A Book of Caricatures*, 1907
OWNER Piccadilly Gallery

1525★ [Walter Richard Sickert 1910]
Bending over in front of a blank wall with a curtain on it. Title, signature and date are all in the hand of Albert Rutherston.
OWNER David Rutherston

1526 [Ambrosial Nights at the London County Council Westminster Technical Institute]

[Mr Walter Sickert: 'Fi, donc, p'tite insupportable! If one saw this drawing by daylight one would be almost able to distinguish the outlines of the model.']

W. S.'s picture 'Noctes Ambrosianae', which shows a music-hall audience almost in darkness, was exhibited at the N.E.A.C. in 1906.

EXHIB N.E.A.C. Summer 1910

1527★ Duke of Westminster Divorced 1919

The title is a pasted-on cutting from 'The Times' of 18 June 1919, which goes on: 'THE QUESTION OF DESERTION. Counsel cited · and discussed on this point . . . Sickert v. Sickert (1899).' W. S., labelled The Man who Turned the Scale, stands in a bare studio, where he has been interrupted in painting a picture of a jug and basin on a wash-hand stand. On the wall are three framed texts: [EX]EGI MONUMENTUM ETC; NOT MARBLE NOR THE GILDED ETC; NOT FOR AN AGE BUT ETC. *He is approached on one side by the Duke, saying* 'How can we ever thank you enough?' *and on the other by the Duchess, saying:* 'But for YOU –'. *Sickert's divorce in 1899 produced a new legal definition of 'Constructive Desertion', from which the Duke benefited.*

OWNER University of Texas

1528★ The Old and the Young Self 1924

Old Self: 'No, you didn't think you were going to become a Master and an Oracle, did you? You thought Jimmy Whistler was the last of the Oracles and Masters, didn't you, hein, p'tit imbécile?'

EXHIB L.G. 1925, 1952 and 1957
REPRO *Observations*, 1925
OWNER Lord Cottesloe

1529 Walter Sickert, Lion-Sentimentale, with his tear-provoking ditty 'Jack Gibson'. Now appearing in *The Times,* **daily** [1925]

Like the subject of his picture 'Le Lion Comique', W. S. stands on a music-hall stage in seedy evening dress. He is singing:

Then say, was he a sculptor?
 Had he a sculptor's heart?
By acting in this manner, did
 He play the sculptor's part?
It was his earnest wish
 To perpetuate his Queen –
Shan't his and her dear memories
 Be kept for ever green?

On 3 and 7 Jan 1925 'The Times' published letters from W. S. protesting against the plan to remove the statue of

Queen Victoria by John Gibson (1790–1866) from the Prince's Chamber in the House of Lords, to make way for a war memorial. The second one runs: 'Sir, your beautiful illustration of the gracious and touching contemporary monument to Queen Victoria expresses, with an eloquence that no words can reach, the respectful and loyal prayer that his Majesty may see fit to withdraw his consent to its removal.' *Lord Beauchamp and Hamo Thornycroft agreed, but Lord Curzon defended the plan at portentous length. The statue is still in its original place, though the flanking symbolic figures of Justice and Clemency have been removed.*

EXHIB L.G. 1957
OWNER R. A. Bevan

1530★ Walt Sickert [etc, as in 1529 n.d.]

Almost identical with 1529, except for the alignment of the song, in which 'sculptor' is each time 'bungler'.

OWNER Reresby Sitwell

1531 [Mr Walter Sickert]

EXHIB L.G. 1928

1532★ [Untitled] 1929

Pasted-on cutting from 'The Sunday Times' of 3 Nov 1929: 'Some, no doubt, will object that the features of Lazarus are not clearly indicated; but Mr Sickert seems to have embarked on a campaign recently to prove that faces do not matter. And there is a good deal to be said for this point of view. Why should the spectator concentrate his attention on a face when' *etc. etc.*

Richter Waltard, to Lazarus: 'That's all right! Go on! The face doesn't matter.'

A faceless Sickert provides food for a faceless Lazarus. On the wall a faceless portrait hangs crookedly. The reference is to S's picture 'Lazarus breaks his fast'.

EXHIB L.G. 1952
OWNER University of Texas

1533★ 'Walter Sickert and other august elders' (Tonks, MacColl, Furse and Steer are the 'elders') [n.d.]

The title is taken from Max's story 'Enoch Soames' ('Seven Men', 1919, p. 5) and the drawing was intended for the N.Y. edition but not used. See also 1842–60.

EXHIB Grolier 1944
REPRO **Plate 66**
OWNER University of Texas

1534 [Untitled n.d.]

Six heads of W. S.

OWNER Sold at Christie's 24 Jun 1949

1535★ 'Never morbid' [n.d.]

Dressed as sailor on the pier at Dieppe

REPRO Simona Pakenham, *Pigtails and Pernod*, 1961
OWNER Simona Pakenham

1536* **Un dandy singulier** [n.d.]
Wearing a bowler hat and a check suit much too big for him. Title is newspaper-cutting pasted on.
OWNER British Museum (Prints and Drawings)

1537* **Il est avec Whistler le peintre de la nuit** [n.d.]
W. S. and Whistler creeping out at dead of night with a dark lantern. Title is newspaper-cutting pasted on.
REPRO James Thorpe, *English Illustration: the Nineties*, 1935
OWNER British Museum (Prints and Drawings)

1538* **Lit avec délices Martial dans le texte** [n.d.]
Deep in a book. Behind him on a shelf are a gradus, Smith's Latin-English Dictionary, Public School Primer etc. Title is newspaper-cutting pasted on.
OWNER British Museum (Prints and Drawings)

1539* **Les visiteurs, au premier aspect, sont déconcertés par l'uniformité des tons noirâtres répandus dans ses toiles** [n.d.]
Bearded gentlemen gesticulating, and a lady swooning, before three of W. S.'s dark-toned canvases. Title is newspaper-cutting pasted on.
OWNER British Museum (Prints and Drawings)

1540* **[Untitled Unsigned n.d.]**
A slim dandy, in frock-coat, carrying a rolled umbrella, his face almost obscured by large top hat.
OWNER Art Gallery of New South Wales, Sydney

ELIZABETH SIDDAL
1833–62   Wife of D. G. Rossetti
See 1270, 1271, 1279

ARTHUR SIDGWICK
1840–1920   Greek scholar

1541* **Mr Sidgwick as represented in Corpus Coll** [n.d.]
O formose senex nimium ne crede libellis
Non sic Parnassum tangere tu poteris !
[Put not too much trust in your writings, fair old man; not thus will you manage to attain Parnassus !]
The first line is partly a play on Virgil, Eclogues II, 17, with 'puer' (boy) changed to 'senex' (old man). A. S. stands on one foot on a peak whose name has been changed from Parnassus to Corpus. An undergraduate drawing.
OWNER Merton College, Oxford

S. H. SIME
1867–1941   Artist

1542* **Mr Sime** [1900]
Seated at table
REPRO *Idler*, Aug 1900

SIR JOHN SIMON
1873–1954   Lawyer and Liberal politician

1543* **Sir John Simon** 1932
EXHIB L.G. 1952
OWNER All Souls College, Oxford

G. R. SIMS
1847–1922   Journalist and author
See also 386

1544* **[Untitled 1903]**
Standing, hands in pockets, beside a bulldog.
REPRO *John Bull*, 5 Nov 1903

OSBERT SITWELL
1892–1969   Poet and writer

1545* **Mr Osbert, and Mr Sacheverell, Sitwell** 1923
Side by side, in evening dress, leaning against a table. Each holds a parrot: O's is saying 'Bravo, Sacheverell!' and S's 'Well done, Osbert!'
EXHIB L.G. 1923
REPRO *Things New and Old*, 1923
OWNER Reresby Sitwell

1546* **Mr Osbert and Mr Sacheverell Sitwell**
Three-quarter face, heads and shoulders against a dark background.
EXHIB L.G. 1925
REPRO *Observations*, 1925
OWNER Reresby Sitwell

1547 **Mr Osbert and Mr Sacheverell Sitwell**
A copy by Max of 1546.
OWNER Sir Sacheverell Sitwell Bart

1548* **[Untitled n.d.]**
For O and S from M
Pencil sketch for 1546.
REPRO John Lehmann, *A Nest of Tigers*, 1968
OWNER Reresby Sitwell

1549★ 'Talis Amyclaeos non junxit gratia fratres'
[No such grace united the Amyclaean brothers, i.e.
Castor and Pollux] 1925
EXHIB L.G. 1952 and 1957
REPRO **Plate 47**

1550★ [Untitled] 1930
'Is it a purblind prank, O think you,
    Friend with the musing eye
    Who watch us stepping by?'
(Thomas Hardy's 'Song of the Soldiers', September
1914)
*O. S. stands watching as a procession of eminent
Victorians file past.*
REPRO Margaret Barton and Osbert Sitwell, *Victoriana*, 1931
OWNER Reresby Sitwell

SACHEVERELL SITWELL
b. 1897   Poet and writer
See 1545-9

OTIS SKINNER
1858–1942   American actor

1551 [Otis Skinner]
OWNER Private (Yale)

F. E. SMITH
1872–1930   Lawyer and Conservative politician
See also 71, 335, 365, 672, 1443

1552★ Mr F. E. Smith 1907
*Sitting on a low stool, very high collar, hands clasped
round leg.*
EXHIB Carfax 1907
REPRO *A Book of Caricatures*, 1907

1553★ [Mr F. E. Smith, K.C., M.P.]
Three-quarter-length profile, facing left.
EXHIB L.G. 1911
REPRO *Daily Mail*, 22 Apr 1911

1554 [F. E., K. C., M.P., P.C. 1912]
EXHIB L.G. 1952, where dated as above

1555★ [Untitled] 1912
*Reclining on a bench in the House of Commons, wearing
top hat.*
REPRO *Bystander*, 15 May 1912

LOGAN PEARSALL SMITH
1865–1946   American writer
See also 612, 703, 1839

**1556★ The author of 'Trivia' submitting his latest
MS to the conductors of 'The London Mercury'**
1921
*He is handing a minute scrap of paper to J. C. Squire,
while Edward Shanks stands by.*
EXHIB L.G. May 1921
REPRO *A Survey*, 1921

LEONARD SMITHERS
1861–1907   Publisher

1557★ [Untitled Unsigned 1947]
Head and shoulders, sent by Max to owner in Sep 1947.
REPRO *London Magazine*, Sep 1956
OWNER Sir John Betjeman

PHILIP SNOWDEN
1864–1937   Socialist politician
See 1749, 1750

ALEC SORBE

1558 Mr Alec Sorbe [n.d.]
*Known only from Winifred A. Myers catalogue 382,
1955.*

JOHN PHILIP SOUSA
1854–1932   American composer and bandmaster

1559★ Mr Sousa [c. 1902]
Back view, head in profile, conducting.
EXHIB L.G. 1957
REPRO *Artist*, Feb 1902
OWNER Alan Bott

MARQUIS LUIS DE SOVERAL
1862–1922   Portuguese Ambassador in London
1897–1910
See also 335, 514, 515, 1423, 1443

1560★ M. de Soveral [1899]
Standing in frock-coat and top hat in front of a railing.
REPRO *Butterfly*, Jan 1900

1561★ M. de Soveral [1900]

Sitting in an armchair in evening dress.

REPRO *World*, Christmas No, 1900
OWNER Sold at Sotheby's 26 Apr 1972

1562 [Marquis de Soveral 1901]

EXHIB Carfax 1901

1563★ [The Eloquence of the Backs of Necks Unsigned c. 1903]

Eight heads, in each of which the face is lightly pencilled in, and the back of the head more firmly delineated. The heads are of Soveral, Kipling, Lord Halsbury, Sir William Harcourt, King Edward VII, Hall Caine, Joseph Chamberlain and Rostand.

REPRO *Cassell's Magazine*, Feb 1903, where captioned as above

1564★ [Untitled 1903]

Full-length profile facing left, right hand extended.

REPRO *John Bull*, 8 Apr 1903

1565★ Tout passe. The Marquis de Soveral standing on the site once occupied by the statue of John Brown, and meditating [1907]

EXHIB Carfax 1907
REPRO *Daily Mirror*, 20 Apr 1907
OWNER Mrs David Karmel

1566★ [Untitled Unsigned 1907]

[Unlike Wilkes, who was only half-an-hour behind the handsomest man in Europe, M. de Soveral is usually a minute or two ahead of him. By 'Ruth']
Standing, elegant in evening dress, beside a tall column. For explanation of the signature, see note to 1485.

REPRO *Vanity Fair*, 2 Oct 1907, where captioned as above; *A Book of Caricatures*, 1907

1567★ [Untitled] 1908

S and two other Ambassadors: Mensdorff and Benckendorff.

EXHIB Carfax 1908, where catalogued as 'A Triad'
OWNER Malcolm Borthwick

1568★ [Untitled Unsigned n.d.]

Rough pencil sketch for 1567

OWNER University of Texas

1569 [M. de Soveral]

EXHIB L.G. 1928

1570★ Another Memory for Ralph Wood 1944

'We think he's so very handsome' (Queen Mary)
Full length, evening dress, opera hat in right hand.

OWNER Ernest Ruffer

1571★ Monsieur de Soveral [n.d.]

Very similar to 1570, but no opera hat

EXHIB L.G. 1952
OWNER Anthony Powell

1572 [M. de Soveral in the afternoon]

EXHIB L.G. 1957

1573★ Marquis de Soveral 'Near the Rose' [n.d.]

Half-length, day clothes.

OWNER Miss Olga Lely

1574★ Soveral [n.d.]

Half-length profile facing left.

EXHIB Grolier 1944
OWNER Harvard College Library

E. F. SPENCE
1860–1932   Lawyer and writer

1575★ Mr Spence [n.d.]

REPRO *Folio Society Journal*, no 11, 1962

THE FIFTH EARL SPENCER
1835–1910   Politician and viceroy

1576★ [Untitled 1895]

REPRO *Pick-Me-Up*, 9 Mar 1895; *Max's Nineties*, 1958

THE SIXTH EARL SPENCER
1857–1922   Lord Chamberlain
See also 114, 612, 679, 1443

1577★ Lord Althorp [n.d.]

Full-length profile facing left, collar up to chin.

OWNER Picadilly Gallery

1578★ Lord Althorp [1907]

Full length, three-quarter face, collar up to moustache.

EXHIB Carfax 1907
REPRO *A Book of Caricatures*, 1907

1579★ Lord Althorp 1908

Full length, full face, collar up to chin.

REPRO *Observer*, 4 Dec 1966
OWNER Malcolm Borthwick

1580★ Lord Spencer 1912

Full-length profile. The collar reaches to the top of the head, and has holes cut to see through. Cf. 114.

EXHIB L.G. May 1921

SPENCER (continued)

REPRO *A Survey*, 1921, where captioned 'Lord Spencer, still seeing'
OWNER Miss Joan Wilson

1581 [Lord Spencer]
EXHIB L.G. 1945 (Guedalla)

HERBERT SPENCER
1820–1903 Philosopher
See 595

SIR EDGAR SPEYER
1862–1932 Pioneer of electric railways and patron of the arts
See also 1083

1582★ Insatiate. Sir Edgar Speyer strenuously planning ways to a yet wider control of our traction 1913
He is considering a bath-chair, a perambulator and a toy horse.
EXHIB L.G. 1913
REPRO *Fifty Caricatures*, 1913

'SPY' (LESLIE WARD)
1851–1922 Caricaturist

1583★ 'Spy' [c. 1894]
EXHIB L.G. 1928, where dated as above
OWNER Keith Mackenzie

J. C. SQUIRE
1884–1958 Poet and critic
See 616, 1556

H. M. STANLEY
1841–1904 Explorer

1584★ Sir H. M. Stanley [1897]
EXHIB L.G. 1928, where dated as above
OWNER National Portrait Gallery

PHILIP WILSON STEER
1860–1942 Painter
See also 614, 615, 679, 1054, 1423, 1434, 1443, 1533

1585★ Mr P. W. Steer, prospecting – and the landscape beginning to fidget under his scrutiny [1904]
EXHIB Carfax 1904; New York 1912; L.G. 1945 (Guedalla)
REPRO *Caricatures by Max*, 1958
OWNER Ashmolean Museum, Oxford

1586★ [The N.E.A.C. 1906 Vanity Fair]
Title and date are in the hand of Albert Rutherston. Steer sits in the middle, and round him are grouped Sickert, Orpen, Conder, Augustus John, MacColl, Tonks, Will Rothenstein, Roger Fry, L. A. Harrison, Walter Russell, and Albert Rutherston.
EXHIB L.G. 1957
REPRO *A Book of Caricatures*, 1907
OWNER Sir John Rothenstein

1587★ N.E.A.C. 1907
Revised version of 1586. Conder and Fry are replaced by W. G. de Glehn and Sargent. The long necks of Tonks and MacColl now form an arch over Steer.
EXHIB L.G. 1911 and 1952
REPRO L.G. 1957 catalogue (in error for 1586)
OWNER Tate Gallery

1588★ [Untitled Unsigned n.d.]
Rough and torn sketch for 1587, with the arched necks, but with characters of 1586.
OWNER University of Texas

1589★ Chelsea, and Mr Steer, by moonlight 1907
EXHIB Carfax 1907; L.G. 1952
REPRO *A Book of Caricatures*, 1907
OWNER Piccadilly Gallery

1590 Mr P. Wilson Steer [n.d.]
Full face, three-quarter-length.
EXHIB L.G. 1911
OWNER Christopher Medley

1591★ Annual Banquet. A suggestion to the New English Art Club 1913
Steer stands to read his speech. On his right are seated the Prince of Wales, Sickert, Asquith and Augustus John; on his left the Archbishop of Canterbury (Davidson), Tonks, the Duke of Argyll and Walter Russell.
EXHIB L.G. 1913
REPRO *Fifty Caricatures*, 1913
OWNER Tate Gallery

1592★ Mr Wilson Steer [n.d.]
Very similar to 1590.
OWNER Piccadilly Gallery

G. W. STEEVENS
1869–1900 Journalist and writer

OWNER Picadilly Gallery
1593★ **Mr G. W. Steevens** [n.d.]

COUNT STANISLAUS ERIC STENBOCK
1860–95   Swedish poet and eccentric

1594★ **Count Stenbok** [n.d.]
OWNER Picadilly Gallery

SIR HERBERT STEPHEN
1857–1932   Lawyer

1595★ **Sir Herbert Stephen, talking enthusiastically**
[1907]
EXHIB Carfax 1907; L.G. 1911
REPRO *A Book of Caricatures*, 1907

JAMES STEPHENS
1882–1950   Irish poet

1596★ **A Master of Speech – a Lord of Language – but a Poet** 1930
Max to J. S.
OWNER Mrs Iris Wise

1597★ [**Untitled Unsigned** n.d.]
EXHIB   Achenbach 1964
REPRO   **Plate 45**
OWNER U.C.L.A. (Clark)

ROBERT LOUIS STEVENSON
1850–94   Poet and writer

1598★ **R. L. S. – W. E. H. 'Out, out, brief candle'**
[Macbeth, V, 5] [1901]
A small W. E. Henley attempting to extinguish the flame of a large candle bearing R. L. S.'s features. Refers to H's attack on S in the 'Pall Mall Magazine' of Dec 1901, and probably replaced an idea that Max described in a letter to Robert Ross, of 'Henley as Brutus, in the tent-scene of Julius Caesar, *with R. L. S. as the ghost, and Whibley as the sleeping Lucius'.*
EXHIB   Carfax 1901
REPRO   *Tatler*, 4 Dec 1901

1599★ **Revisiting the Glimpses** 1911
Shade of R. L. S.: 'And now that you have shown me the new preachers and politicians, show me some of the men of letters.'

Mr Gosse: 'But, my dear Louis, these *are* the men o letters.'
The authors, tub-thumping and orating in all directions, are Cunninghame Graham, Wells, Chesterton, Galsworthy, Shaw, Zangwill, Hewlett, Belloc, and Kipling.
EXHIB   L.G. 1911 and 1952
REPRO   *Illustrated London News*, 10 May 1952
OWNER Robert H. Taylor

L. M. STEWART
Charterhouse master
See 664, 665

THE HON. HARRY STONOR
1859–1939   Courtier

1600 [**Mr Harry Stonor** 1909]
EXHIB N.E.A.C. Winter 1909

1601 **Mr Harry Stonor** 1912
EXHIB   L.G. 1928
OWNER Lord Camoys

LYTTON STRACHEY
1880–1932   Writer
See also 614–616

1602★ **Mr Lytton Strachey trying hard to see her with Lord Melbourne's eyes** November 1920
In the L.G. catalogue Max added an asterisk after 'hard' and a footnote: '– and contriving – M. B. 1921', when L. S.'s 'Queen Victoria' was published.
EXHIB   L.G. May 1921
REPRO   *A Survey*, 1921
OWNER National Gallery of Victoria, Melbourne

1603★ **Echo** 1923
'Why, Uncle Lytton, oh why . . .'
An echo of 37, and a similar design.
EXHIB   L.G. 1923 and 1957
REPRO   *Things New and Old*, 1923
OWNER City Art Gallery, Birmingham

1604★ **Lytton Strachey** [c. 1925]
Three-quarter-length profile, facing left.
EXHIB   L.G. 1925 and 1957
REPRO   *Observations*, 1925
OWNER Ashmolean Museum, Oxford

1605★ **Mr Belloc on British Literature** October 1927
Title pasted on from newspaper, above the following:

'We had two men carrying on the traditions of English prose – Sir Edmund Gosse and Dr Inge – and two others who were doing good constructive prose were Mr Max Beerbohm and Mr Strachey, but they were not recognised as national figures.'

[L. S.:] 'Belloc says we are not recognised as national figures'
[Max:] 'Roman Catholics will say anything'

EXHIB L.G. 1952
REPRO *Bandwagon*, Jun 1952
OWNER Yale University Library

1606* **L. S. A The Prince of Prose-Writers** [1929]
EXHIB L.G. 1952
REPRO *Manchester Guardian*, 30 Mar 1929; **Plate 42**

1607* **Mr Lytton Strachey** 1931
Sitting on edge of hard chair, legs crossed, holding a tiny cup of tea.
EXHIB L.G. 1952 and 1957
OWNER Joseph Scott-Plummer

1608 [**Mr Lytton Strachey** 1931]
EXHIB L.G. 1952, where dated as above

WILLIAM STRANG
1859–1921   Painter and etcher

1609 [**Mr William Strang** 1907]
EXHIB Carfax 1907

EUGENE STRATTON
1861–1918   Music-hall singer
See 1307

G. S. STREET
1867–1936   Journalist and writer
See also 335, 614

1610* **Garge Ztreet** 1901
Full length as country bumpkin, in smock, gaiters and wide hat. A foaming tankard in right hand, cart-whip in left.
OWNER Piccadilly Gallery

[**Untitled** 1903]
A series of six numbered drawings occasioned by an article by G. S. S. in the 'Quarterly Review' of May

1903, *in which he defended his move from London to Brighton. Each drawing has an appropriate text from the article:*

1611* I. 'As for living in the provinces nowadays, we(!) think a cultivated and thoughtful man is to be congratulated on the fact'
Shows G. S. S. on the front at Brighton.

1612* II. 'Only very exceptional circumstances can prevent his visiting . . . his intellectual peers'
[*Maid, carrying G. S. S.'s card with Brighton address:*] 'Mr Street is below, Sir'
[*Max, in armchair:*] 'Not at home'

1613 III. [*missing*]

1614* IV. 'and the thought of his age is easily accessible in print'
G. S. S. reading the 'Daily Mail' in a draught

1615* V. 'He is no more apart from the movement or the crisis of his day than the man in the city.'
[*G. S. S., speaking into primitive telephone:*] 'On no account, Arthur, must you remit the Corn Tax. It would be a confession of weakness.'
[*Arthur Balfour, the Prime Minister:*] 'Oh George, do you really mean that? Very well. I leave myself entirely in your hands.'

1616* VI. 'And he has readier to his sympathies the homely humanising interests and anxieties of common life outside his own house.'
G. S. S. with flashy Brighton riff-raff.
OWNER Stephen Greene (all five)

[**Untitled** c. 1903]
A series of seven numbered drawings, as follows:

1617* 1. George dreams that he will some day meet a Russian Prince
The Prince, tall, imposing and richly dressed, towers above the sleeping G. S. S.

1618* 2. George's dream is fulfilled – in the foyer of His Majesty's Theatre. Tuesday, December 29th, 1903
G. S. S., bowing low, is introduced by a super-elegant Max to a very ordinary-looking Prince.

1619* 3. George's rage and anguish on hearing that it wasn't a Russian Prince at all.
Stamping on his top hat and weeping.

1620* 4. George is assured that it *was* a Russian Prince . . . But how is he to know?
[*Max, to a stern-faced G. S. S.:*] 'No but *really* . . . really and *truly* . . . Oh George, do listen . . . I'm

so sorry, so ashamed, dear George . . . I didn't know how much it meant to you . . . I never again will jest on sacred subjects . . . It *really* was a *real live* Prince – a cousin of Tolstoi, the Johnny that writes those novels . . . etc, etc.'

1621* 5. George is somewhat comforted, at the Hôtel Metropole, by [A. B.] Walkley's demonstration that the joke (if joke it was) does not conform with the rules laid down by Aristotle περὶ τοῦ γελοίου (Walkley retires to his bedroom and dreams that he himself will one day meet a Russian Prince)
A. B. W. and G. S. S. sitting at table.

1622* 6. But the comfort passes; and George, inwardly lacerated by the eternal doubt whether it *was* a Russian Prince or not, pines slowly and surely away.
G. S. S., very thin, broods in an armchair.

1623* 7. *Labuntur anni*; and we (the Prince and I), who were young and careless, become old and crabbed; yet never, year after year, do we leave unpaid our visit, on the anniversary of George's demise, to the little cemetery in Kemp Town.
Hand in hand a stout elderly whiskered Max and an aged Prince, both in top hats and overcoats, carry wreaths inscribed HAD HE BUT KNOWN *and* TO THE GREAT COMMONER *towards a tombstone engraved* IN MEMORIAM G. S. STREET. 'PUT NOT YOUR TRUST IN PRINCES'.
REPRO (2) D'Offay Couper catalogue, Oct 1968
OWNER D'Offay Couper Gallery

1624 **'What ails us to fear overmeasure?' George Street 1 a.m.** 1907
'The implacable beautiful tyrant' still going on with his recitation.
'Wilt thou smile as a woman disdaining
⠀⠀The light fire in the veins of a boy?
But he comes to thee sad, without feigning,
⠀⠀Who has wearied of sorrow and joy;
Less careful of labour and glory
⠀⠀Than the elders whose hair has uncurled,
And young, but with fancies as hoary
⠀⠀And grey as the world.'
G. S. S. huge in evening dress, with cigar, reciting on sofa with Marjorie Battine, who is bored and languid. All the quotations are from Swinburne's 'Dolores'.
OWNER Dr I. O. Macaulay

1625* **Mr William Toynbee and Mr G. S. Street deploring the twentieth, and the latter part of the nineteenth, century** 1908
A large piece has been torn off the corner.
EXHIB Carfax 1908
OWNER University of Texas

1626* **[Untitled Unsigned** n.d.]
Outline pencil sketch for 1625.
OWNER University of Texas

1627* **[Untitled Unsigned** n.d.]
Another pencil sketch for 1625, with the position of the figures transposed.
OWNER University of Texas

1628* **Mr G. S. Street** 1910
Three-quarter face, head and shoulders, facing left.
EXHIB L.G. 1911
OWNER Piccadilly Gallery

1629 **A Dulcified Autocracy** 1913
Mr G. S. Street (to the Tsar): 'Aha! Wouldn't *you* like to have a colleague, and all responsibility taken by a nice Lord Chamberlain?'
G. S. S. had just been appointed Joint-Reader of Plays to the Lord Chamberlain.
OWNER Athenaeum Club

1630* **G. S. S. 'Alone with God'** [n.d.]
G. S. S., sitting nervously on the edge of a chair and holding his bowler hat, faces the terrifying figure of a heavily bearded God, who is saying: 'Have you seen Mr Girdlestone lately?' F. K. W. Girdlestone was Max's and G. S. S.'s house-master at Charterhouse.
EXHIB L.G. 1945 (Guedalla)
OWNER Ashmolean Museum, Oxford

1631* **Mr George Street** [n.d.]
Full-length profile facing right, holding pint-sized glass to his mouth.
OWNER Mrs Eva Reichmann

1632* **[Untitled Unsigned** n.d.]
Three-quarter-length profile facing left, in evening dress, lighted cigar in right hand. Another, almost full-face, head of G. S. S. below. Titled 'George Street' in another hand.
OWNER Douglass Debevoise

STIRLING STUART-CRAWFORD
See 823, 824

HOWARD OVERING STURGIS
1855–1920 Writer

1633* **Mr Howard Sturgess** [n.d.]
OWNER Mrs Clarissa Higginbotham

THE HON. HUMPHREY STURT
See Lord Alington

THE FIFTH LORD SUFFIELD
1830–1914   Courtier

1634   **Lord Suffield** 1911
EXHIB   L.G. 1928
OWNER   Maxwell Halliday

SIR ARTHUR SULLIVAN
1842–1900   Composer

1635   [**Sir Arthur Sullivan** c. 1896]
EXHIB   L.G. 1928, where dated as above

1636★   **Sir Arthur Sullivan** [n.d.]
REPRO   **Plate 28**
OWNER   Mrs M. E. Yates

MILLICENT DUCHESS OF SUTHERLAND
1867–1955   Wife of the fourth Duke
See 1366

ALFRED SUTRO
1863–1933   Playwright
See also 335, 679, 769, 1443

1637★   [**Mr Alfred Sutro** 1907]
Tiny body, huge pear-shaped head. Large cigar in hand.
EXHIB   Carfax 1907
REPRO   *Daily Mirror*, 20 Apr 1907

1638   [**Mr Alfred Sutro**]
EXHIB   L.G. 1957

1639★   [**Untitled Unsigned** n.d.]
Full-length profile facing left, tiny body, large forward-jutting head. On verso four full-face heads of A. S., the last one turning into a mouse.
OWNER   University of Texas

1640★   [**Untitled Unsigned** n.d.]
Tiny body and huge full-face head.
OWNER   University of Texas

SIR FRANK SWETTENHAM
1850–1946   Proconsul and writer
See also 612, 679

1641★   **Sir Frank Swettenham** 1914
EXHIB   L.G. May 1921
OWNER   Robert Beloe

ALGERNON CHARLES SWINBURNE
1837–1909   Poet
See also 281, 595, 838, 857, 858, 1268, 1275, 1276, 1281-3, 1744, 1829

1642★   **Mr Swinburne** June 1899
EXHIB   L.G. 1945 (Guedalla)
REPRO   **Plate 44**
OWNER   Mrs Philip Guedalla

1643★   **Riverside Scene. Algernon Swinburne taking his great new friend Gosse to see Gabriel Rossetti** 1916
EXHIB   Grosvenor 1917; L.G. Sept 1921
REPRO   *Rossetti and his Circle*, 1922
OWNER   Tate Gallery

1644★   **2 The Pines** 1921
Believed to be Max's only etching, this shows A. C. S. (back view) and Watts-Dunton (profile) in front of a book-lined wall. On the mount Max wrote 12 copies No. . . .
EXHIB   L.G. 1957
OWNER   No 1 Ronald Searle; No 5 Sir Rupert Hart-Davis; No 7 Merton College, Oxford

1645★   **No 2 The Pines** [1926]
Max lunching with A. C. S. and Watts-Dunton, as in Max's essay in 'And Even Now', 1920.
EXHIB   L.G. 1928, where dated as above

1646★   **Sophia** 1928
For Philip
In 'Bonnet and Shawl', 1928, Philip Guedalla included a brief imaginary account of A. C. S. marrying a barmaid called Sophia. The drawing shows her big and beautiful behind the bar, across which a tiny A. C. S. greets her over his half-pint of beer.
EXHIB   L.G. 1945 (Guedalla)
OWNER   Mrs Philip Guedalla

1647★   **At the Pines** [n.d.]
A. C. S. and Watts-Dunton standing before a large Pre-Raphaelite portrait.
EXHIB   L.G. 1945 (Guedalla) and 1952
REPRO   *Caricatures by Max*, 1958
OWNER   Ashmolean Museum, Oxford

G. S. C. SWINTON
1859–1937   Lyon King of Arms

1648* **Captain Swinton** 1907

REPRO *A Book of Caricatures*, 1907
OWNER Robert Beloe

1649 **[Captain Swinton]**

EXHIB L.G. 1911

ARTHUR SYMONS
1865–1945   Poet and critic

1650* **Some Persons of 'the Nineties' little**
imagining, despite their Proper Pride and Ornamental Aspect, how much they will interest Mr Holbrook Jackson and Mr Osbert Burdett 1925

A. S. prominent in foreground. Also present, Le Gallienne, Sickert, George Moore, John Davidson, Henry Harland, Conder, Oscar Wilde, Will Rothenstein, Max, Yeats, Beardsley, and (just showing) perhaps Enoch Soames. Jackson's 'The Eighteen Nineties' appeared in 1913, Burdett's 'The Beardsley Period' in 1925.

EXHIB L.G. 1925, 1945 (Guedalla), 1952 and 1957
REPRO *Observations*, 1925; *Caricatures by Max*, 1958
OWNER Ashmolean Museum, Oxford

T

ROBERT TABER
1866–1904   Actor

1651* **Robert Taber** [n.d.]

OWNER Mrs Eva Reichmann

RABINDRANATH TAGORE
1861–1941   Indian poet
See also 1311

1652* **[A recollection of Rabindranath Tagore and Bernard Shaw, at the Hyde Park Hotel, on an afternoon in 1931]**

For East is East and West is West,
And ~~never~~ the twain shall meet
        [Kipling, 'The Ballad of East and West']

EXHIB L.G. 1952
REPRO *Sketch*, 7 May 1952

THE REV. J. A. A. TAIT
Charterhouse master
See 664, 665

THE FIRST DUKE OF TECK
1837–1900   Father of Queen Mary
See 473

PRINCE FRANCIS OF TECK
1870–1910   Soldier

1653 **Prince Francis of Teck laying the ghost of the Venetian Republic** 1908

He is looking out of a (presumably Venetian) window.

EXHIB Carfax 1908
OWNER Ford Motor Company

FREDERICK TEMPLE
1821–1902   Archbishop of Canterbury
See 478

REGINALD TEMPLE
1868–1953

1654* **Mr Reginald Temple** 1908

OWNER Piccadilly Gallery

1655 **Reginald Temple** [n.d.]

OWNER Sir Richard Temple Bart

ALFRED TENNYSON
1809–92   Poet Laureate
See also 595

1656★ **Mr Tennyson reading 'In Memoriam' to his Sovereign** 1904

For Nicholsons, William and Mabel [*on mount*]

REPRO *The Poets' Corner*, 1904 and 1943
OWNER Robert H. Taylor

1657★ **Woolner at Farringford, 1857** 1917

Mrs Tennyson: 'You know, Mr Woolner, I'm the most un-meddlesome of women, but – when (I'm only asking) *when* do you begin modelling his halo?'

Woolner's bust of T is now in Trinity College, Cambridge.

EXHIB L.G. Sept 1921
REPRO *Rossetti and his Circle*, 1922
OWNER Tate Gallery

BRANDON THOMAS
1857–1914   Actor and playwright

1658★ **Mr Brandon Thomas** [c. 1898]

EXHIB Carfax 1901; L.G. 1928, where dated as above
REPRO Jevan Brandon-Thomas, *Charley's Aunt's Father*, 1955
OWNER Jevan Brandon-Thomas

DAVID CROAL THOMSON
1855–1930   Art expert and writer
See 679

LORD ALEXANDER THYNNE
1873–1918   Soldier and Conservative M.P.

1659★ **Lord Alexander Thynne enchanting the Labour Party** 1913

EXHIB L.G. 1913
REPRO *Fifty Caricatures*, 1913
OWNER Mark Birley

LITTLE TICH
1868–1928   Music-hall comedian
See also 386

1660 **[Little Tich]**

OWNER Sold at Sotheby's 26 Apr 1961

JAMES TIMEWELL
1857–1926   Fabian Socialist tailor
See 1482

A. H. TOD
Charterhouse master
See 664, 664A

LEO TOLSTOY
1828–1910   Russian writer
See 1484

HENRY TONKS
1862–1937   Painter and teacher
See also 614, 615, 679, 1054, 1443, 1533, 1586-8, 1591

1661★ **Mr Tonks** [n.d.]

Half-length, full face, very long neck.

EXHIB L.G. 1911
OWNER Piccadilly Gallery

1662★ **Tonkscape by Max. Landscape by C. Conder** [n.d.]

Head and shoulders, profile facing left, by Max. Two little models and an easel, the second part of the title, and probably Tonks's hand, by Charles Conder. Cf. 36.

OWNER The Hon Mrs Lyle

JOHN TOOLE
1832–1906   Actor
See 1781

PAOLO TOSTI
1846–1916   Italian composer and pianist
See also 1423

1663★ **Signor Tosti** [1907]

Full length, three-quarter face, holding a lighted cigar.

EXHIB L.G. 1952
REPRO *A Book of Caricatures*, 1907
OWNER Lady Beddington-Behrens

1663A **[Signor Tosti** 1908]

EXHIB Carfax 1908; L.G. 1928

1664★ **[An Audition, or, Les Chanteurs au Salon]** 1908.

Shows a tiny Tosti at the piano, smoking a cigar. Behind are grouped the singers Edouard de Reszke, Mario Sammarco, and Antonio Scotti. On each side a stout female lay-figure listening. In the foreground a stout tenor singing. The title has been added in another hand. See also 1963.

REPRO John Russell, *From Sickert to 1948*, 1948
OWNER British Museum (Prints & Drawings)

1665★ [Untitled Unsigned n.d.]
Sketch for 1664. Slightly different grouping, and without Sammarco.
OWNER Roy Huss

1666★ [Untitled Unsigned n.d.]
Another rough sketch for 1664, with all its characters, also another singer and a stout lady sketched in at back.
OWNER University of Texas

1667★ [Untitled Unsigned n.d.]
Rough pen-and-ink sketch of T playing piano on high stool and smoking cigar. Another sketch for 1664, with vague outlines of tenor and females.
OWNER Sir Rupert Hart-Davis

WILLIAM TOYNBEE
1849–1942 Writer
See 1625-7

H. D. TRAILL
1842–1900 Journalist and author

1668★ Mr H. D. Traill [1898]
Full-length profile facing right, holding cigarette.
REPRO *Sketch*, 18 May 1898
OWNER Victoria & Albert Museum

1669★ Mr H. D. Traill [n.d.]
Full length, full face, hands in trouser pockets.
OWNER Mrs Eva Reichmann

HERBERT BEERBOHM TREE
1853–1917 Actor-manager. Max's half-brother

1670★ Herbert Beerbohm Tree by H. M. Beerbohm November 1893
Full length, head in profile facing left, small bowler hat, right hand raised to chin, left holding stick on ground.
OWNER Peter Lister

1671★ Mr Beerbohm Tree [1895]
Full length, head in profile facing left, top hat, stick in left hand.
EXHIB F.A.S. 1896
REPRO *Savoy*, Jan 1896; *Twenty-Five Gentlemen*, 1896

1671A★ Mr Beerbohm Tree 1898
To Bobbie [Robert Ross] some days after his birthday '98
Full length, right hand scratching head, left hand on hip.
OWNER Mrs George Hayes

1672 [Mr Herbert Beerbohm Tree 1901]
EXHIB Carfax 1901

1673★ [Untitled 1903]
Full-length back view. Stick in right hand, letters falling from top hat in left, overcoat pockets stuffed with documents.
REPRO *John Bull*, 25 Jun 1903

1674★ Mr H. Beerbohm Tree 1908
Full length, three-quarter face to left, evening dress, left hand behind head.
EXHIB Carfax 1908; L.G. 1911
REPRO *Graphic*, 29 Apr 1911

1675★ [Untitled Unsigned n.d.]
Three-quarter length outline drawing. Pose almost identical with that of 1674. Perhaps a sketch for it.
EXHIB L.G. 1945 (Guedalla)
OWNER Ashmolean Museum, Oxford

1675A [Untitled] 1909
Back view of H. B. T. and Max.
OWNER Mrs Olivia Wigram

1676★ Sir Herbert Beerbohm Tree [?c. 1928]
For Viola and Alan [Parsons] with Max's love 1928
Full length, three-quarter face, in overcoat, right hand on forehead, left holding hat and stick.
REPRO Frances Donaldson, *The Actor-Managers*, 1970
OWNER David Tree Parsons

1677 [Herbert Beerbohm Tree]
Full length in grey frock-coat and blue cravat.
EXHIB L.G. 1952

1678★ Mr Beerbohm Tree [n.d.]
Full-length back view in black silhouette.
OWNER Victoria & Albert Museum

1679★ Genus Beerbohmiense [n.d.]
[Shows H. B. T.:] Species Herbertica Arborealis, *[and Max:]* Species Maximiliana.
EXHIB American Academy 1952
REPRO Hesketh Pearson, *Beerbohm Tree*, 1956
OWNER Robert H. Taylor

HERBERT TRENCH
1865–1923 Poet and playwright

1680 [**A Repertory Theatre. The Struggle for Life, and Mr Herbert Trench wishing he had never been born** 1909]

H. T. was artistic director at the Haymarket Theatre 1909–11.

EXHIB N.E.A.C. Summer 1909; L.G. 1911

R. C. TREVELYAN
1872–1951 Poet

1681★ **Scholar Poet R. C. T.** 1941

REPRO R. C. Trevelyan, *Selected Poems*, 1953

REGINALD TURNER
1869–1938 Journalist and author
See also 367 ,400, 514, 515, 1974

1681A★ **The Industrious Apprentice** [**Signed with monogram** n.d.]

Two drawings: No 1 showing R. T. on the river seated in a punt called 'The Stubbs', with a paddle on his shoulder, reading Stubbs's [?'Charters']. *In No 2 all has sunk except for R. T.'s straw hat.*

OWNER Robert H. Taylor

1682★ [**Untitled Unsigned** n.d.]

Full-length profile facing left. Smoking cigarette in holder and reading a document.

OWNER Miss Mary Parker

1682A★ [**Titled as below Unsigned** n.d.]

Dignified, bland and very, very tactful, perched aloft in this presidential arm-chair so that his feet can never touch the ground, sits Tudsbury Turner
The chair stands on a small dais, on the side of which is written SUAVITER IN MODO CUM FORTITER IN RE [*Gentle in manner but resolute in action*]. *William Tudsbery Tudsbery was a Merton contemporary of Max and R. T.*

OWNER Robert H. Taylor

1683★ **Mr Reginald Turner** 1907

Full-length profile facing left, line of forehead and huge nose almost horizontal.

EXHIB Carfax 1907
REPRO *A Book of Caricatures*, 1907, where subtitled 'A Psychologist'
OWNER Mrs Tania Jepson

1683A★ **Mr Reginald Turner** [n.d.]
Very similar to 1683, but nose more up-tilted.

OWNER Piccadilly Gallery

1684★ [**Untitled**] 1908
Full length, three-quarter face, lighted cigarette in mouth.
OWNER Mrs Mary Hyde

1684A★ **Regie** [n.d.]
Full-length profile facing left, hands in trouser pockets. Three other heads of R. T. on same sheet.
OWNER Robert H. Taylor

1685★ **Mr Reginald Turner** [n.d.]
Three-quarter face, huge head facing left, tiny body, hands on hips.
REPRO Max Beerbohm, *Letters to Reggie Turner*, 1964

1685A★ **English Fiction currying favour with the Reviewer** [**Unsigned** n.d.]
E. F., an elderly lady, is kissing the hand of R. T., who stands on a rostrum labelled D[aily] T[elegraph]. *R.T.*
OWNER Robert H. Taylor

1686★ **Mr Reginald Turner** [n.d.]
REPRO **Plate 81**
OWNER Philippe Jullian

1687★ **Sir Reginald Turner (1st baronet)** [n.d.]
Dressed as a Regency buck.
OWNER Irving Drutman

1687A★ **The Author complimenting his Leading Lady** [n.d.]
R. T., backed by a man and a woman in deep mourning, faces another lady similarly dressed. Behind her hangs a notice saying R.I.P.
OWNER Robert H. Taylor

1688★ **Portrait of Regie – as *I* see him** [n.d.]
A tall slim elegant figure in check trousers, eyeglass, buttonhole and a very small nose. Cf. 1937.
OWNER D. Coombs

1688A★ **'And Private Means!'** . . . [**Unsigned** n.d.]
Full-length profile facing left, cigarette in mouth.
OWNER Robert H. Taylor

MARK TWAIN (S. L. CLEMENS)
1835–1910 American author

1689★ **'Mark Twain'** 1908
EXHIB Carfax 1908
REPRO **Plate 50**
OWNER University of Texas

1690★ **'Mark Twain'** [n.d.]
Cigar in mouth, light background.
OWNER Wadsworth Athenaeum, Hartford, Conn.

THE SECOND LORD TWEEDMOUTH
1849–1909 Liberal politician

1691★ **Lord Tweedmouth** 1907
EXHIB Carfax 1907
REPRO *A Book of Caricatures*, 1907
OWNER New Club, Edinburgh

UNIDENTIFIED
(but probably real)

1692★ The New Helen [n.d.]

An almost epicene figure, winking, on edge of pavement. Outline of policeman in distance. An early drawing.

OWNER Private (Yale)

1693★ [Untitled n.d.]

Full length, full face, of woman in fur-collared coat. An early drawing.

OWNER Private (Yale)

1694★ [Untitled Unsigned 1894]

Full-length drawing of an actor, mistakenly supposed to be Edward Terry.

REPRO *Pall Mall Budget*, 26 Jul 1894; **Plate 90**

1695★ The Chief Croupier (Baccarat) [?c. 1908]

Officiating, bearded and goggle-eyed, among regular gamblers. Probably at Dieppe.

EXHIB L.G. 1957
OWNER Armand G. Erpf

1696★ [Untitled] 1908

Behind the head and shoulders of the croupier of 1695 are a long-nosed man, possibly a waiter, and an older man walking with a stick. Again probably Dieppe.

OWNER M. S. J. Montgomery

1697★ [Untitled Unsigned n.d.]

de la part d'un Anglais qui aime beaucoup le Restaurant Labo

Full-length profile of head waiter, with two other waiters scurrying in background. Again probably Dieppe.

OWNER Piccadilly Gallery

1698★ Souvenir de Dieppe 1908

A stout, upstanding, whiskered man in a nautical cap striding along the front. Pencil caricature of Frank Richardson on verso.

OWNER Sir Rupert Hart-Davis

1699★ [Untitled] 1908

A stern, Germanic, completely bald man standing behind a seated lady, who is wearing an elaborate hat.

OWNER A. M. Hamilton

1700 [As I had supposed them to be 1910]

[For names of figures, see margin of drawing]

EXHIB N.E.A.C. Summer 1910

1701 [Untitled] 1919

For Egan [Mew] Souvenir de Jack Straw March. 30 1919

Full-length profile of a dinner-jacketed man with moustache, eyeglass and a huge nose.

OWNER Mrs Viva King

1702★ L'Onorévole Meda, Acqui 1927

A stout man in a straw hat, smoking a cigar and striding along with a stick.

OWNER Mrs Eva Reichmann

1703★ Lancaster Gate in the 'Nineties. 'O, That We Two Were Maying!' 1929

For Richard Pryce from Max – à la Recherche du Temps Perdu

Two Jewish gentlemen, almost identically dressed, sharing a music-score and singing lustily.

OWNER Mrs Eva Reichmann

1704★ [Untitled n.d.]

Rough sketch of man's head and shoulders in profile, cigar in mouth. Drawn on Haymarket Theatre paper.

EXHIB Grolier 1944, where wrongly described as W. L. Courtney
OWNER Harvard College Library

1705★ [Untitled n.d.]

EXHIB Cincinnati 1965
REPRO **Plate 91**
OWNER Lilly Library

1706★ [Untitled Unsigned n.d.]

REPRO **Plate 92**
OWNER Jay Hall

1707★ [Untitled Unsigned n.d.]

Pencil sketch, half-length, of a powerful-looking man with jutting eyebrows.

OWNER University of Texas

1708★ [Untitled n.d.]

Half-length profile facing left, of a lugubrious man in moustache and spectacles, with a flat top to his head.

OWNER Mrs David Karmel

1708A★ [Untitled n.d.]

Almost identical with 1708, but full length.

REPRO **Plate 93**
OWNER Piccadilly Gallery

1709* [**Untitled Unsigned** n.d.]

Rough pencil sketch, half-length profile facing right, of a smartly dressed man with a pointed beak-like nose, and a parrot on his wrist.

OWNER University of Texas

1710* [**Untitled Unsigned** n.d.]

Head and shoulders of the man of 1709, with a large cockatoo above him. Two more cockatoos on verso.

OWNER University of Texas

1711* [**Untitled Unsigned** n.d.]

Large man, of plebeian appearance, sitting at a table playing cards. Drawn on paper of Enborne Lodge, Newbury, Berks.

OWNER University of Texas

1712* [**Untitled Unsigned** n.d.]

REPRO **Plate 94**
OWNER Malcolm Borthwick

1713* [**Untitled Unsigned** n.d.]

Profile head of a spectacled, chinless man, smoking a curved pipe.

OWNER Arents Collection (N.Y.P.L.)

1714* [**Untitled Unsigned** n.d.]

Big-nosed man in evening dress, speaking from a stage. Has been wrongly taken for Reggie Turner.

EXHIB Achenbach 1964
OWNER U.C.L.A. (Clark)

1715* [**Untitled Unsigned** n.d.]

REPRO **Plate 95**

1716* [**Untitled Unsigned** n.d.]

Pencil sketch, full-length profile facing left, of stocky double-chinned man, lighted cigar in hand. Known only from a photograph in Max's papers.

1717* [**Untitled Unsigned** n.d.]

REPRO **Plate 96**
OWNER Sir Rupert Hart-Davis

1718* **Vague Memory of Some Gentlemen of the Household. July 13th 1939**

This was the day on which Max received the accolade of Knighthood. The drawing shows an elderly man in morning dress giving orders to three exquisitely dressed younger men. Although presumably based on real people, they have so far defied identification.

OWNER Merton College, Oxford

1719* [**Untitled Unsigned** n.d.]

REPRO **Plate 98**
OWNER University of Texas

1720* [**Untitled Unsigned** n.d.]

Half-length full face of red-haired man with bow tie.

OWNER University of Texas

1721* [**Untitled Unsigned** n.d.]

Pencil sketch, full-length profile facing left, of serious-looking man with hair standing on end.

OWNER University of Texas

1722* [**Untitled Unsigned** n.d.]

Pen sketch, full-length profile facing left of a man, not unlike Lord Rosebery, wearing top hat with mourning band.

OWNER University of Texas

1722A* [**Untitled Unsigned** n.d.]

REPRO **Plate 97**
OWNER Robert Lescher

V

PAUL VERLAINE
1844–96 French poet

1723* **Paul Verlaine – Usher in private school at Bournemouth – Sunday morning** [c. 1904]

EXHIB Carfax 1904; N.Y. 1912; L.G. 1945 (Guedalla)

REPRO *The Poets' Corner*, 1904 and 1943
OWNER Mrs Philip Guedalla

1724 [**Verlaine in bed**]

Known only from letter of Will Rothenstein in 'Times Lit. Sup.', 22 Apr 1926, asking for its whereabouts.

KING VICTOR EMANUEL III
OF ITALY
1869–1947
See 186, 1079, 1080

QUEEN VICTORIA
1819–1901
See also 438, 490, 503, 517, 1086, 1656

1725★ Four generations of Royalty from an instantaneous photograph by Messrs Downey (Ebury Street) [Unsigned c. 1894]

Framed alongside the photograph, which shows the future Kings Edward VII, George V and Edward VIII, the last in the arms of Queen Victoria.

EXHIB L.G. 1945 (Guedalla)
OWNER Mrs Philip Guedalla

1726★ [Untitled c. 1900]

The Queen holds in her arms a bearded, naked Prince of Wales, with a fleur-de-lys in his hand. Beneath is this letter to Robert Ross:

Dear Bobbie, Perhaps you will often wonder why this peevish-looking Madonna, conformed to no acknowledged or obvious type of beauty, attracts you more and more, and often comes back to you when Bassano and Herr von Angeli are forgotten. At first, contrasting it with those, you may think there is in it something loud or vulgar even, for the abstract lines of the face have little nobleness, and the colour is crude. For with Beerbohm she too, though she holds in her hands the 'Undesirable of all nations,' is one of those who are neither for Kruger nor for His enemies, and her choice is on her face. The red light on it is laid on hard and cheerful with a brush, as when claret is spilt on the shirt-front, and the hostess looks up with surprise at the strange redness of the guest's face. The trouble is in the very caress of the mysterious child, whose gaze is always far from her, and who has already that sweet look of intoxication which men have never been able altogether to love, and which still makes the born drunkard an object almost of suspicion to his earthly brethren. Once indeed, he guides her hand to transcribe with a Remington the words of her exaltation, the 'God Save,' and the 'Revered, Beloved' and the 'Widder o' Windsor.' And the Indian servants, glad to rouse her from her dejection, are eager to play the bag-pipes and to dance the reel. But the machine is out of order, and the high-flown words have no meaning for her, and her true children are those others, among whom, in her Highland home, the dubitable honour came to her, with that look of wistful inanity on their irregular faces which you see in over-fed animals – female children, such as those who, in the four-mile radius, still drive out in landaus to bow to us, but at Balmoral become '*bourgeoises du home*', with their thick brown *toupées* nicely put away, and no white powder on their drooping noses. I hope you have been having a good time in Italy, and are soon coming back. Yours affectionately Max

OWNER A. D. Peters

1727 [Untitled n.d.]

Shows the Queen with the Prince and Princess of Wales and the Emperor and Empress of Russia, based on a photograph, which is framed on the back of the drawing.

EXHIB L.G. 1945 (Guedalla)
OWNER Mrs Winifred Mackintosh

W

A. B. WALKLEY
1855–1926 Dramatic critic
See also 95, 1443, 1479, 1483, 1488, 1509, 1621

1728★ Mr A. B. Walkley [1898]
Tiny bearded figure with enormous bald forehead.
REPRO *Academy*, 24 Dec 1898; *Max's Nineties*, 1958

1729 [Mr A. B. Walkley c. 1904]
Upholding bust of Aristotle on a tall pedestal. On 30 May 1904 A. B. W. wrote to Max: 'I have just bought your caricature of Aristotle – but who is the midget clinging to A's pedestal?'
OWNER Sold at Sotheby's 13 May 1959

1730★ Dramatic Critics arboricultural and otherwise 1907
A. B. W. showing Max neatly espaliered fruit-trees.

WALKLEY (continued)

EXHIB Achenbach 1964
REPRO Achenbach catalogue, 1964
OWNER U.C.L.A. (Clark)

1731 [In Mr Walkley's Garden 1908]
[G. B. S. 'So these are your pear-trees? Now I see
why you don't like my plays']
EXHIB Carfax 1908

1732* [Untitled Unsigned n.d.]
*Three joined sketches for 1731 in pen and pencil, showing
back view of G. B. S. and A. B. W. in front of espaliered
trees.*
OWNER University of Texas

1733* A. B. Walkley – Pomologist
Full length, full face, in front of espaliered trees.
EXHIB L.G. 1911
REPRO *Bookman*, Aug 1911
OWNER Sold at Sotheby's 14 Dec 1960

FRANK WALLACE

1734* Mr Frank Wallace [n.d.]
OWNER Mrs Eva Reichmann

LEWIS WALLER
1850–1915   Actor-manager

1735* Mr Lewis Waller [n.d.]
REPRO *Theatre Notebook*, Winter 1966–67
OWNER Victoria & Albert Museum

MRS HUMPHRY WARD
1851–1920   Novelist
See 37

LESLIE WARD
See 'Spy'

HUGH WARRENDER
1868–1926   Soldier

1736* Mr Hugh Warrender [1909]
REPRO *English Review*, Oct 1909

H. B. MARRIOTT WATSON
1863–1921   Writer

1737* Mr Marriott Watson [c. 1896]
EXHIB L.G. 1928, where dated as above
OWNER Mrs Leonard Marsili

MALCOLM WATSON
1853–1929   Dramatic critic and playwright

1738* Mr Malcolm Watson [n.d.]
REPRO *Theatre Notebook*, Summer 1967
OWNER Mrs Raymond Lister

WILLIAM WATSON
1858–1935   Poet

1739* [Untitled 1900]
*Lord Salisbury offers W. W.'s head on a charger to the
Sultan of Turkey.*
REPRO *World*, Christmas No, 1900

1740* [Mr William Watson, secretly ceded by the
British Government to Abdul Hamid, but, in
the nick of time, saved from the trap-door to the
Bosphorus by the passionate intercession of Mr
John Lane c. 1904]
In the 1943 edition Max noted: At the time of the
Armenian atrocities in 1896, William Watson wrote
several sonnets denouncing the Sultan, Abdul Hamid.
One of them ended with the words 'Abdul the
damned, on his infernal throne.'
EXHIB Carfax 1904
REPRO *The Poets' Corner*, 1904 and 1943

1741 [Mr William Watson drilling his Muse]
['A little more rigid, please. Don't look out of the
window at Nature. And don't think of *me*. Think
hard of Milton and Wordsworth; and also of
Liberty – but only in the national sense, mind you.
And then you may go. I shall not be writing to-day.']
EXHIB L.G. 1913

1742* Mr William Watson [n.d.]
*Full length, holding quill pen in front of nose; long
protruding waxed moustache.*
OWNER Sir John Rothenstein

1743* Mr William Watson [n.d.]
*Full-length profile facing left, in check knickerbocker suit,
hands behind back.*
OWNER Princeton University Library

THEODORE WATTS-DUNTON
1832–1914   Journalist and author
See also 1268, 1277, 1644, 1645, 1647

1744 [Theodore Watts-Dunton]
['Who saved Swinburne?']
EXHIB L.G. 1928

1745★ Mr Theodore Watts-Dunton [n.d.]
OWNER Mrs Katharine Stonehill

THE FIRST LORD WEARDALE
1847–1923   Liberal politician

1746★ Lord Weardale [1907]
'No! Once and for all: I am *not* Lord Rosebery.'
EXHIB Carfax 1907; L.G. 1911 and 1957
REPRO *A Book of Caricatures*, 1907
OWNER A. J. Blackett-Ord

SIDNEY WEBB
1859–1947   Fabian reformer and writer

1747★ Mr Sidney Webb on his birthday 1914
Kneeling on the floor arranging toy people symmetrically. On the wall behind him hang a geometrical composition titled HUMAN NATURE *and a picture of a pretty girl titled* THE STATE
EXHIB L.G. 1945 (Guedalla) and 1957
REPRO *A Survey*, 1921; *Caricatures by Max*, 1958
OWNER Ashmolean Museum, Oxford

1748★ Mr Sydney Webb on his birthday [Unsigned n.d.]
Rough sketch for 1747 marked SPOILT.
OWNER Alan G. Thomas

1749★ 'Tout peut se rétablir' 1920
Urgent Conclave of Doctrinaire Socialists, to decide on some means of inducing the Lower Orders to regard them once more as Visionaries merely.
S. W. in foreground, gesticulating to H. G. Wells. Also present: Shaw, Cunninghame Graham, H. M. Hyndman, Philip Snowden, and five supposedly lay-figures.
EXHIB L.G. May 1921, 1945 (Guedalla), 1952 and 1957
REPRO *A Survey*, 1921; *Caricatures by Max*, 1958
OWNER Ashmolean Museum, Oxford

1750★ 'Tout peut se rétablir' [Unsigned n.d.]
Rough sketch for 1749, with different grouping and one extra figure.
OWNER Cornell University

1751 The Wrong Man in the Right Place [Unsigned n.d.]
S. W. in the House of Lords.
OWNER London School of Economics

1752 [Lord Passfield 1931]
EXHIB L.G. 1952, where dated as above

SIR RICHARD WEBSTER
See Lord Alverstone

THE REV. C. H. WEEKES
Charterhouse master
See 664, 664A

JAMES WELCH
1865–1917   Actor

1753★ Mr James Welch [n.d.]
OWNER William Bealby-Wright

H. G. WELLS
1866–1946   Writer
See also 133, 134, 338, 339, 896, 1599, 1749, 1750

1754 [Mr H. G. Wells c. 1901]
EXHIB L.G. 1928, where dated as above

1755★ Mr H. G. Wells and his patent mechanical New Republic; and the Spirit of Pure Reason crowning him President (View of Presidential Palace in background) [1903]
The forbidding Spirit is pressing a button, by which an elaborate machine will place a bowler hat on H. G. W.'s head. The Palace is a huge rectangular skyscraper.
EXHIB L.G. 1911
REPRO *Sketch*, 21 Oct 1903; *Bookman*, Aug 1911
OWNER Yale University Library

1756★ Mr H. G. Wells, prophet and idealist, conjuring up the darling Future 1907
Through a trap-door appears a grim lady, holding in one hand an even grimmer baby, and in the other a geometrical instrument.
EXHIB Carfax 1907
REPRO *A Book of Caricatures*, 1907

1757 [Mr H. G. Wells 1912]
EXHIB L.G. 1945 (Guedalla), where dated as above

1758* **The Old and the Young Self** 1924

Young Self: 'Did you ever manage to articulate the bones of that microglamaphoid lizard?'

Old Self: 'I'm not sure. But I've articulated the whole past of mankind on this planet – and the whole future, too. I don't think you know very much about the past, do you? It's all perfectly beastly, believe me. But the future's going to be all perfectly splendid . . . after a bit. And I must say I find the present very jolly.'

EXHIB L.G. 1925
REPRO *Observations*, 1925

1759* **Mr H. G. Wells foreseeing things** [1931]

REPRO *Spectator* Supplement, 14 Feb 1931
OWNER *The Spectator*

1760* **Mr H. G. Wells** [n.d.]

Full length three-quarter face, hands in trouser pockets.

OWNER Dan H. Laurence

REBECCA WEST
b. 1892 Author and journalist

1761* **Miss Rebecca West as I dimly and perhaps erroneously imagine her** [c. 1917]

She appears as a young female Shaw in a trouser suit, and the drawing is surrounded by this letter:

12 Well Walk Hampstead N.W.3, June 28 1918
My dear G. B. S. This is a drawing which I found today in an old portfolio. It was done a year or two ago; and at that time I meant to send it to you, thinking it might amuse you; but I forgot. Here it tardily is. It was the result of my having read in the *Star*, now and again, some very brilliant articles by Miss West. I had marvelled much at her skill in catching your tone of mind and the hang of your sentences. Very wonderful it all seemed to me, and not quite sufferable – rather a monstrous birth. I remembered that when I was a small boy I went to a concert in the Town Hall of Folkestone, to hear a lady who had been billed all over the place as *La Femme Grossmith*. Well, here, after all these years, was La Femme Shaw. . . . The former lady, when I saw her, was not young; so that (very clever though she too was) I felt she would have no great future. The latter lady, I am sure, is young; and I have little doubt that in the past year or two she has been strenuously shaking off her likeness to you, and becoming her own self, and making this portrait 'date' duly. I haven't yet read her novel. Your quoted declaration that it is one of the best stories in the language gives me to fear that perhaps

after all she is still very Shavian – cool, frank, breezy, trenchant, vain, swift, stern, frivolous, incorruptible, kind, accurate, and all the rest of it!

Yours ever Max Beerbohm

REPRO British Museum (Add. MSS. 50529, ff. 57–58)
OWNER Dame Rebecca West

DEAN OF WESTMINSTER
See Ryle

THE SECOND DUKE OF WESTMINSTER
1879–1953 Soldier and landowner
See also 335, 1382, 1527, 1822, 1823

1762* **The Duke of Westminster** 1908

Full-length profile facing left, wearing bowler hat, mackintosh and field-glasses, smoking cigar. Racecourse background.

EXHIB Carfax 1908; L.G. 1952

1763* **[Untitled Unsigned** c. 1908]

Pencil sketch for 1762.

OWNER University of Texas

1764* **[Untitled Unsigned** c. 1908]

Another rough pencil sketch for 1762, but facing right.

OWNER University of Texas

CHARLES WHIBLEY
1859–1930 Author and journalist
See also 1598

1765 **[An Authority on the Dandies. Mr Charles Whibley** c. 1900]

EXHIB L.G. 1928, where dated as above

1766* **Mr Charles Whibley consoling Mr Augustine Birrell for the loss of the Education Bill, by a disquisition on the uselessness of teaching anything, sacred or profane, to children of the non-aristocratic class** 1907

EXHIB Carfax 1907
REPRO *A Book of Caricatures*, 1907

1767 **Mr Charles Whibley** [n.d.]

OWNER Mrs T. S. Eliot

JAMES McNEILL WHISTLER
1834–1903 American artist
See also 151, 241, 457–9, 595, 1149, 1268, 1528, 1537, 1829

1768* **A Nocturne. Mr Whistler crossing the Channel** [1898]

Seated on a broomstick.

REPRO *Idler*, Feb 1898; *Max's Nineties*, 1958

1769* **Mr James McNeill Whistler** [1901]

Tiny full-length profile facing left, eyebrows above brim of large hat, white lock of hair protruding through hole in hat, high coat-collar, left hand extended, cane in right, rounded pedestal instead of feet.

EXHIB Carfax 1901
REPRO **Plate 57**
OWNER D'Offay Couper Gallery

1770* **The Mercilessness of Youth** 1920

Post-Impressionist: 'No man with any *real* talent could have behaved like that.'

He is looking at a portrait of Whistler signed W[alter] Greaves.

EXHIB L.G. May 1921
REPRO *A. Survey*, 1921

1771* **The Mercilessness of Youth** [n.d.]

Virtually identical with 1770, marked SPOILT, presumably because of a blot on the legend.

OWNER University of Glasgow

1772* **Mr Whistler giving evidence in the case of Pennell v. The Saturday Review and Another** [n.d.]

In April 1897 Joseph Pennell successfully sued the 'S. R.' for libel, on account of an article by W. R. Sickert which said that J. P.'s prints were not true lithographs. Whistler gave evidence for J. P.

EXHIB L.G. 1928, 1952 and 1957
REPRO Hesketh Pearson, *The Man Whistler*, 1952
OWNER City Art Gallery, Birmingham

1773* **Mr Whistler** [n.d.]

Full length, three-quarter face. Long black coat, black gloves, stick in left hand, eyebrows curling above brim of tall black hat and white lock protruding, as in 1769.

EXHIB Grolier 1944; American Academy 1952
REPRO A. E. Gallatin, *Sir Max Beerbohm: Bibliographical Notes*, 1944; *Fin de Siècle*, ed. Nevile Wallis, 1947
OWNER Harvard College Library

1774* **[Untitled** n.d.]

Four drawings during which the tiny figure of W. in black hat and overcoat, with pedestal for feet as in 1769, turns progressively into an extinguished candle in a candlestick.

REPRO **Plate 58**
OWNER University of Glasgow

1775 **Mr James Whistler** [n.d.]

Full-length profile, facing left. Usual hat, stick and overcoat reaching to ground.

OWNER Mrs Albert Ehrman

WALT WHITMAN
1819–92   American poet

1776* **Walt Whitman, inciting the bird of freedom to soar** [c. 1904]

EXHIB Carfax 1904
REPRO *The Poets' Corner*, 1904 and 1943

FREDERIC WHYTE
1867–1941   Journalist and author

1777 **Mr Frederic Whyte** [n.d.]

OWNER Mrs Helen Stutchbury

OSCAR WILDE
1854–1900   Poet and playwright
See also 595, 1307, 1322, 1650, 1796

1778* **[Untitled Signed with monogram** n.d.]

A page of undergraduate drawings. Head of O. W. in centre, broad full-length back view on left. Round the edge tiny vignettes illustrating: 'Disappointed with the Atlantic;' He has lectured in America; His style of dress has somewhat changed; Was once editor of 'The Woman's World'; Mr Whistler rather worsted him in 'Truth'; Dorian Gray; He is what the newspapers call an unrivalled raconteur.

REPRO **Plate 5**
OWNER John Bryson

1779* **Oscar Wilde** [1894]

Half length, full face, day clothes, huge buttonhole.

EXHIB L.G. 1945 (Guedalla)
REPRO *Pick-Me-Up*, 22 Sep 1894; *The Poets' Corner*, 1943; *Max's Nineties*, 1958; *Caricatures by Max*, 1958
OWNER Ashmolean Museum, Oxford

1780* **[Untitled Unsigned** ?c. 1894]

Three-quarter length, full face, evening dress, cloak on arm. The face, hair, collar and general shape are so like those of 1779 as to make 1894 seem its likely date. Known only from a photograph in the Witt Library, Courtauld Institute.

1781* **Oscar Wilde and John Toole – Garrick Club – '93** 1898

EXHIB Grolier 1944
OWNER Princeton University Library

1782★ Oscar Wilde: a memory 1909

Three-quarter-length profile facing left, cigarette in mouth. Right hand held out, matching huge buttonhole.

EXHIB L.G. 1952 and 1957
REPRO *Bandwagon*, Jun 1952
OWNER Hugh Beaumont

1783★ [Untitled ?c. 1911]

Three-quarter-length profile facing left, in frock-coat and top hat, stick in left hand. Sending this drawing to Stuart Mason on 4 Feb 1911, Max wrote:

It gives a much more *essential* view of Oscar. The other one [from *Pick-Me-Up*] showed only the worse side of his nature. At the time when I did that other one, and even when it was published, I hardly realised what a cruel thing it was: I only realised that after Oscar's tragedy and downfall. I shouldn't at all like it to be perpetuated in your book. This caricature that I am sending to you shows Oscar in a light that won't pain posterity, and is, as I have said, much more really true.

REPRO Stuart Mason, *Bibliography of Oscar Wilde* [1914]

1784★ The name of Dante Gabriel Rossetti is heard for the first time in the Western States of America. Time: 1882. Lecturer: Mr Oscar Wilde 1916

EXHIB Grosvenor 1917; L.G. Sep 1921
REPRO *Rossetti and his Circle*, 1922; *The Poets' Corner*, 1943
OWNER Tate Gallery

1785 For Marie [Beerbohm] – a memory of O. W. as he was in 1893-1894 1922

Head and shoulders, full face.

OWNER Sir Anthony Hooper Bart

1786★ Willie and Oscar Wilde 1926
1787★ Oscar and Willie Wilde 1926

A pair of drawings, each showing one facing and one back view.

EXHIB L.G. 1928
REPRO Terence de Vere White, *The Parents of Oscar Wilde*, 1967
OWNER University of Texas

1788★ Willie and Oscar Wilde 1946

Both in profile, face to face.

OWNER David Tree Parsons

1789★ Oscar Wilde [n.d.]

Three-quarter-length profile facing left. Hair stretching back over collar, cigarette in hand.

REPRO *Sixteen Letters from Oscar Wilde*, ed. Rothenstein, 1930 (frontispiece)
OWNER Richard Attenborough

1790★ [Untitled Unsigned n.d.]

Full-length profile facing left, wearing short coat and top hat, cigarette in mouth.

EXHIB L.G. 1957
REPRO *Sixteen Letters from Oscar Wilde*, ed. Rothenstein, 1930
OWNER Sir John Rothenstein

1791★ [Untitled Unsigned n.d.]

O. W. and Lord Alfred Douglas sitting opposite each other at a table.

REPRO Lord Alfred Douglas, *Oscar Wilde and Myself*, 1914

1792 [Untitled n.d.]

Full-face head and shoulders in pencil. Smoking cigarette with long smoke-spiral. Big drooping bow tie.

EXHIB L.G. 1952
OWNER Mrs Yehudi Menuhin

1793★ Oscar Wilde [n.d.]

Half-length profile facing left, bare-headed, left hand resting on tasselled cane.

OWNER Oliver R. W. W. Lodge

1794 [Oscar Wilde]

EXHIB L.G. 1945 (Guedalla)

1795 [Oscar Wilde]

EXHIB L.G. 1945 (Guedalla)

WILLIAM WILDE
1852–99 Journalist brother of Oscar
See also 1786-88

1796★ [Untitled n.d.]

Full length, full face, with lightly pencilled head of Oscar over W's shoulder.

EXHIB L.G. 1945 (Guedalla)
OWNER Ashmolean Museum, Oxford

KAISER WILHELM II
1859–1941 Emperor of Germany
See also 186, 575, 1415

1797★ Dawning of a horrid doubt as to the Divine Right

The K in an armchair regards his son and heir, the Crown Prince.

EXHIB L.G. 1913
REPRO *Fifty Caricatures*, 1913

1798★ The Old Adam 1920

Count von Hohenzollern rehearsing, on the fond off-chance that he might yet be extradited, his Demeanour in the Dock.

Posturing before a full-length looking-glass.

EXHIB   L.G. May 1921 and 1945 (Guedalla)
REPRO   *A Survey*, 1921
OWNER   Ashmolean Museum, Oxford

E. S. WILLARD
1853–1915   Actor

1799★ [Untitled 1903]

Full length, face obscured by hair.

REPRO   *John Bull*, 27 Aug 1903

1800★ Mr Willard [n.d.]

Full-length back view, top hat at jaunty angle.

OWNER   D'Offay Couper Gallery

CAPTAIN WILLIAMS

1801★ Captain Williams [n.d.]

OWNER   Mrs Eva Reichmann

SIR HEDWORTH WILLIAMSON BART
1867–1942

1802★ Sir Hedworth Williamson, approaching the Presence 1907

EXHIB   Carfax 1907; L.G. 1911
REPRO   *A Book of Caricatures*, 1907
OWNER   Sir Hedworth Williamson Bart

THE NINETEENTH
LORD WILLOUGHBY DE BROKE
1869–1923   Soldier, landowner and M.F.H.
See 898

WOODROW WILSON
1856–1924   President of the United States

1803★ President Wilson visiting Congress 1914

EXHIB   L.G. 1945 (Guedalla)
REPRO   *A Survey*, 1921
OWNER   Princeton University Library

1804★ Woodrow Wilson's Peace . . . 1920

Mr Lloyd George, to M. Clemenceau: 'Thought he was going to get the better of you and I!'

EXHIB   L.G. May 1921
REPRO   *A Survey*, 1921
OWNER   City Art Gallery, Manchester

SIR GEORGE WOMBWELL BART
1832–1913   Veteran of Balaclava charge

1805★ Sir George Wombwell [c. 1896]

EXHIB   Carfax 1901; L.G. 1928, where dated as above
REPRO   Sotheby catalogue, 14 Dec 1960
OWNER   Sold at Sotheby's 14 Dec 1960

PEGGY WOOD
b. 1892   Actress

1806★ Miss Peggy Wood as Sarah Millick [c. 1931]

REPRO   *Heroes and Heroines of Bitter Sweet*, 1931
OWNER   Lilly Library

1807 Miss Peggy Wood as Sarah Millick [c. 1931]

Apparently a copy of 1806 by Max.

OWNER   Miss Peggy Wood

RALPH WOOD
1870–1945   Chartered Accountant
See also 1034

1808 An attempt at Mr Ralph Wood 1943

OWNER   Mrs Marguerite Ruffer

THOMAS WOOLNER
1826–92   Sculptor and poet
See 1657

WILLIAM WORDSWORTH
1770–1850   Poet Laureate

1809★ [Untitled 1900]

W. W. taking notes of a sailor's conversation.

EXHIB   Achenbach 1964
REPRO   *World*, Christmas No, 1900
OWNER   U.C.L.A. (Clark)

1810★ Wordsworth in the Lake District, at cross purposes [c. 1904]

EXHIB Carfax 1904
REPRO *The Poets' Corner*, 1904 and 1943
OWNER Municipal Gallery of Modern Art, Dublin

CHARLES WYNDHAM
1837–1919 Actor-manager
See also 335

1811★ Mr Charles Wyndham [1901]

EXHIB Carfax 1901
OWNER Victoria & Albert Museum

1812 Sir Charles Wyndham defying Time 1907

Time on the left, with hour-glass and scythe. C. W., arms folded, staring him out of countenance.

OWNER Robert H. Taylor

1813★ Sir Charles Wyndham bearding Time 1908

C. W. is histrionically plucking the beard of Time, who drops his hour-glass in horror.

EXHIB Carfax 1908
OWNER Mr and Mrs Daniel Longwell

1814★ [Untitled Unsigned n.d.]

Rough pencil sketch for 1813.

OWNER University of Texas

1815★ London's Leading Ladies. No. 1. Miss Mary Moore [n.d.]

Shows M. M. as tiny, blue-eyed, yellow-haired, pink-sashed doll, with C. W. looming large above her. She had been his leading lady since 1885 and married him in 1916.

Specimen dialogue

Miss M. M.: 'Papa!'

Sir C. W.: 'Yes, look on me as though I were your father. If I were twenty years younger, I should dare to ask you to be my wife. But "Anno Domini" – ha, ha, ha! "Anno Domini"! I can but offer you the wisdom the years have taught me.'

Miss M. M.: 'Mamma!'

Sir C. W.: 'Go home to her. Can't you see that you're compromising yourself in the eyes of the world? Ah, don't fly in the face of Mrs Grundy. I knew a girl once – her name was Arabella. And we loved each other – Arabella and I' – etc. etc. etc.

OWNER Victoria & Albert Museum

GEORGE WYNDHAM
1863–1913 Conservative M.P. and author
See also 8, 9, 63, 71, 335

1816★ [The Perfidious Devotee 1900]

From the Bard a young man's fancy lightly turns into Pall Mall.

Shows G. W. pushing a bust of Shakespeare off a pedestal and replacing it with the bust of a toy soldier. On the pedestal WILLIAM has been struck out in favour of THOMAS [ATKINS]. In 1898 G. W.'s edition of Shakespeare's Poems appeared, and he forsook literature to become Parliamentary Under-Secretary for War.

EXHIB Achenbach 1964
REPRO *World*, Christmas No, 1900, where captioned as above
OWNER U.C.L.A. (Clark)

1817★ Mr George Wyndham [1901]

Three-quarter-face, full length, huge collar, hands in pockets.

EXHIB Carfax 1901
REPRO *Candid Friend*, 26 Oct 1901

1818★ [Untitled 1903]

Seated on bench in House of Commons in evening dress.

REPRO *John Bull*, 16 Jul 1903

1819★ Mr George Wyndham, reciting [c. 1906]

EXHIB L.G. 1928, where dated as above
OWNER Reresby Sitwell

1820 [Mr George Wyndham and Prof. Walter Raleigh speaking of Shakespeare 1908]

EXHIB Carfax 1908; L.G. 1911

1821★ [Untitled] 1908

Pencil sketch for 1820, very much torn and smudged. G. W. is talking up to W. R., whose head is bent forward horizontally.

OWNER University of Texas

1822 ['Great Possessions']

[Mr George Wyndham (to ducal step-son): 'Life is real, my dear boy, life is earnest. Why not write an opera, like Howard de Walden?']

G. W.'s step-son was the second Duke of Westminster. H. de W's opera 'The Children of Don' was produced in London in 1912.

EXHIB L.G. 1913

1823 'Great Possessions' 1951

Mr George Wyndham (to ducal step-son): 'Life is real, my dear boy, life is earnest. Why not write an opera, like Howard de Walden?'

A pencil copy from memory of 1822.

OWNER Jim Rose

1824★ Mr George Wyndham [n.d.]

Sitting on a table in evening dress.

EXHIB L.G. 1945 (Guedalla) and 1957
REPRO *Caricatures by Max*, 1958
OWNER Ashmolean Museum, Oxford

Y

W. B. YEATS
1865–1939   Irish poet
See also 144, 616, 748, 1046, 1650

1825* **Celtades Ambo [Both of them Celts. Cf.** *Arcades Ambo* **(both of them denizens of Arcady) in Virgil, Eclogue VII, 4]** [1899]
W. B. Y. and Edward Martyn.
REPRO *Daily Chronicle*, 26 May 1899; *Max's Nineties*, 1958
OWNER Robert H. Taylor

1826 **[Mr W. B. Yeats** 1901]
EXHIB Carfax 1901

1827* **Mr W. B. Yeats presenting Mr George Moore to the Queen of the Fairies** [c. 1904]
EXHIB Carfax 1904
REPRO *The Poets' Corner*, 1904 and 1943
OWNER Municipal Gallery of Modern Art, Dublin

1828* **W. B. Yeats** [n.d.]
REPRO **Plate 48**
OWNER National Gallery of Ireland

1829 **[Shades of Rossetti, Ruskin, Swinburne, Pater and Whistler wondering that so much space has been devoted to this other later Romantic – and whether even he is the 'Last one']**
W. B. Y. is the later Romantic. Cf. 'We were the last romantics' in his poem 'Coole Park and Ballylee', 1931. Known only from G. F. Sims catalogue 53, Spring 1962.

C. T. YERKES
1837–1905   American railway magnate

1830* **Mr Yerkes. One of Our Conquerors** [1903]
EXHIB L.G. 1928
REPRO *John Bull*, 20 May 1903
OWNER Oliver Stonor

THE HON. ALEXANDER YORKE
1847–1911   Courtier

1831 **Mr Alexander Yorke** [1901]
EXHIB Carfax 1901
OWNER The Earl of Leven

FILSON YOUNG
1876–1938   Journalist and author

1832* **Mr Filson Young** 1913
EXHIB L.G. May 1921
REPRO *A Survey*, 1921

Z

ISRAEL ZANGWILL
1864–1926   Jewish writer
See also 1423, 1443, 1599

1833* **Mr I. Zangwill** [1901]
EXHIB Carfax 1901
REPRO *Candid Friend*, 14 Dec 1901
OWNER Sold at the Parke-Bernet Galleries, N.Y.

1834 **At last! Mr Zangwill leading the way into Zion** 1908
For Alice and Will [Rothenstein], with love. 1912
I. Z., lean and spectacled, riding a little donkey through an imposing portal into a compound. I.Z. leans back and looks towards the hills.
EXHIB Carfax 1908; L.G. 1911
OWNER Joseph Gold

PART TWO

Imaginary People and Allegorical Subjects

ZULEIKA DOBSON, 1911

1835 Zuleika Dobson [1912]

Full length, against background of college buildings.

EXHIB L.G. 1928, where dated as above
OWNER L. J. Cadbury

1836 'May I boast myself the first possessor of your heart?' *Zuleika Dobson* **p. 216 (Tauchnitz)**

For E[dward] G[ordon] C[raig] from Max. Rapallo 1920

Depicts the scene between the Duke of Dorset and Katie Batch in Ch. XVII.

OWNER Lord David Cecil

1837★ [Untitled Unsigned 1922]

An oval fresco depicting Zuleika, the Duke of Dorset and Katie Batch. For Max's three other frescoes, see 514, 515, 614, 615, 1281–3 and 1838.

OWNER Merton College, Oxford

1838★ [Untitled Unsigned 1922]

A perfect sketch for 1837, the four blank corners filled with this letter to John Rothenstein:

Rapallo Oct. 1922. My dear John, As you are at Oxford (which is the next best place to Rapallo) and as the Duke of Dorset and Miss Z. Dobson and the daughter of the Duke's landlady were there before you, perhaps it might amuse you to have this sketch. I call it a sketch, but it is really a cartoon for a fresco – which sounds much grander and is the title which I advise you to use in speaking of it, if you ever do speak of it. On the walls of the little house where Florence and I live I have recently done two frescoes on eligibly blank architectural spaces that seemed to be crying out loud for something upon them. Not frescoes in the *strict* sense – not things painted on plaster which is added on in bits by pupils while the master feverishly works. But mural painting done in tempera and Indian ink on plaster that has been laid on by a local workman and has since dried. The design that I send will be 'executed' at just double this size, and in a flatter, more mural fashion – the figures all white, with slight modelling, against the sort of background you here perceive. You must make your family bring you out here to see the enlarged version, and to see Florence and me again. We are just exactly the same as ever; but I suppose you are alarmingly different, with an Oxford manner that would frighten us both out of our wits. Knowing, however, that behind the manner was our well-remembered young friend all the time, we should be able to control our tremors and to cope with you very happily. Yours ever, Max Beerbohm.

EXHIB L.G. 1957
REPRO John Rothenstein, *Summer's Lease*, 1965
OWNER Sir John Rothenstein

1839★ Miss Dobson 1905 Oxford 1929

For Logan [Pearsall Smith] Rapallo

REPRO **Plate 83**
OWNER The Hon. Mrs Lyle

1839A★ Zuleika Dobson [Unsigned n.d.]

Same hat and background as 1839, but different dress and pose. A rough sketch, perhaps for 1835 or 1839.

OWNER Robert H. Taylor

1840★ Zuleika Dobson [n.d.]

Head and shoulders in round frame.

REPRO *Zuleika Dobson*, 1947

1841★ Le Jeune Duc fut-il séduit? Instantément, inexorablement 1952

I meant to send this to the translator, and inscribed it to him – but never posted it!

These words written over erased inscription. The drawing shows the first meeting of Zuleika and the Duke of Dorset in Ch. III. 'Was the young Duke bewitched? Instantly, utterly.'

EXHIB L.G. 1957

NOTE – *Max had a special copy of 'Zuleika' which, through the years, he elaborately illustrated with line-drawings, water-colours, vignettes, pasted-on items etc. This is now in the possession of Mrs Eva Reichmann, and in 1966 ten of the illustrations were reproduced in the Folio Society edition of the book.*

SEVEN MEN, 1919
See also 709, 1533, 1650

1842★ 'Negations' Seen at the Café Royal [n.d.]

Page of sketches of Enoch Soames, standing and sitting, also a head of Will Rothenstein. 'Negations' was E. S.'s first book of poems. Of this, and the other five illustrations that appeared in the N.Y. edition of 'Seven Men', Max wrote to the Century Company: 'I have executed what look like old sketches of these several persons – convincingly untidy-looking attempts, mostly.'

EXHIB Grolier 1944; American Academy 1952
REPRO *Seven Men* (N.Y.), 1920
OWNER University of Texas

1843 'You don't remember me,' he said in a toneless voice [n.d.]

Max and Enoch Soames (1919 edition, p. 7). Intended for N.Y. edition but not used.

EXHIB Grolier 1944; American Academy 1952
OWNER Alfred A. Knopf

1844★ [Untitled n.d.]

For Will [Rothenstein] from Max affectionately

Enoch Soames standing in front of his portrait by W. R. (1919 edition, p. 21).

OWNER University of Glasgow

1845 'Fame had breathed on him' [n.d.]

Enoch Soames at the N.E.A.C. exhibition (1919 edition, p. 21). Probably very similar to 1844. Intended for N.Y. edition but not used.

EXHIB Grolier 1944; American Academy 1952
OWNER Alfred A. Knopf

1846 'The Vingtième [restaurant] in its hey-day 1896' [n.d.]

1919 edition, p. 23. Intended for N.Y. edition but not used.

EXHIB Grolier 1944; American Academy 1952
OWNER Alfred A. Knopf

1847★ ' "Excuse – permit me," he said softly' [n.d.]

The Devil introduces himself to Max and Enoch Soames in the restaurant (1919 edition, p. 27). Intended for N.Y. edition but not used.

EXHIB Grolier 1944; American Academy 1952
REPRO **Plate 84**
OWNER University of Texas

1848★ 'I had a suspicion, I had a certainty' [n.d.]

Max reading newspaper opposite Enoch Soames in the restaurant (1919 edition, p. 33). Intended for N.Y. edition but not used.

EXHIB Grolier 1944; American Academy 1952
OWNER University of Texas

1849★ Enoch Soames and myself [n.d.]

A more finished version of 1848, and almost identical.

EXHIB L.G. 1952
OWNER Piccadilly Gallery

1850★ 'The bringer of that inevitable ending filled the door-way' [n.d.]

The Devil reappears to claim Soames (1919 edition, p. 41). Intended for N.Y. edition but not used.

EXHIB Grolier 1944; American Academy 1952
OWNER University of Texas

1851★ 'I was miserably aware that I nodded and smiled to him' [n.d.]

Max meeting the Devil in Paris (1919 edition, p. 47). Intended for N.Y. edition but not used.

EXHIB Grolier 1944; American Academy 1952
OWNER University of Texas

1852 Enoch Soames 1947

For Dennis Arundell

Full-length profile facing left.

OWNER Dennis Arundell

1853★ 'Ariel' 1895

Full-length drawing of Hilary Maltby. The date is as fictional as the character.

EXHIB Grolier 1944; American Academy 1952
REPRO *Seven Men* (N.Y.), 1920
OWNER University of Texas

1854★ 'A Faun' 1895

Head and shoulders of Stephen Braxton. The date is fictional.

EXHIB Grolier 1944; American Academy 1952
REPRO *Seven Men* (N.Y.), 1920
OWNER University of Texas

1855★ [Untitled Unsigned n.d.]

A pencil sketch of James Pethel playing baccarat, with other people around him.

EXHIB Grolier 1944; American Academy 1952
REPRO *Seven Men* (N.Y.), 1920
OWNER University of Texas

1856★ [Untitled Unsigned n.d.]

Half-length profile facing right of A. V. Laider in cap, muffler and overcoat, drawn on a sheet of paper headed The Beach Hotel, Linmouth, Sussex, *which Max had specially printed by a local stationer.*

EXHIB Grolier 1944; American Academy 1952
REPRO *Seven Men* (N.Y.), 1920
OWNER University of Texas

1857 Poor A. V. Laider [Unsigned n.d.]

Three-quarter-length profile facing left, walking by sea in cap and overcoat.

OWNER Mrs Viva King

1858★ Savonarola Act II. Slow but Sure [n.d.]

One large sketch, and several small ones, of 'Savonarola' Brown.

EXHIB Grolier 1944; American Academy 1952
REPRO *Seven Men* (N.Y.), 1920
OWNER University of Texas

1859★ In piam memoriam 'Savonarola' Brown 1936

REPRO **Plate 85**
OWNER Merton College, Oxford

1860★ **Felix Argallo and Walter Ledgett** [n.d.]
EXHIB Achenbach 1964
OWNER U.C.L.A. (Clark)

NOTE – *Six drawings of the characters with which Max illustrated his own copy of 'Seven Men' (now at Merton College, Oxford) were reproduced in the World's Classics edition of the book, 1966.*

THE DREADFUL DRAGON OF HAY HILL, 1928
1861★ **Thia and Thol – B.C. 39,000** 1928

EXHIB L.G. 1952
REPRO *The Dreadful Dragon of Hay Hill*, 1928
OWNER Anthony Rye

1862★ **Thia and Thol – B.C. 39,000** 1928
Almost identical with 1861
OWNER Berg Collection (N.Y.) P.L.

MAINLY ON THE AIR, 1957
See 1284

(2) THE SECOND CHILDHOOD OF JOHN BULL, 1901

A series of fifteen drawings as follows:

1863★ [1] **The Ideal John Bull** – 1901
'I'm going to see this thing through'

1864★ [2] **The Real J. B.** 1901
'Ah well, but I ain't doin' so badly neither. There's Boney under lock an' key at St Helena. An' Drake he have stopped that there Armada. An' Burgoyne's goin' to teach them Colonists a lesson. Just you wait. What I say is "Old England's Old England still",' etc. etc. etc.

1865★ [3] **Lest we forget ourselves**
Kimberley – Ladysmith – Mafeking
J. B.: 'What I shay ish thish: A man'sh ash young ash 'e feelsh, an' ash dignified.'
'We are often taunted with being a phlegmatic and unemotional race; but the nature and extent of the recent rejoicings will convince even our neighbours' etc., etc. (See Contemporary Historians, passim.)
J. B. lies drunk in gutter while foreigners look on.

1866★ [4] **An Errand of Mercy**
J. B.: 'Out-patient? *Me?* Imperence! I've just stepped round to leave a few flowers for them poor decaying Latin races. (Drat these 'ere couple o' steps).'
He is hobbling up to a door marked EUROPEAN HOSPITAL.

1867★ [5] **Saint George and the Dragon (revised version)**

The Dragon is swallowing Saint George, whose horse gallops away.

1868★ [6] **Colenso – Magersfontein – Spion Kop**
'The admiration and envy of the whole civilised world has been excited by the exemplary fortitude and self-control with which, during that dark week, the public received the news of the disasters – a fortitude and a self-control which (and we speak in no mere spirit of vaingloriousness) no other nation,' etc., etc. (See Contemporary Historians, passim.)
J. B. asleep in bed, with a Union Jack bedspread.

1869★ [7] **[Untitled]**
J. B.: 'Not another word about that Kroojer telegram. I don't deny as 'ow at the time I may 'ave been a bit 'urt and 'uffy-like. But by your affable be'aviour since, you've bin and gone and made hample atonement. So what I say is, let bygones *be* bygones. 'Ock * to you, Sir.' * ?Hoch
A helmeted German soldier is extracting a bundle marked TRADE *from J. B.'s tail-pocket.*

1870★ [8] **To Brother Jonathan**
J. B.: 'O Sir, please Sir, *do* let us young Hanglo-Saxons stand shoulder to shoulder agin the world. Think of our common tongue. Think of that there Mayflower. O Sir, Sir, ain't blood thicker than water?' etc., etc. (B. J. guesses the At-lantic is not com-posed of blood.)
J. B. on his knees clasps the coat-tails of B. J., who has stars on his shirt and stripes on his trousers.

1871★ [9] Ireland

J. B.: ''Tain't no manner o' use you goin' on a-talkin' to me. I be that 'ard o' 'earin, I don't ketch one blessed word o' your jabbering. You lemme alone, or I'll give you in charge again, I will.'

He is addressing a ragged beggar-girl with a harp on her back.

1872★ [10] The Crusade against Ritualism

J. B. (from his pew): 'Why, this is better than cock-fightin', any day; and there ain't no croolty involved. 'Ooray! Don't no one interfere with 'em. Let 'em fight it out. I'm a lover of fair-play, I am. Go it, you with the umberella! Stick to it, you with the censer!'

1873★ [11] De Arte Theatrali

J. B.: 'Melpomene, *you're* dismissed. I ain't so young as I was, and that gloomy face of yours is more than I can stand about the 'ouse. Thalia, you can stay on. Not as 'ow I've been puffectly satisfied with you, either, o' late. Don't let me 'ave to make any more complaints about you tryin' to get *Ideas* into your 'ead. You keep to your station; or, I cautions you, *you'll* 'ave to go too, my girl.'

J. B. sits at a desk, before which stand the two Muses, dressed like hospital nurses and wearing appropriate masks.

1874★ [12] De Arte Pictoria

J. B.: 'Two-ought-three-seven: "David playing before Saul"' (pause). '*There's* Saul – 'im with the crown on 'is 'ead. Saul what was also called Paul. And there's young David with the 'arp' (pause), 'And there's the evenin' star in the middle' (pause). 'Lor'! what a lesson to all of us' (pause). 'Colourin' very fine. Somethin' *like* a picter, that is!' (marks it in R.A. catalogue and totters to next canvas).

Saul in the picture bears a strong resemblance to God in 1630.

1875★ [13] De Arte Poetica

J. B. to R[udyard] K[ipling]: 'Yes, I've took a fancy to you, young feller. 'Tain't often I cottons to a Pote, neither. 'Course there's Shakespeare. 'E was a wonder, 'e was.' (Sentimentally) ' "Swan of Avon," *I* calls 'im. Take 'im for all in all we shall not look upon 'is likes agin. And then there was Tennyson – 'im as wrote the ode to Balaclavy. '*E* was a master-mind, too, in his way. So's Lewis Morris. Knows right from wrong like the palm of 'is 'and, and ain't afraid to say where one begins and 'tother ends. But most Potes ain't like that. What I say is, *they ain't wholesome.* Look at Byron! Saucy 'ound, with 'is stuck-up airs and 'is stuck-down collars, and 'is oglin' o' the gals. But *I* soon sent 'im to the right about. "*Outside,*" said I, and out 'e went. And then there was that there friend o' his, went by the name o' Shelley, 'ad to go too. '*E* was a fair caution, was Shelley. Drownded hisself in a I-talian lake, and I warrant that was the first bath '*e* ever took. Most of 'em is like that – *not wholesome,* and can't keep a civil tongue i' their 'eads. You're different, you are: don't give yourself no 'aughty airs, and though you're rough (with your swear-words and your what-nots) I will say as 'ow you've always bin wery civil an' respec'ful to myself. You're one o' the right sort, you are. And them little tit-bits o' information what you gives me about my Hempire – why, Alf 'Armsworth 'imself couldn't do it neater, I do believe. Got your banjo with you tonight? Then empty that there mug, and give us a toon.'

R. K., wearing a schoolboy's cap, is holding a foaming tankard and smoking a clay pipe. Beside him a little dog sits begging. Some think it represents Alfred Austin, the Poet Laureate.

1876★ [14] Darby and Joan at Dover Castle

J. B. looks through a defective telescope at the setting sun. Behind him sits Britannia, glum and old, her battered trident sheathed in an umbrella. 'H.M.S. Obsolete' steams by.

1877★ [15] The Twentieth Century pressing the English rose between the pages of History

The T. C. is a young girl. See also 2047.

EXHIB Carfax 1901 (all 15): L.G. 1945 (Guedalla), nos 2, 4, 7, 8 and 9 only

REPRO *Daily Mail,* 7 Dec 1901 (nos 2, 7 and 8 only); *The Second Childhood of John Bull,* 1911

1878 Nil

(3) 'DOUBLES'
(arranged alphabetically)

[They] were done in 1917. They may be called 'doubles'. You fold a sheet of paper in half, you make some random blotch on it, fold it again instantly, unfold it, see what possibility it suggests, and proceed to make blotches of a more calculated kind. A little cheating – a very little of it – is within the rules of the game.

Max's Note to L.G. catalogue, May 1921

1879* **Ariadne in Naxos** 1917
EXHIB L.G. May 1921
OWNER Mrs Hamilton Cottier

1880 **[Belle Bergère** 1917]
EXHIB L.G. May 1921

1881 **[A Brontë** 1917]
EXHIB L.G. May 1921

1882* **Café Chantant** 1917
REPRO **Plate 88**
OWNER D'Offay Couper Gallery

1883* **Cassandra** 1917
EXHIB L.G. May 1921
REPRO *Illustrated London News*, 21 May 1921

1884 **[Design for costume of Macduff (by Gordon Craig)** 1917]
EXHIB L.G. May 1921

1885* **Esmeralda** 1917
EXHIB L.G. May 1921
REPRO **Plate 86**
OWNER Mrs Hamilton Cottier

1886* **Incognita** 1917
EXHIB L.G. May 1921
OWNER Dr A. Herxheimer

1887* **Japanese Girl** 1917
OWNER D'Offay Couper Gallery

1888 **[Louise de la Vallière** 1917]
EXHIB L.G. May 1921

1889* **Merlin** 1917
EXHIB L.G. May 1921
OWNER D'Offay Couper Gallery

1890* **Mr Arnold Dolmetsch** 1917
EXHIB L.G. May 1921
REPRO **Plate 87**
OWNER D'Offay Couper Gallery

1891 **[Mrs Holmes Grey** 1917]
Mrs H. G. was the subject of a long fictional narrative poem by W. M. Rossetti.
EXHIB L.G. May 1921

1892* **Nero** 1917
EXHIB L.G. May 1921
REPRO **Plate 89**
OWNER D'Offay Couper Gallery

1893* **Pantomime Fairy** 1917
OWNER D'Offay Couper Gallery

1894* **Portrait of a Lady** 1917
EXHIB L.G. May 1921

1895* **Professional Beauty 1880** 1917
EXHIB L.G. May 1921
OWNER D'Offay Couper Gallery

1896* **The Queen of Hawaii – a Memory** 1917
EXHIB L.G. May 1921

1897* **Richard II** 1917
OWNER D'Offay Couper Gallery

1898* **Saturday Afternoon** 1917
OWNER D'Offay Couper Gallery

1899 **[Scaramouch** 1917]
EXHIB L.G. May 1921

1900* **Souvenir de Kate Greenaway** 1917
EXHIB L.G. May 1921
OWNER Mrs Hamilton Cottier

1901* **Study of a Chinese Princess** 1917
EXHIB L.G. May 1921
OWNER D'Offay Couper Gallery

1902* **Study of a Sprite** 1917
OWNER D'Offay Couper Gallery

1903* **Study of an Egyptian Dancer** 1917
OWNER D'Offay Couper Gallery

A series of sixteen drawings as follows. Their dates are part of the joke, and they were probably drawn between 1921 and 1923.

1904★ [1] **Mr Ashby Blount-Williamson** 1873
Was an intimate friend of Count Metternich, has been sought in counsel by a long line of our Prime Ministers, and possesses the finest Guido Reni in England

1905★ [2] **Mr Sergeant Gibbs** 1875
His eloquence, though rude, wrings verdicts

1906★ [3] **Count Zariocinski** 1874
His Excellency has everywhere owed much, though not more than he acknowledges, to feminine interest and influence

1907★ [4] **Mr Alfred Nixon** 1876
Almost the last repository and exponent of the great tradition of English acting, he survives to shame the brood of inarticulate amateurs who have jostled him from the boards

1908★ [5] **Admiral Sir Japhet Kenway, K.C.B., etc.** 1873
Without recanting his famous apothegm that Steam tolls the knell of Seamanship, he continues to be personally the cheeriest and pleasantest of men

1909★ [6] **Mr Thomas MacGrath, M.P.** 1874
A rigorous opponent of all the doctrines preached by Mr Carlyle, he has nevertheless failed hitherto to catch the ear of the House of Commons

1910★ [7] **General Sir George Rawlinson, V.C., G.C.M.G., etc.** 1873
He is convinced, rightly or wrongly, that the abolition of the Purchase System must entail the instant surrender of England to whatever foreign Power shall first attack her

1911★ [8] **Mr Jacob Stanning, R.A.** 1874
Let the pundits argue about the technical merits of his work: posterity will hold that no painter of our time has shown a deeper insight into the character and career of Mary Queen of Scots

1912★ [9] **Sir Archibald Boyd, M.D., F.R.S., etc. etc. etc.** 1875
Has rendered noble service to medical science, and is generally acknowledged to be the best *raconteur* in London

1913★ [10] **Mr Ambrose Hart** 1875
Having adapted already upwards of one hundred and twenty comedies, dramas, farces and melodramas from the French, he bids fair to raise English theatrical art from that slough of despond in which it has so long lain submerged

1914★ [11] **Sir Herbert Vansittart** 1873
Ah, did you once see 'Prinny' plain,
    And did he stop and speak to you?
And did you speak to him again?
    How strange it seems, and new!
The first stanza of Browning's 'Memorabilia', with 'Shelley' changed to 'Prinny' (George IV).

1915★ [12] **Father Vernon** 1873
Amidst all that he has suffered for the Faith of his adoption, he has the comfort of knowing that ladies of even the highest fashion have professed to find no flaw in his dialectics

1916★ [13] **Viscount Westerville** 1876
In these days, when statesmanship has given place to glibness, his break-down in seconding the Address last week is an earnest of the great services that he is destined to render to this country

1917★ [14] **Mr Justice Blethlake** 1874
In his ninety-fifth year he still charges juries with not less of vigour and with far more of wisdom than Don Quixote charged windmills

1918★ [15] **The Hon. and very Rev. the Dean of Hippister** 1876
Albeit the warmest of his admirers did not claim for him in his famous controversy with Professor Tyndal a more than moral victory, his simple dignity and force of character are such that whenever he occupies the pulpit of the Cathedral with which he has so long been connected even the most thoughtful among his hearers are often listeners also

1919★ [16] **Lord Pentham of Lithway** 1874
In an age of hucksters and chapmen he has done nothing to tarnish the great name he bears, and honourably remains almost as poor as the majority of his creditors

EXHIB L.G. 1923 (all sixteen) and 1957 (fourteen only)
REPRO *Things New and Old*, 1923
OWNER Osbert Lancaster (all but nos 8 and 11); Denys Parsons (no. 8)

1920★ **Sketches of the New Boys' Exam [Signed with monogram** 1887]

A page of drawings of boys, masters and parents.

REPRO *Greyfriar,* Aug 1887

1921★ **Exeat Sketches [Signed with monogram** 1889]

A page of drawings, mostly of boys.

REPRO *Greyfriar,* Aug 1889

1922★ **[A Bedesman Unsigned** 1889]

REPRO *Greyfriar,* Dec 1899, where captioned as above

[Charterhouse Types. Signed with monogram 1890]
1923★ 1. The Photographer
1924★ 2. The Debater
1925★ 3. The Vocalist

REPRO *Greyfriar,* Apr, Aug and Dec 1890

1926★ **[Club Types Unsigned** 1892]

Thirty-six drawings representing typical members of the following clubs:

1. Playgoers', Savage, National Liberal, Amphitryon, White's, Jockey, Reform, Beefsteak, Garrick, Junior United Service, Devonshire, Senior United Service, Arts, St James's, Junior Carlton, Travellers', Lyric, Carlton
2. Green Room, Isthmian, Bachelors', St Stephen's, Marlborough, Constitutional, Corinthian, Savile, Athenaeum
3. Gardenia, Union, Brooks's, Albemarle, Maison Dorée, Junior Athenaeum, Turf, Guards', Press

REPRO *Strand Magazine,* Sep, Nov and Dec 1892; *Max's Nineties,* 1958 (9 drawings only)

1927★ **Typical of almost *any* Club nowadays** 1946

A postscript to 1926, showing a scruffy nondescript man.

REPRO *Strand Magazine,* Oct 1946

1928★ **[Untitled Unsigned** 1946]

Rough sketch for 1927.

OWNER Merton College, Oxford

1929★ **Boulevard Types [Signed with monogram** 1892]

A page of seven drawings.

REPRO *Greyfriar,* Dec 1892

1930 **The New Culture [Signed with monogram** 1893]

REPRO *Oxford Magazine,* 18 May 1893

1931★ **[Oxford at Home Unsigned** 1894]

Eight drawings illustrating 'Oxford at Home' by Harold George: A Speaker at the 'Union'; 'Blood'; 'Smug'; A Member of the Bullingdon; A Student of Somerville Hall; The Lady Novelist's Ideal; The Dilettante; Dons, New School and Old School.

REPRO *Strand Magazine,* Jan 1895

1932★ **[Untitled Unsigned** *c.* 1894]

A Don of the New School: 'Oh, I am so glad that the Era of Platitude and Port Wine is past!'
A Don of the Old School: 'Alas that I should live to see Alma Mater pass into the hands of a pack of puny free-thinkers in billicock hats!'

Very similar to the last drawing in 1931.

OWNER John Sparrow

1933★ **[Seen on the Towpath Unsigned** 1895]

A young man in a striped suit and straw hat, holding a lighted cigar behind his back.

REPRO *Octopus,* Oxford, 29 May 1895, where captioned as above

1933A★ **Recreations of the Rabelais Club. Mr John Bull à la Française [Signed with monogram** n.d.]

Done at Oxford. Three other similar 'Recreations' are in Mr Taylor's collection.

OWNER Robert H. Taylor

[Political Types *c.* 1896]

Eleven drawings as follows:
1934★ The Old-Fashioned Tory
1935★ One of the Few Members who care about the Indian Budget
1936★ The Professional Member, whose fame is outside the House
1937★ The Ordinary Tory
1938★ The Irish Member
1939★ The Ordinary Radical
1940★ The Scotch Member
1941★ The Old-Fashioned Liberal
1942★ The Labour Member
1943★ The Tory who has subscribed much to the Party Funds
1944★ The Welsh Member

'The Ordinary Tory' is almost identical with 1688

EXHIB L.G. 1945 (Guedalla), where dated as above
OWNER Art Gallery of New South Wales, Sydney

1945★ **[The 'Smug' and the 'Blood' Unsigned** 1898]

An *elaborated version of 1329, illustrating a doggerel poem by Max called 'Eudaemonia'.*

REPRO *Isis*, Oxford, 28 May 1898, where captioned as above
OWNER Sold at Sotheby's 11 Dec 1968

1946★ **An American Humourist** [c. 1900]
Seated at table, smoking a cigar. May conceivably represent a real person, but a generic type seems more likely.
REPRO *Butterfly*, Feb 1900

1947★ **A ministering Angel? Thou?** [1900]
An amateur nurse in the Boer War.
EXHIB Achenbach 1964
REPRO *World*, Christmas No, 1900
OWNER U.C.L.A. (Clark)

1948★ [**Untitled** 1900]
Head and shoulders of bored soldier with rifle.
EXHIB Achenbach 1964
REPRO *World*, Christmas No, 1900
OWNER U.C.L.A. (Clark)

1949★ [**Untitled** 1900]
A volunteer, with fixed bayonet, attacking sea-serpent called EUROPE which is threatening Britannia, chained on a tiny island.
EXHIB Achenbach 1964
REPRO *World*, Christmas No, 1900
OWNER U.C.L.A. (Clark)

1950★ [**Untitled** 1900]
A Chinaman with pigtail and umbrella, representing the Yellow Peril.
EXHIB Achenbach 1964
REPRO *World*, Christmas No, 1900
OWNER U.C.L.A. (Clark)

1951★ **'Nec spes opis ulla dabatur'** [**Nor was any hope of help offered. Virgil, Aeneid, II, 803.**] [1900]
Back-view of three Boer delegates walking towards the setting sun.
REPRO *World*, Christmas No, 1900

1952★ **The unsuccessful decoy** [1900]
A lady representing the Paris Exhibition.
EXHIB Achenbach 1964
REPRO *World*, Christmas No, 1900
OWNER U.C.L.A. (Clark)

1953★ [**Untitled** 1900]
'The girl he left behind him' – a dockside scene.
EXHIB Achenbach 1964
REPRO *World*, Christmas No, 1900
OWNER U.C.L.A. (Clark)

1954★ **Controllers of our Naval Policy** [1900]
Three 'patriots of the music-halls'.

EXHIB Achenbach 1964
REPRO *World*, Christmas No, 1900
OWNER U.C.L.A. (Clark)

1955★ [**Untitled** 1900]
A big fish caught on hooks in the form of a soldier and a sailor.
EXHIB Achenbach 1964
REPRO *World*, Christmas No, 1900
OWNER U.C.L.A. (Clark)

1956★ **Messrs Carfax** [1901]
A monstrous head, with two kiss-curls, three eyes and four Jewish noses, appearing from a groundwork labelled PERCENTAGES.
EXHIB Carfax 1901
OWNER J. F. McCrindle

[**The visit of the English M.P.'s to Paris** 1903]
Three drawings:
1957★ [1. The English member as foreseen by the French deputy]
1958★ [2. The French deputy as foreseen by the English member]
1959★ [3. Each, as met by the other]
REPRO *Sketch*, 2 Dec 1903 and Christmas No, 1958, where captioned as above

1960★ **Everyman** 1907
A nondescript man in flashy riding clothes.
REPRO Geoffrey Keynes, *Bibliotheca Bibliographici*, 1964
OWNER Sir Geoffrey Keynes

1961 **Jeunesse Dorée** 1907
OWNER Sold at Sotheby's 14 Dec 1960

1962★ **A Study in Democratic Assimilation** 1908
Two joined drawings, the first showing Scion of Proletariat and Scion of Nobility in 1868, dressed as you would expect; the second showing them indistinguishably dressed in 1908.
EXHIB L.G. 1911 and 1957
REPRO *Fifty Caricatures*, 1913
OWNER Mrs Dilys Sullivan

1963★ [**Untitled Unsigned** c. 1908]
Rough sketch for the tenor in 1664.
OWNER Roy Huss

1964 **Nil**

1965★ **The Horny Hand** 1909
The huge hand of Labour descends on an obese and coroneted peer, nakedly counting his money-bags on a hilltop within sight of his ancestral home.
EXHIB N.E.A.C. Winter 1909
REPRO **Plate 82**
OWNER Fitzwilliam Museum, Cambridge

1966* Effect of Lady Cardigan's Book 1909

Early-Edwardian Era (to Early-Victorian Era): 'So! Now at last we see you in your true colours!'

Lady C's 'My Recollections' caused a sensation when they were published in Sep 1909.

EXHIB N.E.A.C. Winter 1909
REPRO *Daily Mail*, 20 Nov 1909
OWNER Ben Glazebrook

1967 [What's to be done with our Drama? 1909]

EXHIB L.G. 1952, where dated as above

1968 [The Artist]

EXHIB L.G. 1911

1969 [A Dream for Eugenists . . . the Cecil brow, the Churchill eye, the Campbell hair, the Somerset nose, and the Cavendish under-lip]

EXHIB L.G. 1911

1970 [Noblemen's Memoirs]

[Industrious Anonyma: 'I saw a good lot of the Prince of Wales – afterwards Edward VII – in those days, and I must say that a better sportsman – and, I may add, a better pal – never stepped in shoe-leather. I remember once after I had been having rather a rotten day at Newmarket he came up to me and, slapping me on the back, said,' etc., etc.]

EXHIB L.G. 1913

1971* [Untitled Unsigned c.1913]

Pompous man, crowned with laurel-wreath, about to be struck in the back by an arrow.

REPRO Binding-case of *Fifty Caricatures*, 1913

1972* Myself according to Longmans Greene & Co. Shame! [n.d.]

For John Barrymore Rapallo Jan. 1935

Very similar to 1971, but without arrow. The date seems likely to be that of the inscription rather than the drawing. Known only from a photograph at Merton College, Oxford.

1973 The Olympic Affair [1912]

British (to American) Athlete: 'I say, hang it, look here, you know, I tell you what it is, damn it: you're not a gentleman.

The Englishman fat and smoking a cigar, the American lean and dressed in running kit. The Olympic Games were held in Stockholm in 1912.

EXHIB L.G. 1913
OWNER Dr E. V. Bevan

1974* In John Bull's Servants' Hall ('Punch', 'The Daily Telegraph', and 'The Spectator') 1913

'Above the mantelpiece hangs a little oleograph of John Bull. Facing it stands the house-keeper, a middle-aged, sad, smug 'treasure' (the *Spectator*), gazed at by a *very* old and decrepit footman (*Punch*), while between them, leaning against the mantelpiece, haughtily, is the large and wildly Semitic butler (*Daily Telegraph*).' (*Max to Reggie Turner, 22 Apr 1913*)

EXHIB L.G. 1913 and 1957
OWNER Mrs Jill Hirschmann

1975* Such Good 'Copy' [1913]

Our Yellow Press: 'Aoh, light up yer torch and come along, Bellona, do! Hingland and Germany's *got* ter fight it aht!'

EXHIB L.G. 1913
REPRO *Fifty Caricatures*, 1913
OWNER Yale University Library

1976* And only just thirteen! 1913

The Grave Misgivings of the Nineteenth Century, and the Wicked Amusement of the Eighteenth, in watching the Progress (or whatever it is) of the Twentieth

EXHIB L.G. 1913
REPRO *Fifty Caricatures*, 1913
OWNER Lady Barlow

1977* Night-Life in London. No. 1. The Wits and Beaux of the Garrick Club 2.30 a.m. 1914

Retired Military Man: 'My dear feller, what I say is this: let's stick to the point. Agreed. Very well. Well then, what I say is what I said just now: if Jesus Christ wasn't a Messiah, donchersee, then what the Hell was 'e?'

A row of dullards at a long table, in full evening dress and smoking cigars. Waiter stifling yawn in background.

EXHIB Cincinnati 1965
OWNER Lilly Library

1978* The Wits and Beaux of the Savile Club [n.d.]

A standing group of scruffy lay-figures, one holding a cup of tea.

EXHIB L.G. 1957
OWNER Lt Col C. J. G. Meade

1979 [Titled as below] 1917

In Memory of dear old charming days. Whig Nobleman, imprescient of Death Duties, Motor Cars, Labour Members, the War of 1914–19?? or *anything* of that kind. To William [Rothenstein] from Max, affectionately

OWNER Mrs Rachel Ward

1980* Cinderella 1917

OWNER Piccadilly Gallery

1981 An English working-class family 1919

'We are realising that education, as a Latin poet said, is something that changes mind and will. On all sides this doctrine of education is being preached today. We are busy in deflecting the mind and will of adults and children alike from the paths of ignorance into those of instructed reasonableness. Girls are learning house-craft, mothers the art of keeping children healthy, boys the use of their hands, men the use of books.' (*Times:* leading article Monday, Mar 31, 1919)

The drawing shows the parents and eight children. Dad sits comfortably smoking his pipe and reading a novel by William Le Queux. Behind him two small boys are fighting fiercely. Three daughters are resentfully swabbing and sweeping the floor. Mum is doing physical jerks with three very small children.

OWNER Maxwell Halliday

1982★ 'Si Vieillesse Pouvait' 1920

Scene: A Room in the War Office. Time: The Present.
Eminent Scientist (explaining chemical formula): 'One ounce of this powder, dropped from an aeroplane, would destroy all human and other animal life throughout an area of 500 square miles.'
Eminent Soldier (Sudan Campaign. Medal with clasps. Despatches twice): 'Would it though? Good gracious me, you don't say so! Marvellous! . . . Have the other Powers got anything of the sort, d'ye think?'
Eminent Scientist: 'Nothing *quite* so good at present, I think. But of course——'
Eminent Soldier: 'Well, it's perfectly marvellous. But – gad! – how one wishes one was a youngster, and *sure* of being in the Next Great War!'

EXHIB L.G. May 1921
REPRO *A Survey*, 1921

1983★ The Future, as beheld by the Eighteenth Century 1920

A topical worthy contemplates a faded version of himself.

EXHIB L.G. May 1921 and 1952
REPRO *A Survey*, 1921
OWNER Fitzwilliam Museum, Cambridge

1984★ The Future, as beheld by the Nineteenth Century 1920

A topical worthy contemplates a larger version of himself.

EXHIB L.G. May 1921 and 1952
REPRO *A Survey*, 1921
OWNER Fitzwilliam Museum, Cambridge

1985★ The Future, as beheld by the Twentieth Century 1920

A topical worthy contemplates a question-mark.

EXHIB L.G. May 1921 and 1952

REPRO *A Survey*, 1921
OWNER Fitzwilliam Museum, Cambridge

1986★ A Translethean Soliloquy 1920

[Damsel of the 'Keepsake' Time:] 'I do wonder what the young gentlemen saw in *me*!'

She is contemplating a blasé-looking girl dressed in the extreme fashion of 1920.

EXHIB L.G. May 1921 and 1957
REPRO *A Survey*, 1921, where the speaker is identified as above
OWNER Victoria & Albert Museum

1987★ A Study in Temptation. Our Labour Delegates in Russia 1920

EXHIB L.G. May 1921 and 1945 (Guedalla)
REPRO *A Survey*, 1921
OWNER Lilly Library

1988★ Blame the Cloth 1920

A Captain of Industry declaring [to a curate] that the desire of the manual workers to be paid exorbitant wages for doing the least possible amount of work is a sure sign that they have lost their faith in a future life

EXHIB L.G. May 1921
REPRO *A Survey*, 1921
OWNER Mrs Ronald Wells

1989★ The Reaction towards a more Judicial Method of Criticism 1920

Elder Critic: 'And what is *that*–er–rather peculiar object?'
Younger Critic: 'My hat, sir.'

He points to a lawyer's wig.

EXHIB L.G. May 1921
REPRO *A Survey*, 1921

1989A★ [Title and dialogue similar to 1989, but partially torn off Unsigned n.d.]

Pencil sketch for 1989, but figures transposed.

OWNER U.C.L.A. (Clark)

1990★ Politics 1920

'M'dyah, doncher think Trotsky must be *rarther* a darling? Doncher think it would be *rarther* divine if we had some one *rarther* like him here? Isn't there something *rarther* touching about him? Of co'rse a Red Terror would be *rarther* awful while it larsted. Bur orl the same, I do think,' etc.

One bright young female addresses another in a jazzy décor.

EXHIB L.G. May 1921
REPRO *A Survey*, 1921
OWNER The Earl of Antrim

1991★ The Patron 1920

(a drawing dedicated – with all possible sympathy and good-will, heaven knows! – to those of our young poets who, not knowing very much – why *should* they know very much? – about politics and the deplorable part which human nature plays in politics, imagine that under the domination of LABOUR the liberal arts might have quite a decent chance.)

Minister of Education: 'Wot? You'll dedicate your mon-you-mental translation of Pett Rark's sonnits to me if I'll get you out-door relief for six months? Oh, really! And you say *you*'re one o' the Workers yourself? Worker? Blackmailer – that's what *you* are! . . . *Outside!*'

(Exit Poet, inwardly composing (*mutatis mutandis*) some such letter as was written by Samuel Johnson to the fourth Lord Chesterfield.)

EXHIB L.G. May 1921
REPRO *A Survey*, 1921

1992 Our Complex World 1920

Proletariat: 'And if I destroyed *them* [two Edwardian exquisites] I should destroy myself *with* 'em!'

EXHIB L.G. May 1921
REPRO *Sketch*, 1 Jun 1921
OWNER Alistair Cooke

1993★ Author, Publisher, and Printer 1920

[A] In the dear old recent time
[B] At the present time

Two joined drawings. In [A] the thin author stands hat in hand while the fat and prosperous publisher patronisingly hands a parcelled manuscript to a thin and obsequious printer. In [B] the author, still hat in hand, is a skeleton, and the shrunken publisher is begging the fat rich printer to accept the parcel.

EXHIB L.G. May 1921
OWNER Miss Mary Parker

1993A★ Author, Publisher and Printer [Unsigned n.d.]

Sketches for 1993 on two sides of the paper, one subtitled Nineteenth Century.

OWNER Robert H. Taylor

1994 Author, Publisher, and Printer [n.d.]

[A] Eighteenth Century
[B] Nineteenth Century

Probably a sketch for 1993.

OWNER A. H. Perrin

1995★ Independent Liberalism's desire for some means whereby it and Labour shall not clash in electoral contests 1921

Labour: 'Well, I won't say it mightn't be for what you've called the national good. But you see, Guvnor, the *goods* are what *I*'m out for.'

The gross figure of Labour holds the tiny earnest Liberal on the palm of his hand.

EXHIB L.G. May 1921
REPRO *A Survey*, 1921
OWNER Piccadilly Gallery

1996★ The Independent Liberals' desire for some means whereby they and Labour shall not clash in electoral contests [Unsigned n.d.]

A sketch for 1995, from which Labour's words have been partially erased.

OWNER Miss Julia K. Williams

1997★ St James's Street 1921

[A] a few years ago
   The Marquess of Pantagruel believing (quite rightly) that the sight of him cheers and pleases the populace
[B] to-day
   The Marquess of Pantagruel fearing (rightly or wrongly) that the sight of him embitters the populace

Two drawings of the same club window. In [A] the Marquess in top hat and frock coat, smokes a cigar. In [B], in very ordinary clothes, he smokes a pipe.

EXHIB L.G. May 1921
REPRO *A Survey*, 1921

1998 [L'Entrée au Bal (painting by Georges Nastreau 1879) 1921]

EXHIB L.G. 1952, where dated as above

1999★ The Average Secretary of State 1921

Two joined drawings

(1) as he once was – how rightly!
   For Philip Guedalla
(2) as he soon must be.
   Dear P. G. I leave this drawing in a rough, crude, bald condition. I haven't the nerve to linger over it. And yet – who knows? – time works such wonders, time casts such glamours – 100 years hence or so this very drawing *may* strike sentimental deep wistful chords in such breasts as yours and that of Yours sincerely M.B.

(1) *is a finished drawing of a slim and elegant aristocrat.*
(2) *is an outline drawing of a coarse plebeian.*

EXHIB L.G. 1945 (Guedalla)
OWNER Mrs Philip Guedalla

The Theatre of the Future 1922

Five pages as follows:

2000★ (1) The Managing Director addressing the cast on the prime importance of civic conscience
   A long beard, three pairs of spectacles, carpet slippers

2001★ (2) The Call-Boy
   A spectacled, egg-headed boy, running

2002★ (3) The Acting Manager (front of house)
Spectacled and bearded, in seedy evening dress

2003★ (4) Orlando . . . Ex-Seminarist Smith
Rosalind . . . Ex-Seminarist Robinson
Both solemn, spectacled and highbrow

2004★ (5) The Public
A blank page

For Harley [Granville Barker], these five drawings done after reading his book [*The Exemplary Theatre, 1922*] with keen delight in the power and charm of his exposition, but with a Philistine lack of reverence for what practical results may come hereafter. Max. Rapallo. 1922

REPRO (1 and 4 only) S. N. Behrman, *Portrait of Max*, N.Y., 1960

OWNER Robert H. Taylor (all five)

2005★ **Communist Sunday School** 1923
Pupils learning that they must not shrink from shedding blood in order to achieve starvation

EXHIB L.G. 1923
REPRO *Things New and Old*, 1923
OWNER J. C. Thomson

2006★ **Reciprocity** 1923
Dame Europa: 'And now, young man, now that you've bought up all *my* art-products, I shall be happy to acquire all *yours*, and I am willing to pay a generous price'
Brother Jonathan: 'Name it, Marm'
Dame Europa: 'Twopence-halfpenny'
(Brother Jonathan is slightly hurt, but, like a sensible fellow, closes with the offer.)

EXHIB L.G. 1923
REPRO *Things New and Old*, 1923

Tales of Three Nations 1923
Nine drawings, each showing varying figures representing England, France and Germany, as follows:
2007★ I. in the early years of the nineteenth century
2008★ II. 1815
2009★ III. in the eighteen-forties
2010★ IV. in the eighteen-sixties
2011★ V. in the eighteen-seventies
2012★ VI. in the early years of the twentieth century
2013★ VII. 1914
2014★ VIII. 1919
2015★ IX. January 1923

EXHIB L.G. 1923
REPRO *Things New and Old*, 1923
OWNER L. J. Cadbury

2016★ **English Fiction – Ancient and Modern** 1923
Two joined drawings:

I Ancient
The Hero trying to control a guilty passion (Quite dramatic and interesting, this)
II Modern
The Hero trying to muster up a guilty passion (Less dramatic, surely, and less interesting)

EXHIB L.G. 1923
REPRO *Things New and Old*, 1923
OWNER Mrs David Karmel

2017★ **[Untitled]** 1923
My dear Evans, I think I told you that my immense enjoyment of 'Nash' was really rather a tribute to you because I had never overcome an innate prejudice against boys as a human product. Anyhow, that is so. I dislike the shape of their heads, and the shape of their boots. Their very boot-laces displease me; but not so much as the furtive malevolence of their eyes; and the impudence of their noses. And yesterday I found in a drawer here a picture which I send to you because it explains my point of view so clearly. This is Nash as *I* see him. But of course I don't offer it as a frontispiece for the delightful book. Yours very sincerely, Max Beerbohm. Rapallo. August 26th, 1923.
A horrible little boy illustrating 'Nash and Some Others' a book of stories by C. S. Evans.

REPRO *Bermondsey Book*, Jun 1925
OWNER A. Dwye Evans

2018★ **The Private Secretary of a Minister of State – new school** January 1924
Aoh nao, you can't see the Boss to-d'y – 'e's up to 'is naose in work. If Keir-'Ardie 'imself was to rise from the grive, 'e couldn't see the Boss to-d'y.

OWNER Mrs Eva Reichmann

2019 **Theatrical Manager (London, W.C.1.)** [1924]
'Vot ith all thith Mahthk?'
For Ted [Gordon Craig]. See p. 96, *The Mask*, July 1924, from Max
Full face, Jewish, white mask on black face. 'The Mask' was a periodical edited and largely written by E.G.C.

REPRO *Mask*, Oct 1924

2020★ **Two Dear Little Sisters** 1924
Ulster armed with a shillelagh, Eire with a gun.

EXHIB L.G. 1925 and 1952
REPRO *Observations*, 1925

2021★ **The Poor Relation** 1924
[John Bull:] 'It's only me, Jonathan, with another little cheque on account. And – and – asking your pardon, Jonathan; if you *could* seem a bit chatty-like with me in the street sometimes, it would do me such a deal of good among my neighbours.'

EXHIB L.G. 1925
REPRO *Observations*, 1925

2022* **The Governing Classes and Communism**
1924

Too proud to fight? – or too tactful? – or too short-sighted? – or too liberal-minded? – or what?

A militant worker with torch and knife rushes up to a figure representing the Establishment, dressed in riding breeches, naval tunic, crucifix round neck, judge's wig and top hat.

EXHIB L.G. 1925
REPRO *Observations*, 1925
OWNER Mrs C. E. Cater

2023* **Things in General** 1924

The Principle of Good: 'How is it that you always seem to get the best of it?'
The Principle of Evil: 'Because I'm *active*, my dear!'

EXHIB L.G. 1925 and 1957
REPRO *Observations*, 1925
OWNER Lady Marks

2024* **Parerga of Statesmanship** 1924

Two drawings:
[I] Statesman of the Olden Time, making without wish for emolument a flat but faithful version of the Georgics, in English hexameters
[II] Statesman of To-Day, doing one of the articles in his powerful series, 'Men I've Been Up Against', for *The Sunday Rumpus* (Terms, £75 a line. Grammar and style touched up in the Office.)

EXHIB L.G. 1925 and 1957
REPRO *Observations*, 1925
OWNER J. C. Thomson

2025* **'Class-Consciousness'** 1924

'Now, that's the sort of class-consciousness *I*'d like ter have!'

Young worker regarding portrait of eighteenth-century aristocrat.

EXHIB L.G. 1925 and 1945 (Guedalla)
REPRO *Observations*, 1925
OWNER Mrs Philip Guedalla

2026* **Miniature design for colossal fresco commemorating the International Advertising Convention (Wembley, July 1924) and the truly wondrous torrents of cant and bunkum that were outpoured from it.** [1924]

A group of tough businessmen, all fitted with haloes and in attitudes of mock piety. Above are their comments:
All for Each; Ter-rewth; Know-ledge; Umbleness; Service; Elpfulness; Each for All; Etcetera

EXHIB L.G. 1925
REPRO *Observations*, 1925
OWNER L. J. Cadbury

2027* **The Insurgence of Youth** 1924

She: 'What I say is: it's a —— putrid shame that Europe should be run by a gang of —— old beavers without an Idea or an Ideal between 'em. If I'd my way, I'd hoick 'em all out of their —— billets, and then there might be some hope for the Nations.'
He: 'I think you're —— well right.'

EXHIB L.G. 1925
REPRO *Observations*, 1925
OWNER Victoria & Albert Museum

2028* **Civilisation and the Industrial System** 1924

He: 'No, my dear, you may've ceased to love me, but you took me for better or wuss in younger and 'appier days, and there'll be no getting away for you from me, ever.'

EXHIB L.G. 1925
REPRO *Observations*, 1925
OWNER L. J. Cadbury

2029 **[Untitled]** 1924

Two joined drawings:
[1] Did Adam and Eve, leaving the Garden, really cut quite such abject figures as all the painters would have us believe?
[2] Is it not likelier that they tried to carry off the situation with a certain *hauteur*?

OWNER Viscount Norwich

2030* **Marianne's Creditors** December 7, 1924

Brother Jonathan: 'Oh, him [John Bull]? He's a darned sight too dellacut-minded for *this* world. Just you start paying *me*, Miss!'

EXHIB L.G. 1925
REPRO *Observations*, 1925
OWNER Columbus Gallery of Fine Arts, Ohio

2031* **Recurrent Alarms** [1925]

Eleven small ovals. In each of the first eight are the head and shoulders of a worried man, suitably dressed according to his date, and saying:
1831 The treacherous opportunism of Lord Grey has tolled England's knell
1848 Thrones everywhere totter. The Chartists are on the march. O, my Country!
1867 A 'leap in the dark'? *I* call it a plunge in broad daylight into a bottomless pit
1870 The Sovereign seems to grow less and less popular. The Republicans are increasingly vocal. The end is at hand
1885 The Lords have passed the Franchise Bill. This is the last nail in Britannia's coffin. And she will have a pauper's funeral
1911 Frenzied Budgets have bled us white. And now the Constitution is to be wrecked by the sinister and malign Asquith
1919–1922 Strikes – strikes – nothing but strikes. The yawning jaws of the proletariat will close on us with a horrid clash tomorrow at latest

1923 A Socialist Government in power! Roll up the map of England: there will be no further use for it

In the ninth oval optimism prevails

1925 Well, really now, I seem to have had a great many foolish false alarms! Henceforward I'll placidly rely on the inherent sound good sense of the British People

To which a tiny Max at the bottom of the drawing interjects: Oh, my dear Sir, don't do that! You'll look a far greater fool if —— or if ——

pointing to the last two ovals, in which the optimist is submerged by bureaucracy and blown to pieces

EXHIB L.G. 1925
REPRO *Observations, 1925*

2032 ['A Prinsish, that she is']

Known only as having been sold at L.G. in 1925.

2033★ Some [Charterhouse] Masters of To-Day 1928

Fourteen imaginary faces, with the names of real masters attached to them. A companion piece to 664.

REPRO *Greyfriar, Dec 1928*
OWNER Charterhouse School

2034★ [Titled as below] 1929

Prevision of a painting which, in 1940 or so, will enrage all elderly critics but be fervently acclaimed by all the young bloods of Chelsea and of Bloomsbury. – 'Here,' they will cry, 'here at last is the happy ending to the divine Fildes's masterpiece.'

The drawing shows, in an elaborate frame, a picture of a strapping young countryman advancing across a field with open arms towards an aged man with two sticks and saying: 'You saved my life, Sir, when I was a kid!' Refers to Luke Fildes's picture 'The Return of the Penitent', 1879.

OWNER Merton College, Oxford

2035 [Untitled] 1935

Two joined drawings:
(1) The Dandy of 1895 [immaculate in top hat etc]
(2) The Dandy of 1935 [messily dressed]
For Virginia [Parsons], who, I am sure, prefers the right-hand side of the picture

OWNER The Marchioness of Bath

2036★ Literary Society in the Eighteen-Nineties 1938

A married couple ready to start for a Soirée at the Douglas Sladens'. The parlour-maid is on the door-step, whistling for a four-wheeler. The wife is taking an anxious look at herself in the mirror. There is a strong smell of camphor. But there is a hope of meeting some publishers and of making a good impression.

For Siegfried [Sassoon] from Max

OWNER George Sassoon

2037★ Charlie Parr, O.B.E. 1939

A clue in 'The Times' crossword of 22 Feb 1939, to which the anagram-answer was 'Irreproachable'.

REPRO *The Times, 25 Feb 1939*

2038★ 'The Intelligentsia' Bloomsbury [1940]

2039★ The Eupepsian Bayswater [1940]

Two drawings illustrating Max's article 'From Blooms-bury to Bayswater'.

REPRO *World Review, Aug 1940*

2040★ La France de Demain [n.d.]

Heroes of the Sandwich Bar (Their honoured names escape me)

A very tall thin man, and a very small fat one, drinking through straws.

OWNER Yale University Library

2041★ Happy Sabbath-Breakers [n.d.]

A dismal procession of men in pouring rain, carrying a banner asking SHALL SUCH THINGS BE?

OWNER Mrs Eva Reichmann

2042★ An Imaginative Man [n.d.]

Full-length profile, facing left, mostly in silhouette

OWNER Private (Yale)

2043★ Studies in Guelph. No 1. A Young Princess [n.d.]

REPRO **Plate 19**
OWNER Piccadilly Gallery

2044★ Jermyn Street [n.d.]

Full-length three-quarter-face drawing of a smartly dressed Jew.

OWNER Piccadilly Gallery

2045 [Extract from R.A. Catalogue]

['When the sun sets low o'er the violet hill,
And the tettix chirps to his mate,
And the olives beside the sacred rill,
Ilyssus, are desolate.' *Anon*]
['Unbidden For'. The last lot in the Attic Slave-Market]

EXHIB L.G. 1945 (Guedalla)

2046★ The Hornton Street Conspiracy [Unsigned n.d.]

Full-length back view of two long-haired men in overcoats and Homburg hats. Robert Ross's friend More Adey lived in Hornton Street, but so did many others.

OWNER Private (Yale)

2047 **'Keepsake'** [n.d.]

The Twentieth Century pressed the brown rose of England between the pages of history.

A variant of 1877, with a picture of a young man on the wall.

OWNER Douglas Cleverdon

2048★ **Lord Runcorn – sketched from life** [n.d.]

Certainly fictional, but from where?

REPRO **Plate 99**
OWNER Sir Rupert Hart-Davis

2049★ **[Untitled Unsigned** n.d.**]**

Three-quarter-length profile facing left, of woman wearing a fur boa and big hat which obscure her face.

OWNER Mark Birley

2050★ **[Untitled** n.d.**]**

Half-length of grotesque woman. Large bosom, necklace. No top to her head. Feather sticking up from hair.

OWNER David Drey

2051 **[Miss Gibbs, the Governess, giving Notice]**

Max's interpretation of a piece of statuary owned by Mr and Mrs Ellis Roberts. Known only from a friend's description.

2052★ **Venice [Unsigned** n.d.**]**

Pencil sketch of three solid Germanic tourists, two male and one female, walking in single file beside the Grand Canal, the leading male reading a guide-book.

OWNER University of Texas

Plates

*The captions are not always exact transcriptions. For these, and all
other particulars, see the catalogue-number in brackets.*

3 Mr Gladstone
Piccadilly Gallery (583)

4 The Warden of Merton
Merton College, Oxford (172)

TWO EARLY DRAWINGS

5 Oscar Wilde
John Bryson (1778)

An undergraduate drawing.

Ar Max Beerbohm receives an influential, though biassed, deputation, urging him, — the cause of our common humanity, and of good taste, to give over.

6 Mr Max Beerbohm receives an influential, though biassed, deputation, urging him, in the cause of our common humanity, and of good taste, to give over. 1908
Art Institute of Chicago (1423)

The deputation consists of Soveral (as spokesman), Lord Burnham, Hall Caine, Carson, Chesterton, Haldane, Henry James, Kipling, George Moore, Northcliffe, Pinero, Will Rothenstein, Sargent, Shaw, Steer, Tosti and Zangwill.

7 Lord Salisbury leading the nation. 1901
Owner Unknown (1359)

8 Lord Rosebery. 1905
Ashmolean Museum, Oxford (1252)

9 Campbell–Bannerman
Jeremy Thorpe (239)

10 Lloyd George. *c.* 1908
National Portrait Gallery (947)

11 The Treasury Bench (while the
Secretary for War still was on it). 1911
Lord Conesford (43)

*Left to right: Lloyd George, Asquith,
Churchill, Haldane, L. V. Harcourt, Birrell,
John Burns.*

12 *Ditto*
Jeremy Thorpe (44)

13 'Porro Unum Est Necessarium': Mr Asquith, having kissed hands on his
appointment, sets to work, with characteristic industry and determination, to
acquire personal magnetism. 1908
Mrs Marie Strang (42)

14 A Solution

Mr Arthur Balfour: '. . . And so – though of course it is quite possible that you are none of you at all restive really – I have prevailed on dear Gerald to return to public life and lead you in my stead.'

Piccadilly Gallery (71)

Left to right: Lord Hugh Cecil, F. E. Smith, George Wyndham, Carson, Austen Chamberlain, Henry Chaplin, Walter Long, A.B., and Gerald Balfour.

15 Once a proconsul, always a proconsul. [Lord Curzon] 1909
All Souls College, Oxford (387)

16 Mr Henry Chaplin
National Portrait Gallery (299)

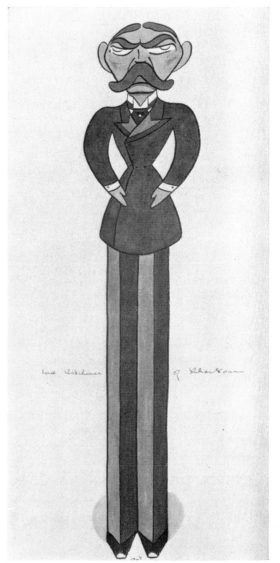

17 Lord Kitchener of Khartoum. 1900
Piccadilly Gallery (865)

18 Mr Joseph Chamberlain,
doing his best. 1901
Merton College, Oxford (274)

19 Studies in Guelph. No 1.
A Young Princess
Piccadilly Gallery (2043)

20 What Had She Expected?
'He [Napoleon III] is excessively kind in private, and so very quiet' (Extract from
letter written by Queen Victoria in Paris, September 1, 1855, to Baron Stockmar).
Mrs Philip Guedalla (1086)

21 King Edward VII is duly apprised of his accession. *Mrs Rau* (478)

22 Illustrating the force of ancient habit
King Edward's visit to the Convent of Dom Successio [1903]
King Edward: 'Enfin, Madame: faites monter la première à gauche.'
Mrs David Karmel (495)

23 A Sailor King [George V]. 1914
Mrs Philip Guedalla (576)

24 Mid-Term Tea at Mr Oscar Browning's. 1908
King's College, Cambridge (186)

Among O.B. and the undergraduates the crowned heads of Europe are, from left to right, Franz-Josef of Austria-Hungary, Gustav V of Sweden, Nicholas II of Russia, George I of Greece, Alfonso XIII of Spain, Abdul Hamid II of Turkey, Wilhelm II of Germany, Victor Emanuel III of Italy, and Leopold II of the Belgians.

25 Mr William Archer Really Conversing. 1904
University of Texas (27)

The initials at the top represent A. W. Pinero, Sidney Lee, George Alexander, William Heinemann, Thomas Hardy, Stephen Phillips, and George Moore.

26 'Rival Beauties' With acknowledgments
to Mr George Wyndham and Mr George
Alexander. 1907
Piccadilly Gallery (8)

27 Mr Clement Scott. 1901
Robert Aickman (1391)

28 Sir Arthur Sullivan
Mrs M. E. Yates (1636)

29 Mr Martin Harvey
Mrs Marie Strang (727)

30 Sir Henry Irving. 1901. *Robert H. Taylor* (788)

31 Edmond Rostand. 1910
D. Coombs (1291)

With Coquelin as Cyrano, Sarah Bernhardt as L'Aiglon, and Lucien Guitry as Chantecler.

32 Mr Shaw's Sortie. 1909
'But this shall be written of our time: that when the Spirit who Denies besieged
the last citadel, blaspheming life itself, there were some – there was one especially
– whose voice was heard, and whose spear was not broken.' Concluding words of
Mr Chesterton's biography of Mr Shaw.
Fitzwilliam Museum, Cambridge (1490)

One Chesterton and two Shaws.

33 Won't it be rather like 'Rep'? 1916
Sir Charles Forte (144)

Augustine Birrell presiding over a class of poets: Yeats, Masefield, Sturge Moore,
Binyon, Hewlett, Belloc, Seaman, and Newbolt.

34 Mr J. M. Barrie in a nursery – telling a story about a little boy who wished –
oh, how he did wish! – to be a mother; and how the fairies sent the stork to
him with a baby; and how he mothered it, and his mother grandmothered it;
with many other matters of a kind to make adults cry and, crying, smile through
their tears. 1908
Haro Hodson (101)

35 Mr Hall Caine
Robert Beloe (227)

36 It is said that [at] a supper given in farewell to Stevenson on the eve of the departure to Samoa, Mr [W. E.] Henley inadvertently upset the salt. 1901
Piccadilly Gallery (741)

37 'The Jolly Corner'. *c.* 1908
George Sassoon (808)

Henry James meets his other self.

38 A memory of Henry James and
Joseph Conrad conversing at an afternoon
party – *circa* 1904. 1926
University of Texas (814)

39 George Moore. *c.* 1916
Miss Jennifer Gosse (1055)

40 Mr Maurice Baring, testing carefully the Russian sense of humour. 1908
Miss Elizabeth Williamson (88)

41 The Nobel Award, 1907. 'Lord God, they ha' paid in full!'
Miss Jennifer Gosse (857)

Kipling carries off the prize, to the envy of Hall Caine, Meredith and Swinburne aloft.

42 L[ytton] S[trachey].
A *The* Prince of Prose-Writers. 1929
Owner Unknown (1606)

43 British Hempire. 1907
Owner Unknown (859)

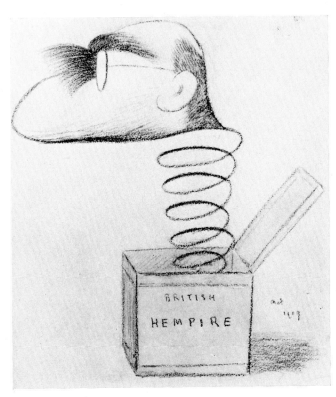

44 Mr Swinburne. 1899
Mrs Philip Guedalla (1642)

45 James Stephens
U.C.L.A. (*Clark*) (1597)

46 Mr Maurice Hewlett. 1908
Ashmolean Museum, Oxford (746)

47 'Talis Amyclaeos non junxit gratia fratres.' 1925
Owner Unknown (1549)

Osbert and Sacheverell Sitwell.

48 W. B. Yeats
National Gallery of Ireland (1828)

49 Mr Ezra Pound. 1934
C. Waller Barrett (1190)

50 'Mark Twain'. 1908
University of Texas (1689)

51 'Had Shakespeare asked me . . .'
S. J. Wingate (720)

52 Mr Frank Harris
presents.
(Frontispiece for that
work of brilliant and
profound criticism
'The Man Shakespeare'.)
1910
J. I. M. Stewart (716)

53 William Shakespeare writing a sonnet. 1907
Mrs Alice Shalvi (1473)

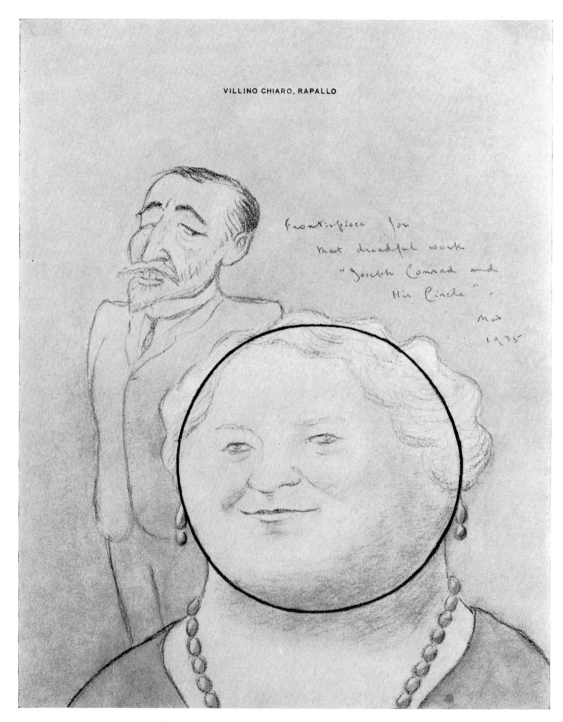

VILLINO CHIARO, RAPALLO

Frontispiece for that dreadful work "Joseph Conrad and His Circle". Mᵒ 1935

54 Frontispiece for that dreadful work 'Joseph Conrad and His Circle'. 1935
Benjamin Sonnenberg (363)

55 Fresco of Swinburne and Rossetti. *Merton College, Oxford* (1281)

56 Sylvester Hethway vainly endeavouring to enlist Rossetti's interest in some
singularly interesting experiment.
A. N. L. Munby (1284)

Mr James McNeill Whistler. 1901
D'Offay Couper Gallery (1769)

58 Whistler into Candlestick.
University of Glasgow (1774)

59 Sir William Eden and Mr Whistler.
University of Glasgow (458)

60 Here are five friends of mine – Mr Nicholson, Mr Rutherston, Mr Craig,
Mr Morrison, and Mr Ricketts. All are designers of fantastic and lovely costumes.
Yet they dress themselves thus:
Birmingham City Art Gallery (382)

61 Why not rather thus?
Birmingham City Art Gallery (383)

62 'Found' (with all acknowledgments to Rossetti). 1911
'Yet I had planted thee a noble vine, wholly a right seed: how then art thou turned into the degenerate plant of a strange vine unto me?' Jeremiah, II, 21.
Johannesburg Art Gallery (1228)

Charles Ricketts attempting to rescue C. H. Shannon from the Royal Academy.

63 Insecurity. 1909
Art-Critic (under his breath): 'How odd it seems that thirty years hence I may
be desperately in love with these ladies!'
National Gallery of Victoria (825)

Augustus John and his models.

64 Mr Aubrey Beardsley. 1896
Newberry Library, Chicago (108)

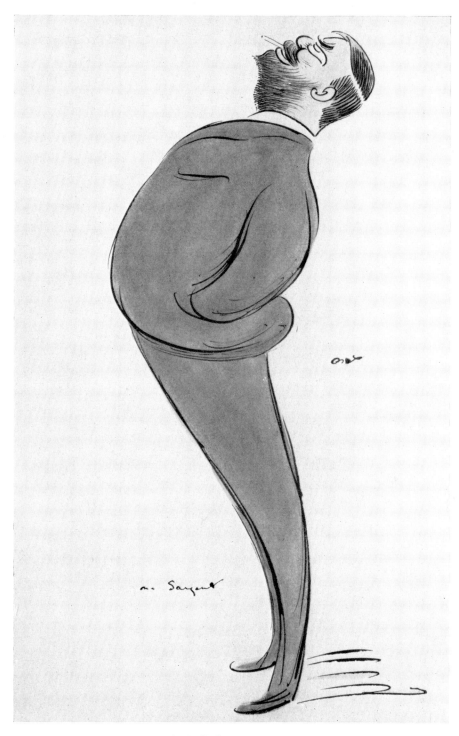

65 J. S. Sargent. 1900
Mrs M. E. Yates (1362)

66 'Walter Sickert and other august elders' (Tonks, MacColl, Furse and Steer
are the 'elders').
University of Texas (1533)

An illustration to Max's 'Enoch Soames'.

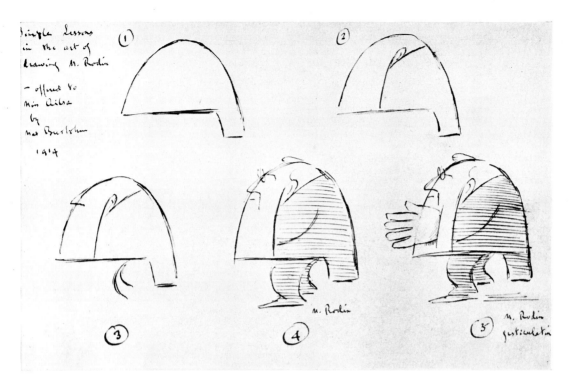

67 Simple Lessons in the art of drawing
M. Rodin. 1914
Merton College, Oxford (1241)

68 Will Rothenstein and
Albert Rutherston. 1906
Herbert D. Schimmel (1349)

69 Sir Hugh Lane producing masterpieces for Dublin. 1909
Municipal Gallery of Modern Art, Dublin (884)

70 Mr William Orpen executing, in his own way, a commission for a portrait.
1909
Sir John Rothenstein (1130)

72 Major Esterhazy
Keith Mackenzie (534)

Forger of the Dreyfus 'bordereau'.

73 A Quiet Evening in Seamore Place.
Doctors consulting whether Mr Alfred [de Rothschild] may, or may not, take a
second praline before bed-time.
David Rutherston (1335)

74 The meeting of Signor D'Annunzio and M. Rostand. 1911
M. Rostand: 'Je trouve qu'il n'a manqué que d'une chose – une: la simplicité.'
Allan Cuthbertson (399)

75 Count Boni de Castellane. 1912
Sir Anthony Hooper, Bart (419)

76 Mr Julius Beerbohm
Piccadilly Gallery (117)

77 Mr Cunninghame Graham
Admiral Sir Angus Cunninghame Graham
(629)

78 Mr Harry Melvill
U.C.L.A. (Clark) (1026)

79 Mr Bernard Posno
Mrs Philip Guedalla (1187)

80 'Charmant et sympathique jeune homme, levez-vous Duc de Guédalla et de la rue du parc d'Hyde!'
Mrs Philip Guedalla (658)

Ennoblement of Philip Guedalla by Napoleon III.

81 Mr Reginald Turner
Phillipe Jullian (1686)

82 The Horny Hand. 1909
Fitzwilliam Museum, Cambridge (1965)

VILLINO CHIARO, RAPALLO

83 Zuleika Dobson. 1929
The Hon. Mrs Lyle (1839)

238

84 '"Excuse – permit me," he said softly.'
University of Texas (1847)

The Devil introduces himself to Max and
Enoch Soames.

85 'Savonarola' Brown. 1936
Merton College, Oxford (1859)

86 Esmeralda
Mrs Hamilton Cottier (1885)

87 Mr Arnold Dolmetsch
D'Offay Couper Gallery (1890)

88 Café Chantant
D'Offay Couper Gallery (1882)

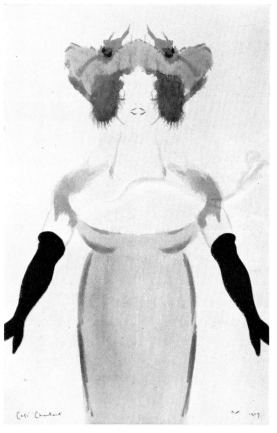

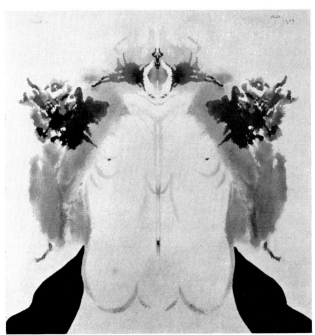

89 Nero
D'Offay Couper Gallery (1892)

90 Unidentified. *Owner Unknown* (1694)

91 Unidentified *Lilly Library* (1705)

92 Unidentified. *Jay Hall* (1706)

93 Unidentified
Piccadilly Gallery (1708A)

94 Unidentified
Malcolm Borthwick (1712)

95 Unidentified
Owner Unknown (1715)

96 Unidentified
Sir Rupert Hart-Davis (1717)

97 Unidentified
Robert Lescher (1722A)

98 Unidentified
*University of
Texas* (1719)

99 Lord Runcorn –
sketched from life
Sir Rupert Hart-Davis (2048)

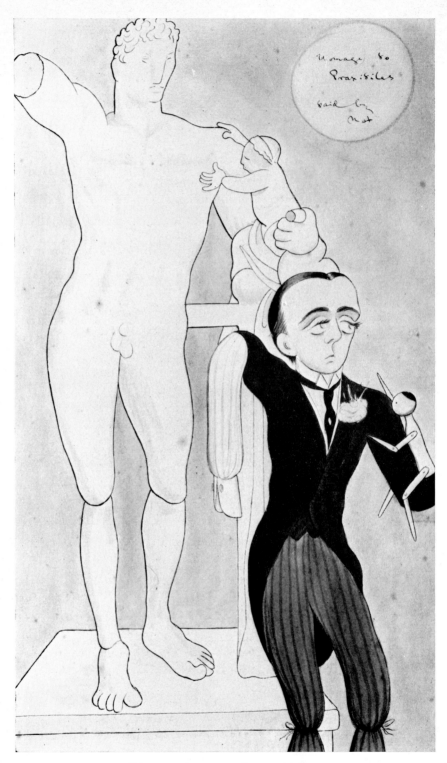

100 Homage to Praxiteles paid by Max
Phillip N. Davis (1425)

Indexes

Index of Titles

EXCLUDING THOSE WHICH CONTAIN THE NAME OF THE SUBJECT

(references are to item-numbers)

247

Index of Books and Periodicals

(references are to item-numbers)

Index of Owners

(references are to item-numbers)

INDEX OF OWNERS